The Origins of the First World War

A second edition of this leading introduction to the origins of the First World War and the pre-war international system. William Mulligan shows how the war was a far from inevitable outcome of international politics in the early twentieth century and suggests instead that there were powerful forces operating in favour of the maintenance of peace. He discusses key issues ranging from the military, public opinion, economics, diplomacy, and geopolitics to relations between the great powers, the role of smaller states, and the disintegrating empires. In this new edition, the author assesses the extensive new literature on the war's origins and the July Crisis as well as introducing new themes such as the relationship between economic interdependence and military planning. With well-structured chapters and an extensive bibliography, this is an essential classroom text which significantly revises our understanding of diplomacy, political culture, and economic history from 1870 to 1914.

WILLIAM MULLIGAN is a lecturer in the School of History and Archives, University College Dublin. He is the author of *The Creation of the Modern German Army* (2005) and *The Great War for Peace* (2014) and is co-editor of *The Wars before the Great War: Conflict and International Politics before the Outbreak of the First World War* (2015).

NEW APPROACHES TO EUROPEAN HISTORY

Series Editors
T. C. W. BLANNING *Sidney Sussex College, Cambridge*
BRENDAN SIMMS *Peterhouse, Cambridge*

New Approaches to European History is an important textbook series, which provides concise but authoritative surveys of major themes and problems in European history since the Renaissance. Written at a level and length accessible to advanced school students and undergraduates, each book in the series addresses topics or themes that students of European history encounter daily: the series embraces both some of the more 'traditional' subjects of study and those cultural and social issues to which increasing numbers of school and college courses are devoted. A particular effort is made to consider the wider international implications of the subject under scrutiny.

To aid the student reader, scholarly apparatus and annotation is light, but each work has full supplementary bibliographies and notes for further reading: where appropriate, chronologies, maps, diagrams, and other illustrative material are also provided.

For a complete list of titles published in the series, please see:
www.cambridge.org/newapproaches

The Origins of the First World War

Second edition

William Mulligan

University College Dublin

CAMBRIDGE
UNIVERSITY PRESS

CAMBRIDGE
UNIVERSITY PRESS

University Printing House, Cambridge CB2 8BS, United Kingdom

One Liberty Plaza, 20th Floor, New York, NY 10006, USA

477 Williamstown Road, Port Melbourne, VIC 3207, Australia

4843/24, 2nd Floor, Ansari Road, Daryaganj, Delhi - 110002, India

79 Anson Road, #06-04/06, Singapore 079906

Cambridge University Press is part of the University of Cambridge.

It furthers the University's mission by disseminating knowledge in the pursuit of education, learning and research at the highest international levels of excellence.

www.cambridge.org
Information on this title: www.cambridge.org/9781316612354

© William Mulligan 2017

First published 2017

Printed in the United Kingdom by Clays, St Ives plc

A catalogue record for this publication is available from the British Library

ISBN 978-1-107-15959-4 Hardback
ISBN 978-1-316-61235-4 Paperback

Contents

Illustrations

All images are used with the permission of the Trustees of the Imperial War Museum, London.

Maps

Preface to the Second Edition

Since the first edition appeared in 2010, a wealth of new scholarship about the origins of the First World War has been published. These works have sparked a renewed debate about numerous issues, including the July crisis, Russian foreign policy, the significance of the Balkan Wars, the relationship between great power politics and globalisation, and the changing normative environment in which international politics was conducted. I have benefited from conversations with friends and colleagues, from reviewers who highlighted questions and problems raised by the first edition, and from readers who alerted me to the odd error.

In particular, I would like to thank Catherine Holmes for encouraging me to write a review article on the new literature that appeared in the *English Historical Review* in 2014 and Jack Levy and John Vasquez, who invited me to participate in a round-table debate at the International Studies Association in 2013, later the basis for an edited volume. I also had the good fortune to co-edit a volume on the Balkan Wars and international politics with Andreas Rose and Dominik Geppert. I would like to thank them and the contributors to that volume for helping me to think through old questions and encounter new ones.

Over the past few years, I have benefited from stints at the Institute of Advanced Study at Princeton and from a EURIAS fellowship at the Wissenschaftskolleg zu Berlin. Although I worked on other projects at these institutes, one project tends to seep into another. The conversations at these institutes were at once far removed from, but resonant with, the debates about the origins of the First World War. Such are the advantages of the inter-disciplinary environment. I would like to thank the staff, members, and fellows of these two institutes for sharing their thoughts.

Acknowledgements

This book, in many respects, is the product of various courses taught at the University of Glasgow and University College Dublin, and I would like to thank students who have taken my courses on the history of international relations for their patience, enthusiasm, and scepticism. Amongst my colleagues in Dublin and Glasgow, I would like to thank especially Phil O'Brien, Simon Ball, Evan Mawdsley, Mark Freeman, Conan Fischer, Declan Downey, Robert Gerwarth, Judith Devlin, Stuart Ward, and Richard Aldous for their support and interest in this project over the last few years. I am also fortunate to have discussed, in the most convivial of places, some of the ideas of the book with Thomas Otte, Paul Readman, and Peter Holquist. I owe Brendan Simms a profound debt for the encouragement he has offered to me since my days as a doctoral student, and I would like to take this opportunity to thank him for his advice and intellectual generosity. The usual rider applies – the mistakes and errors are mine alone.

I am grateful to Michael Watson, the commissioning editor at Cambridge University Press, for giving me the opportunity to write this book, to have my say, as it were, on the origins of the First World War.

In recent years, I have done a good deal of my research in London. I would like to thank my three sisters, Helen, Margaret, and Kate, as well as Kate's husband, Rich, for their kindness and hospitality when I stayed with them in London for extended periods of time. I am grateful for the continued support of my parents, Deirdre and Herbert, over the course of this project.

Most importantly of all, I want to thank my wife, Kate. When I first met her, the argument of this book was but a rough idea in my head. Since then, her support, her interest, and her unceasing patience have been essential in encouraging me to undertake and to complete this project. This book is dedicated to her.

1   Introduction

The American political commentator and an adviser to President Woodrow Wilson, Walter Lippmann, introduced his book on public opinion with the following story: 'There is an island in the ocean where in 1914 a few Englishmen, Frenchmen, and Germans lived. No cable reaches that island and the British mail steamer comes but once in sixty days. In September it had not yet come and the islanders were still talking about the latest newspaper which told about the approaching trial of Madame Caillaux for the shooting of Gaston Calmette. It was therefore with more than usual eagerness that the whole colony gathered at the quay on a day in mid-September to hear from the captain what the verdict had been. They learned that for over six weeks now those of them who were English and those of them who were French had been fighting on behalf of the sanctity of treaties against those of them who were Germans. For six strange weeks they had acted as if they were friends, when in fact they were enemies.'[1] Lippmann used the story to illustrate the way in which public opinion was shaped by the flow and control of information. It also illustrates that war was not widely expected in the summer of 1914.

From the well-connected diplomat to the agricultural labourers in the field, many Europeans were confident that peace between the great powers, which had been tested by a series of severe crises between 1911 and 1913, would endure. At the beginning of 1914, Arthur Nicolson, the permanent under-secretary at the Foreign Office, suggested that the governments of the great powers would have their hands full with domestic affairs. The Home Rule crisis in Britain, the revolving door of government in the French Third Republic, the scandal over military abuse of civilians in Zabern in Germany, and the perennial concerns about the nationalities in the multi-ethnic Habsburg empire meant governments wanted international stability so that they could deal with domestic problems. Only Russia, he thought, had no such internal distractions, but he did

---

[1] Walter Lippmann, *Public Opinion* (New York, 1922), p. 8.

not consider the Tsarist regime a threat to international peace.[2] Whereas Nicolson was writing about the immediate prospects of the international system, others believed that they lived in 'the golden age of security', as Stefan Zweig put it in his memoirs. Peace and stability characterised the permanent condition of life in Europe before 1914, or so many contemporaries believed.

In the town of Mansle, halfway between Limoges and La Rochelle in western France, a teacher, speaking on 1 August 1914, following the German declaration of war the previous day, remained confident that war could still be avoided because nobody would be 'so insane and criminal as to inflict such a scourge'. But within days, even hours, perspectives changed. By August 1914, the stability of the pre-war years seemed superficial. War forced contemporaries to confront and stress the severe tensions in the international system before 1914 and the deep roots of the conflict. Frenchmen pointed to the aggression of German foreign policy in the decade before the First World War. The war was the responsibility of the German government and culture. It was no longer an act of lunacy, but the intended outcome of Germany's war party. 'You can feel how different the attitude would have been', noted one teacher, 'if France had initiated a war of provocation and conquest.' The widely accepted view was that France was fighting a war of national defence against German aggression, a view which, in turn, influenced the interpretations of international relations before 1914.[3]

This shift in perspective was repeated around Europe. The initial shock of war was replaced with attempts to understand how the conflict had come about. This change had important consequences for understanding the history of international relations before 1914. That history was recast by contemporaries as a prelude to the outbreak of war. Of course, there had been writers who predicted that war between the great powers was likely, even inevitable. It is striking, however, how dominant this interpretation of international relations before 1914 was to become once war broke out. The narrative stressing compromise, restraint, and cooperation between the great powers, was replaced with one stressing the causes of war and its inevitability. Indeed, this change of perspective was underpinned by a political imperative. Each side had to justify its entry into the war as a defensive act. To do so, they depicted their opponents as the aggressors. The politicisation of the history of pre-1914 international relations lasted until at least the 1960s. The early accounts produced

[2] Nicolson to Bunsen, 19 January 1914, TNA, FO 800/372, fo. 83.
[3] Jean-Jacques Becker, 'That's the Death Knell of Our Boys', in Patrick Fridenson, ed., *The French Home Front, 1914–1918* (Providence, RI, 1992), pp. 17–34.

during and immediately after the war have shaped questions that continue to feature prominently in debates to the present day. Understanding these debates will enable us to look afresh at the history of international relations before 1914. Nationality, political allegiance, and generational shifts have shaped the writings of historians about the causes of the First World War. The question which has driven almost all research on the history of international relations before 1914 has been 'What caused the First World War?' By privileging the war as the logical culmination of international politics before 1914, the history of the late nineteenth and early twentieth centuries has become framed in a narrative that stresses the increased tensions, confrontations, and crises between the great powers.

The first histories were produced by the belligerent governments in an effort to justify their actions before the tribunal of domestic and world opinion. These histories were found in the famous coloured books, which were rushed into print in August 1914. In the nineteenth century, the British government had come under pressure to publish diplomatic correspondence and to present it to parliament. The result was the publication of what became known as the Blue Books. The Foreign Office made a careful selection, as keen not to embarrass another government as to protect the reputation of Her Majesty's government. Other countries followed suit in the decades before 1914, with each great power choosing its own particular colour – the German White Book, the Austro-Hungarian Red Book, the Russian Orange Book, and the French Yellow Book. There was little pretence that these books constituted a full record of diplomatic correspondence, but they provided the raw material from which the first histories of the July crisis were fashioned. At the end of August, the German Foreign Secretary, Gottlieb von Jagow, instructed officials to prepare a publication presenting German policy in a favourable light, which could be issued in a few days, if necessary. James Wyclif Morley, later Sir James Headlam Morley, was told to 'ensure that the salient points were duly emphasised' in the British Blue Book published in late August.[4]

During the First World War, academics, journalists, and others mobilised to support the war. They published articles, pamphlets, and books. Most intellectuals adopted a patriotic stance, portraying the war as a defensive one. Many moved away from the intricacies of diplomatic interchange to provide a broader perspective on the origins and meaning

---

[4] Imanuel Geiss, *Studien über Geschichte und Geschichtswissenschaft* (Frankfurt, 1972), pp. 113–14; Keith Hamilton, 'The Pursuit of "Enlightened Patriotism": The British Foreign Office and Historical Researchers during the Great War and Its Aftermath', in Keith Wilson, ed., *Forging the Collective Memory: Government and International Historians through the Two World Wars* (Providence, RI, 1996), p. 195.

of the war. The war was no longer the outcome of the twists and turns of diplomacy of the early twentieth century; it was a world historical event, with deep roots in the conflicting cultural values of the great powers. As with government propaganda, the arguments of the intellectual classes ascribed blame to their opponents and portrayed the war as one of self-defence. They also wove cultural and moral categories into the meaning of a defensive war, moving the debate beyond narrowly defined security interests. For many German academics, the war was a defence of German, indeed European, culture against Russian barbarity and British materialism. In France, the war was depicted as 'the struggle of civilisation against barbarism', as Henri Bergson, France's most influential philosopher, put it. A group of Oxford historians defended Britain's declaration of war, on the grounds that Germany was ruled by a militarist caste, which arrogated to itself the right to attack weaker states. British foreign policy was not simply determined by the ugly dictates of the balance of power, but by grander ideals of international law and humanity. War cultures placed great emphasis on the ideological dimension of foreign policy and war aims. This raised the deeper cultural causes of war – German militarism, French revanchism, Russian pan-Slavic ideology, British materialism and commercial interests, and nationalism to name but a few of the issues that remain the subject of historical research.[5]

During and after the war, there was an element of 'patriotic self-censorship' amongst intellectuals. In 1915, Kurt Riezler asked the well-known Munich historian, Karl Alexander von Müller, to write a work, based on carefully selected documents, justifying the case of the German government. Müller, after reviewing the evidence, refused to participate in the project, but he never exposed the responsibility of the German government either during or after the First World War. He went on to become a major critic of the Weimar republic and a supporter of the Nazi party. John Holland Rose, a Cambridge historian working on nineteenth-century European history, was able to gain access to the Foreign Office archives, after Arthur Balfour, Conservative prime minister between 1902 and 1905, pointed out that 'a general conception of the German policy, which has led to the present catastrophe is of public importance and Rose would do it well'.[6] In fact, Rose had briefly opposed British intervention in the war, before writing a number of books on the origins of the war, justifying British policy, another personal example of the rapid shift in perspective in 1914.

---

[5] Isabel Hull, *A Scrap of Paper* (Ithaca, 2014), pp. 16–50.
[6] Hamilton, 'The Pursuit of "Enlightened Patriotism"', p. 196.

Critical voices were rare, but important. In Germany, Prince Lichnowsky, the German ambassador to London between 1912 and 1914, grew increasingly resentful of criticism that he had been duped by the British Foreign Secretary, Sir Edward Grey, and had failed in his mission to keep Britain out of the war. In 1916, he prepared a memorandum, defending his actions during the July crisis and pointing out that he had warned the German government on several occasions that Britain would join in a general European war. He argued that the leaders in Berlin had wilfully disregarded his warnings and ignored the desperate attempts of Grey to resolve the crisis. Lichnowsky sought to rehabilitate his reputation amongst a small elite, but, as luck would have it, his memorandum was leaked to a Swedish newspaper. Allied commentators seized upon it with delight, proof from within the inner circle of German diplomacy of the Reich's guilt for the war. The argument that the French president, Raymond Poincaré, bore considerable responsibility was first articulated within France by pacifists, such as Mathias Morhardt, the Secretary General of the Ligue des droits de l'homme. He argued that Poincaré had progressively surrendered French freedom of manoeuvre to Russia after becoming premier in early 1912. By 1917, the epithet 'Poincaré-la-guerre' was used by critics of the president. His background – he had left his native Lorraine in 1870 following the Prussian invasion – also made it easy for opponents to suggest that his foreign policy was motivated by a personal commitment to revenge for defeat in the Franco-Prussian War.

While most commentators assigned responsibility to one of the belligerent states, other perspectives emerged during the war, which explained the war in terms of the structures of the pre-war international system. These arguments were no less influenced by political interests. In Britain, E. D. Morel, who had campaigned against the atrocities of the Belgian regime in the Congo in the early twentieth century, turned his outrage on the secret diplomacy of the great powers. Morel set up the Union for Democratic Control. He argued that war was the result of a closed system of diplomacy. The mass of the people, he contended, had not wanted war and the answer to preventing future conflicts between the great powers lay in democratising governments and popular control of democracy. 'A secret and autocratic diplomacy . . . is the greatest obstacle to the emancipation of the peoples from the shackles of militarism and war', argued Morel.[7] The failings of secret diplomacy, which culminated in the war, were used by President Wilson, to whom Morel had issued an appeal in his book, to advance his case for open diplomacy.

---

[7] E. D. Morel, *Truth and the War* (London, 1916), pp. 112–13.

1. Charles Ernest Butler, *Blood and Iron*, 1916 (IWM ART 6492). This painting
was exhibited at the Royal Academy in 1917. It offered a clear explanation of
the origins of the war, drawing on Bismarck's famous 'blood and iron' speech,
to suggest that German military aggression was the cause of the war. The
burning of Louvain, which is partly depicted in this painting, reflected the idea
that Britain had gone to war to defend international law and morality, against
which German militarism had offended.

The Bolshevik leader, Vladimir Lenin, also weighed into the debate. He located the origins of the war in the crisis of capitalism and the imperial rivalries of the late nineteenth and early twentieth century. According to Lenin, the struggle between capitalist groups for control of the world's resources intensified after the economic depression of the 1870s. Free competition, the essence of capitalism, had been corrupted by the establishment of monopolies. 'Imperialism', argued Lenin, 'is the monopoly stage of capitalism.' Capitalists, dominating the great powers, partitioned the world, until there was no territory left to divide. 'In the future only redivision is possible', declared Lenin.[8] In this capitalist competition for resources lay the roots of the war. By its nature expansionist, capitalism was incompatible with peace by 1914. Expansion had only warded off the fundamental crisis of an intrinsically unstable capitalist system.

By the end of the war, therefore, governments and intellectuals had set out numerous interpretations of the origins of the war, including the responsibility of individual states, economic rivalries between the powers, the rise of militarism in Europe before 1914, the tensions generated by popular nationalist movements, and the consequences of secret diplomacy and alliances. These issues continue to generate debate amongst historians to the present day.

The politicisation of the debate on the origins of the war was fuelled by the war guilt clause of the treaty of Versailles, which attributed sole responsibility for the war to the German government and her allies. For a variety of reasons, sometimes contradictory, article 231 was inserted into the treaty of Versailles, stating that the war had been 'imposed . . . by the aggression of Germany and her allies'. The need to secure reparations, the hopes for a new world order based on international law, and the pressures of public opinion in the Allied countries informed the war guilt clause. While it was simply a statement of what the Allies and Americans believed about the origins of the war, it provided a starting point for a new round of publications and debates on the origins of the war. The response of the German foreign minister, Count von Brockdorff-Rantzau, demonstrated how categories of political and moral responsibility could blur. Whereas the Allies spoke of responsibility, German commentators denounced the 'war guilt' clause, escalating a debate about political decisions into a conflict about ethics and morality. The moral inflection of the debate has never entirely faded, as subsequent generations of historians have found themselves caught in debates about the present as well as the past of 1914.

[8] V. I. Lenin, *Imperialism, the Highest Stage of Capitalism: Collected Works*, vol. XXII (Moscow, 1964), pp. 187–304.

The German government had already been busy since the armistice, preparing publications on the July crisis. The situation was complicated by the abdication of the Kaiser and the establishment of a republic in November 1918. There was a temptation for the new republic to distance itself from Imperial Germany and to blame the Emperor, his generals, and diplomats for the war. Germany's later defence against the charge of war guilt was almost sunk below the waterline when the new government appointed Karl Kautsky on 18 November to prepare an official selection of documents for publication. Kautsky was a member of the Independent Social Democratic Party and had opposed the war from the outset. Before the war he had condemned the German military and industrialists for promoting the arms race. Kautsky had been appointed to give as full a record as possible of German diplomacy in the July crisis, but the German government thought better of its folly in early 1919. Thereafter, Kautsky's work was hindered. He was denied access to important files, two extra editors were added to his team – Walther Schücking and Maximilian Montgelas, the former a pacifist, the latter a career diplomat – and the publication of the documents was delayed until December 1919. However, damaging extracts of Kautsky's work had already found their way into the public sphere, serving to confirm the Allies' view of German war guilt.

The publication of these documents opened an important new front in the debate about the origins of the war. Governments began to use their archival collections to defend their pre-war diplomacy and blacken that of their former enemies. The German Foreign Office took the lead, publishing over forty volumes of documents in a series entitled *Die Grosse Politik der europäischen Kabinette*. Others followed suit. In 1926, Pierre de Margerie, ambassador to Berlin, told Aristide Briand, the premier, that France would have to respond to the *Grosse Politik* to win the contest for world opinion. The French and German collections started in 1870, the British in 1898, and the Austrian in 1908, the dates suggesting official understandings of the origins of the war. In Russia, the Soviet government published documents that discredited the Tsarist regime. Not surprisingly, these were translated into German, but not into English or French. These documents provided a huge amount of material for contemporary diplomatic historians, and they continue to be used to the present day.

However, governments were not throwing away control of their historical records. Governments normally chose professional academics to put together the collection of documents, but they relied on the patriotism of the chosen, as well as some limits on access, to present a suitable case. Harold Temperley, a British historian who worked on the *British Documents on the Origins of the War*, noted that 'We cannot, of course, tell the whole truth.'[9] In the German Foreign Office, the War Guilt Section, staffed by diplomats, retained control over the flow of documents to the editors. In any case, the editors were committed to defending the record of German diplomacy before 1914. They shortened certain documents and omitted some damaging material, including the crucial meeting with the Austrian diplomat, Alexander von Hoyos, on 5 July 1914.

The 'war of documents' had at least three significant consequences for the study of the origins of the war. First, it pushed the chronology of the origins of the war back to 1870/1. This raised questions which continue to intrigue historians. The continuities between the wars of German uni-fication and the First World War, the consequences of Bismarck's man-agement of the international system, and the enduring tensions between France and Germany were debates stimulated by a study of the German and French documents. Similarly, Britain's decision to start in 1898 high-lighted Anglo-German antagonism as a central theme in the origins of the war. The encirclement of Germany, a common argument during and after the First World War, and the threat from Russia were emphasised in Russian and German documents. Second, the welter of documents from foreign ministries pushed other factors into the background, such as the role of the military, the influence of commercial elites on foreign policy, and the impact of public opinion on the international system. The origins of the First World War, therefore, became inextricably linked with diplomatic history. American historians, such as William Langer, Sidney Bradshaw Fay, and Harry Elmer Barnes, became leading practitioners of diplomatic history and their questioning of the war guilt thesis did much to undermine its credibility. Third, Germany's decision to publish and publish quickly meant that the sole war guilt interpretation came under severe pressure. By the end of the 1920s, academic historians had largely discarded the argument that Germany was solely responsible for the outbreak of the war. This revision of historical interpretations was also part of a wider political process, in which the treaty of Versailles was unravelled, while the former belligerents, Germany, France, and Britain sought to demobilise war cultures in the late 1920s.

By the eve of the Second World War, there was, as Mombauer has put it, a 'comfortable consensus'. Within this consensus, there was room for disagreement, but it was generally accepted that all great powers had had some share in the origins of the war, that the forces at work – the alliance system, the arms race, nationalism – were beyond the control of the statesmen of 1914, and that war had not been planned by any one

---

[9] Cited in Keith Wilson, 'Introduction: Governments, Historians, and "Historical Engi-neering", in Wilson, ed., *Forging the Collective Memory*, p. 17.

person, institution, or state. David Lloyd George, British Chancellor in 1914 and later prime minister between 1916 and 1922, famously declared in his memoirs that Europe had 'slithered into war'. As one Habsburg critic of the Austrian ultimatum to Serbia, Prince Lajos Windischgraetz noted, politicians had come to see the war 'as a tragic event'.[10] It was an event that lay beyond personal responsibility.

The Second World War both marginalised interest in the First World War and also shaped new perspectives on the previous global conflict. On the Allied side, two distinctive narratives of German history emerged, which stressed its militaristic culture as the root of European upheaval for almost a century. This militaristic culture was embodied in the Prussian state, which was abolished by Allied decree in 1947. In the Soviet interpretation, militarism was associated with capitalism, so that the two world wars were the product of a capitalist class system, which, in Germany, was underpinned by military power. As a latecomer to the capitalist struggle for empire, Germany had adopted aggressive methods in its conduct of foreign policy, leading to the two world wars. In the liberal interpretation, favoured in Britain and the USA, Prussian militarism and foreign policy aggression was the product of a flawed historical development, during which constitutional liberties and parliamentary democracy had been fatally compromised by an elite military and agrarian class, whose power was rooted in Prussia. Academic works, such as A. J. P. Taylor's account, pointed to the continuities in German history between the nineteenth century and the Second World War. The Second World War seemed to confirm German responsibility for the First World War.

This narrative of German history, with 1914, 1933, and 1939 as the key staging points in its peculiar historical development, or *Sonderweg*, was challenged by West German historians after 1945. In truth, they were preaching to the converted in their own country, and their work had less impact than they might have wished outside the new Federal Republic. Gerhard Ritter was to become one of the leading protagonists in the most intense debate on the origins of the First World War after 1945. Born in 1888, he had fought in the First World War, briefly supported the Nazi regime in the early 1930s, and ended up in prison in 1944 after the July plot. After the end of the Second World War, he was elected president of the Historians' Association of Germany. 'How infinitely important a task it is for the historian to assure the continuity of our historical thought', he wrote to Friedrich Meinicke, another highly influential post-war historian, 'and thus to prevent a chaos of political

---

[10] Gergely Romsics, *Myth and Remembrance: The Dissolution of the Habsburg Empire in the Memoir Literature of the Austro-Hungarian Political Elite* (New York, 2006), pp. 30–31.

and moral desperation, which could result from the catastrophic and abrupt end of our traditions, and still to possess the necessary flexibility in order to be able to sustain a real new beginning.'[11] Ritter was not blind to the faults of the Kaiserreich, as his four-volume history on German militarism showed. He argued that Schlieffen and his fellow generals had exercised too much influence over German foreign policy, leading to catastrophe in 1914. This interpretation diminished the responsibility of figures such as William II and Bethmann Hollweg. Ritter's view of the Kaiserreich was largely positive, and he saw Nazism as the product of modern mass political culture, rather than the outcome of a specifically German historical development. International politics also shaped judgements. A Franco-German Historians' Commission concluded that the outbreak of the First World War was the collective responsibility of the great powers. The need for a Cold War consensus between the new allies in the western bloc facilitated this judgement, which built on the orthodoxies of the 1930s.

It was in this historiographical context that Fritz Fischer wrote a series of articles and books between 1959 and 1969, which destroyed the consensus about shared responsibility for the First World War. An outsider within the German historical profession in the 1920s and 1930s, the Nazi seizure of power opened up opportunities for the young historian. Only during the Second World War did he turn against the Nazi regime. His transformation was completed by his time as a prisoner of war. His post-war writings marked a reckoning with his own past and served as a contribution to the political re-education of West German citizens. His first book, published in 1959, was on German war aims. This was followed four years later by one on German foreign policy between 1911 and 1914, entitled *Krieg der Illusionen*, or *War of Illusions*. In his first book, he argued that during the war Germany pursued extensive and radical aims. In *War of Illusions*, Fischer argued that these extensive war aims had governed German foreign policy before the outbreak of war and were widely shared, rather than limited to a small section of pan-German opinion. Moreover, he argued that German leaders had brought about the war with their aggressive policy. He pointed to the now famous meeting of William II and his military advisers in December 1912 as the moment when the course was set for war. Further, he argued that war was a response to internal and external weakness, both self-inflicted.

---

[11] Klaus Schwabe, 'Change and Continuity in German Historiography from 1933 into the Early 1950s: Gerhard Ritter (1888–1967)', in Hartmut Lehmann, ed., *Paths of Continuity: Central European Historiography from 1933 to the 1950s* (Cambridge, 1994), p. 104.

In the international system, Germany had brought about its own encirclement, by pursuing imperialist goals, which pushed France, Britain, and Russia into each other's arms. At home, the German elites refused to reform constitutional structures in the face of growing pressures, particularly from the Social Democratic Party, the largest in Germany after the 1912 elections. In a book that was argued as trenchantly as it was well-researched, Fischer placed the blame for the First World War firmly on the shoulders of the Wilhelmine elite.[12]

In West Germany, Fischer's arguments caused controversy. His opponents, notably Ritter, engaged with him at several levels. They argued that the evidence could be read in a less damning way. They noted the lack of a comparative perspective in Fischer's work. By examining only German foreign policy, it was likely that the Kaiserreich would appear as the state most responsible for the war. But contemporary political preoccupations were never far from the surface. Conservative West German politicians and historians were concerned that Fischer's thesis on the origins of the war would revive the war guilt controversy of the 1920s, undermine the political cohesion of the Federal Republic, and give ammunition to Communist propagandists. The Cold War and domestic West German politics exercised an important influence on the course of the Fischer controversy. It rose to such a pitch that the government funded Ritter and other opponents of Fischer. In political debates, the First World War's importance owed much to its relationship to the Third Reich and the Second World War. In particular, Fischer's argument, which traced continuities between the Kaiserreich and the Third Reich, undermined efforts to present German history in a more positive light, in which Hitler was regarded as an aberration, the product of a highly unusual set of circumstances. The charges of his opponents failed to take account of Fischer's own intellectual biography.[13]

By the 1970s, however, Fischer's thesis had emerged as the new orthodoxy on the origins of the First World War. In large part, this was due to the research based on new archival material, which underpinned his arguments. However, his success was also related to the rise of a new generation of West German scholars, who adopted a much more critical approach to their national history. His work stimulated new research into all aspects of German politics before the war, from naval policy to public opinion. Fischer's thesis had important consequences for the historiography of the origins of the First World War. First, it directed

---

[12] Fritz Fischer, *War of Illusions: German Policies from 1911 to 1914* (London, 1975).
[13] Stephan Petzold, 'The Social Making of a Historian in Nazi Germany and the Early Federal Republic: Fritz Fischer's Distancing from Bourgeois-Conservative Historiography', *Journal of Contemporary History*, 48, 2 (2013), pp. 271–89.

the attention of historians to the domestic context of foreign policy. The primacy of foreign policy was replaced by a primacy of domestic policy. According to this approach, foreign policy was the product of domestic political considerations, rather than a response to pressures within the international system. In the work of Hans-Ulrich Wehler, this approach went so far as to reduce politics to a contest between different social groupings. 'German imperialism', argued Wehler, 'can be seen on the one hand as a defensive strategy in domestic politics. On the other hand, it introduced an aggressive component into Germany's foreign relations.' War was the result of the effort of the German elites to stave off the rise of their domestic political opponents, notably the trade unions and SPD.[14]

The second impact of the Fischer controversy was related to the first. If Germany bore the lion's share of the responsibility for the war, this meant that the foreign policies of the other great powers were often depicted as reacting to German ambitions. Moreover, if German policy was the product of the dynamics of its internal politics, then other European states, reacting to German policy, were largely absolved from responsibility for the war. Britain, France, and Russia were defending themselves against the thrusting new arrival in world politics, Germany. The works of Zara Steiner and Paul Kennedy argued that British policy was determined by the German challenge, though Steiner stressed the continued significance of the European balance of power to policy makers in London, whereas Kennedy stressed naval and colonial conflicts. In France, the study of international history before the First World War had almost vanished by the late 1970s, due in part to the robust work during the inter-war period of Pierre Renouvin, a veteran, who attributed the greater degree of responsibility to Germany. Books by the British historian John Keiger and the German historian Gerd Krumeich offered the most cogent new interpretations, based on extensive archival research. Keiger stressed the defensive nature of Poincaré's policy, while Krumeich examined the tensions caused by the different needs of French internal and external politics. Dominic Lieven's book on Russian foreign policy, in the same series as Keiger's and Steiner's, absolved Russia of primary responsibility for the war, while Richard Bosworth analysed the disparity between Italian weakness and her ambitions.

By the mid-1980s, James Joll, professor of international history, was able to write a synthesis, based largely on research produced since the Fischer debate of the 1960s. Joll had introduced Fischer's book on German war aims to an English-speaking public, but while he was generous in his

---

[14] Hans-Ulrich Wehler, *The German Empire, 1871–1918* (Leamington Spa, 1985), pp. 183, 198.

praise of Fischer's work, he did not agree completely with the German revisionist historian.[15] He examined the major themes, which had preoccupied historians for decades, comparing the policies of the great powers, the influence of military planners, the commercial and financial aspects of foreign policy, and the role of public opinion. His approach was comparative, unlike Fischer's. He concluded that the origins of the First World War were complex and varied and he generally eschewed apportioning blame, urging historians to investigate the 'unspoken assumptions' that governed European politics and society before 1914. Only in the conclusion did he ascribe more responsibility to the German leaders, who, in his view, had decided by December 1912 that war was inevitable in order to prevent further decline and to achieve world power status. Once this was decided, the political objective was to choose the best time to strike, rather than to maintain peace. Germany's 'strategic plans became all-important and these had more immediate military consequences than those of any other power'.[16]

By the late 1980s, the debate on the origins of the First World War seemed to have reached an equilibrium, it had lost much of its political relevance, and historical research had moved into other fields, notably social and cultural history, pushing the study of the history of international relations to the margins of the profession.

Yet neither international history nor the debate on the origins of the First World War stood still for long. The centenary of the outbreak of the war was accompanied by a wave of new books that gave rise to a good-tempered, if heated, debate about the degrees of responsibility for the war. These centenary works reflected a quiet transformation in the study of the origins of the war and international history in general that had taken place since the 1990s.[17] Three developments – one in historical research and two in contemporary politics – have helped to revitalise the history of international relations. First historians adopted approaches from cultural history to the study of international relations, while cultural historians reworked old themes in diplomatic and military history. Second, contemporary debates about globalisation have encouraged historians to examine previous eras for evidence of global integration. The chronologies of the history of globalisation do not fit neatly into the boxes of international history, which are conventionally demarcated by

---

[15] James Joll, 'The 1914 Debate Continues: Fritz Fischer and His Critics', *Past and Present*, 34 (July 1966): 100–113; see also his introduction to Fritz Fischer, *Germany's War Aims in the First World War* (London, 1967).

[16] James Joll, *The Origins of the First World War*, 2nd edn (London, 1992), p. 235.

[17] William Mulligan, 'The Trial Continues: New Directions in the Study of the Origins of the First World War', *English Historical Review*, 129, 538 (2014), pp. 639–66.

great power wars. The late nineteenth century has been heralded as the first age of globalisation, which raises questions about the relationship between different forms of globalisation and great power politics. Kevin O'Rourke and Richard Findlay contend that the First World War brought nineteenth-century globalisation to an 'abrupt end', but they also suggest that the war was not the result of inherent tensions in the global economy. Rather, the war 'still appears as somewhat of a *diabolus ex machina*' in their account.[18] In a related but different approach, historians have used transnational approaches to assess the relationships between groups in civil society – businesses, trade unions, students, and churches for example – that span the porous borders of states. The final development was the relatively peaceful ending of the Cold War, in which the Soviet Union surrendered its super-power status without a general great power war. Political scientists and historians have asked whether the Cold War and its ending marked a milestone in the 'waning of major wars' and whether this is part of a long-term historical trend. These developments, in addition to the findings based on new archival evidence, have produced fresh interpretations of international politics before 1914.

The quiet transformation of perspectives arguably began with Jean-Jacques Becker's 1977 path-breaking study of French popular opinion at the outbreak of war. Using detailed reports compiled by prefects throughout France, Becker showed that the majority of citizens greeted war with a sense of stoic patriotism. Enthusiasm for the most part was limited to urban professional and intellectual elites. Fear of death and injury, sorrow at the rupturing of family and community bonds as soldiers left for the front, and concern about the likely catastrophic consequences of war combined with a stoic sense of patriotic duty to defend *la patrie* against invasion. Later studies by Jeffrey Verhey on Germany and Catriona Pennell on the UK demonstrated similar patterns of enthusiasm, fear, anxiety, and patriotism. Demolishing the myth of widespread war enthusiasm raised two questions about existing interpretations of the origins of the war. First, it cast doubt on the significance of militarism and radical nationalism in pushing European states towards war. Once wars broke out, national and military ideals sustained mobilisation, but the evidence of these studies of popular opinion suggested that the bulk of Europeans would have preferred to avoid war in 1914.

Second it placed the myth of the short war within a new context. In the 1990s Stig Förster wrote an important article, arguing that German generals knew that a war against France would likely be a 'war of nations',

[18] Richard Findlay and Kevin O'Rourke, *Power and Plenty: Trade, War, and the World Economy in the Second Millennium* (Princeton, 2007), pp. xxiv–xxv.

16   The Origins of the First World War

not of cabinets, and would certainly last considerably longer than the six weeks foreseen in the Schlieffen plan. The prospect of a long-drawn-out conflict rendered the German decision for war in 1914, according to Förster, 'in the realm of the absurd.'[19] His thesis has not gone unchallenged. More recent accounts accept that German generals recognised the *possibility* of a long war, but considered a short war more probable, not to mention a solution to Germany's geopolitical dilemma.[20] The 'short war' debate has largely concentrated on military planning. The expansion of navies before 1914, within the context of a interdependent global commercial system, also shaped thinking about the next war. Nicholas Lambert's important work on Admiralty planning argued that the British government had developed their own version of a 'short war' myth, designed to cripple the German economy, not by starving the Reich into submission, but by destroying its credit and therefore its capacity to wage war. Nonetheless Lambert's own research as well as other studies of British plans to blockade Germany suggest that contemporaries believed a war would take years, not months, and would end in political, economic, and social upheaval, rather than a decisive battle.[21] Global economic interdependence provided the paradox of creating new ways of fighting wars, while also serving as a restraint on great power conflict due to its immense economic risks.

While the Fischer debate made Germany the magnetic pole of the international system, towards which all other powers orientated their policies, revisionist historians of British foreign policy from the 1980s onwards argued that Russia and empire, rather than Germany and Europe, formed the primary preoccupations of decision-makers in London. Although there are important differences amongst these revisionist historians, they agree that the ententes with France and Russia served British imperial aims, that British policy towards Germany was partly shaped by its concerns about imperial rivalry with Russia in Central Asia, and that European policy was often a function of British global interests.[22] Some

[19] Stig Förster, 'Im Reich des Absurden: die Ursachen des Ersten Weltkrieges', in Bernd Wegner, ed., *Wie Kriege entstehen. Zum historischen Hintergrund von Staatenkonflikten* (Paderborn, 2000), p. 213.
[20] Oliver Stein, *Die deutsche Heeresrüstungspolitik 1890–1914. Das Militär und der Primat der Politik* (Paderborn, 2007), pp. 99–103.
[21] Dirk Bönker, *Militarism in a Global Age: Naval Ambitions in Germany and the United States before World War I* (Ithaca, NY, 2012); Nicholas Lambert, *Planning Armageddon: British Economic Warfare and the First World War* (Cambridge, MA, 2012); Avner Offer, *The First World War: An Agrarian Interpretation* (Oxford, 1989).
[22] Keith Wilson, *The Policy of the Entente: Essays on the Determinants of British Foreign Policy, 1904–1914* (Cambridge, 1985); Keith Neilson, *Britain and the Last Tsar: British Policy and Russia, 1894–1917* (Oxford, 1995); Niall Ferguson, *The Pity of War* (London, 1998); John Charmley, *Splendid Isolation? Britain and the Balance of Power, 1870–1914* (London, 1999).

of these new perspectives owed much to ongoing debates since the 1980s about Britain's place in Europe and the wider world. The revisionist historiography had diverse implications for our understanding of the origins of the war. Anglo-German antagonism no longer appeared fixed nor its outcome in a global war inevitable. It raised questions about the relationship between imperial expansion and the origins of the war. From the vantage point of world politics, the three entente powers – Britain, France, and Russia – appeared as the most expansionist and aggressive powers of the late nineteenth and early twentieth centuries. German aggression within Europe became a response to the blocking of its ill-formed plans for imperial expansion and the sprawling world empires of Britain and Russia.

The sharpest change of perspective resulted from reframing the question about the origins of the First World War. Rather than seeing the war as 'inevitable' or 'probable', historians, primarily Holger Afflerbach, began to ask why a general European war had not broken out earlier, given the anarchic, militarised, expansionist tendencies in the international system. By asking why peace between the great powers was preserved for over four decades – a perspective the first edition of this book adopted and central to the argument of this edition – new insights into the operation of international politics emerged. Take, for example, the issue of alliances. For decades, historians had developed sophisticated arguments to show how the alliances made war likely. Alliances deprived international politics of its flexibility, they transformed bilateral crises into general systemic crises, and they turned from instruments of defensive management into tools of aggressive war. Afflerbach's study of the Triple Alliance, forged between Germany, Austria-Hungary, and Italy in 1882 and lasting until 1914, challenged these arguments. He showed how the alliance facilitated crisis management as members sought to restrain the aggressive instincts of their partners. The alliance created incentives to avoid a war of aggression and partners had considerable flexibility while enjoying a modicum of security. Italy's negotiations with France in the early 1900s and the Anglo-German détente of 1912 and 1913 were just two examples of this flexibility.

More broadly, Afflerbach and others (including this author) claimed that war was improbable. After 1911 tensions in western Europe between France and Britain on the one hand and Germany on the other eased. William II and his civilian advisers consistently rejected war as an instrument of policy, even when the conditions for preventive war favoured Germany. The perceptions of future war were not framed by a dichotomy between a short and long war, but between a decisive and catastrophic war. Contemporaries considered that a war lasting around six months could be catastrophic, which deterred decision-makers from risky policies. Generals, even in the three empires, remained subordinate to civilian decision-makers. Popular opinion throughout Europe was inclined to defensive patriotism and did not push governments into war. Despite the irritations of trade wars, the interdependent European economies served as a structural restraint on war – and in case politicians forgot about this, bankers, merchants, and other businessmen regularly reminded them of the economic benefits of peace.

The advocates of an improbable war thesis have certainly not had it all their own way in recent years, as many historians have produced vibrant new interpretations of a whole series of topics. One of Afflerbach's critics, Volker Ullrich, expressed concerns that these revisionist arguments mark a return to Lloyd George's convenient excuse that Europe 'slithered into war in 1914'. Ullrich asked how the outbreak of war could be explained, if the system was as stable as advocates of the 'improbable war' thesis claim.[23] Broadly speaking, historians have emphasised either structural developments in international politics leading to war or the role of intention and agency – political and military leaders, institutions, states – in bringing about war.[24] Within these broad categories, there is a multitude of approaches, drawing on political, military, cultural, and economic history.

Taking the intentionalist approach first, detailed studies continue to stress Germany's primary responsibility for the outbreak of war, though studies of Austro-Hungarian foreign and military policy underline the significant role Vienna played in the collapse of peace before 1914. The completion of John Röhl's three-volume biography of William II in 2008 marked a formidable addition to this literature. He argued that William II had exercised full control over German foreign policy, launched an aggressive expansionist policy, and, from 1912, had been prepared to risk European war in his attempt to establish German hegemony. William II's military advisers occupy a prominent position in accounts stressing the belligerent intentions of German leaders. Annika Mombauer's biography of the Chief of the German General Staff between 1906 and 1914, Helmuth von Moltke notes that 'the importance and dominance of the military in Imperial Germany is almost proverbial, and their responsibility for bringing about war in 1914 can be clearly demonstrated'.[25] In Mombauer's account, Moltke wielded an important influence in the

---

[23] Volker Ullrich, 'Weltkrieg wider Willen', *Die Zeit*, 2 (2003).

[24] Annika Mombauer, 'The First World War: Inevitable, Avoidable, Improbable, or Desirable? Recent Interpretations on War Guilt and the War's Origins', *German History*, 25, 1 (2007): 78–95, categorises, in part, recent work on this basis.

[25] Annika Mombauer, *Helmuth von Moltke and the Origins of the First World War* (Cambridge, 2001), p. 1.

decision-making processes of the Kaiserreich and he used this influence to push for war before German military strength was eclipsed by Russia. Mark Hewitson rebuts the argument that German leaders were concerned about the prospective deterioration of their position in 1914 in a book that offers a provocative reworking of the argument that Germany adopted a belligerent policy in 1914 because of overwhelming confidence in its own strength.

For decades, the role of Austria-Hungary in the origins of the war had been underplayed in general accounts. The works of Samuel Williamson and Günther Kronenbitter show that the Habsburg empire was not simply a client state of its German ally, but an aggressive actor in its own right. Williamson charted the strengthening of the war party in the second half of 1913 in the Austro-Hungarian leadership, which was able to seize the initiative during the July crisis. Kronenbitter concentrated on the Austro-Hungarian officer corps, arguing that the war resulted from 'the long-term habituation of politicians and public to the use of military threats as a means of diplomacy'.[26]

More critical perspectives on the entente powers have been an important feature of recent debate. The foreign policies of Russia and France have come under increasing scrutiny in recent years. Sean McMeekin offers a challenging account in his study of the Russian origins of the war. He argues that Russian policy before and during the war was driven by expansionist ambitions, directed against the Ottoman Empire. Expansion could only be achieved within the context of a general European war. He identifies an escalation of risk-taking amongst Russian leaders from early 1914, when they developed plans to seize Constantinople and the Straits. The July crisis, according to McMeekin, represented an opportunity for Russia to start a general war and implement these plans. There are some difficulties with this thesis – notably that the Ottoman Empire was not initially a participant in the war and that Russian diplomats considered an alliance with the Young Turk regime in August and September 1914. Moreover the plans developed in early 1914 were not a decision to initiate a war, although the Russian foreign minister Sergei Sazonov favoured a more assertive approach to international politics.[27] Stefan Schmidt's study of French policy during the July crisis places the decision of Raymond Poincaré and others to support Russia within the

[26] Samuel Williamson, *Austria-Hungary and the Origins of the First World War* (Basingstoke, 1991); Günther Kronenbitter, '*Krieg im Frieden': Die Führung der k. u. k. Armee und die Großmachtpolitik Österreichs-Ungarns 1906–1914* (Munich, 2003).

[27] Sean McMeekin, *The Russian Origins of the First World War* (Cambridge, MA, 2012); Mustafa Aksakal, *The Ottoman Road to War in 1914: The Ottoman Empire and the First World War* (Cambridge, 2008).

context of a shifting understanding of the Franco-Russian alliance since 1912. French support for Russia underwrote a more aggressive stance by the alliance in the Balkans, undermined any chance of rapprochement with Germany after the Second Moroccan crisis, and reflected an aggressive turn in French military planning under Joseph Joffre. The increasing willingness to countenance war, rather than an intention to initiate war, characterised policy-making in France and Russia as much as in Germany and Austria-Hungary from 1913.[28]

The broader implications of McMeekin's and Schmidt's work has been a renewed emphasis on systemic factors – if one power or alliance does not bear the overwhelming responsibility for the outbreak of war, then the logical deduction is to examine systemic factors.[29] Systemic approaches concentrate on the interaction between the great powers. The motives behind decisions are less important than their consequences, though one of the criticisms of governments is their failure to take into account the likely consequences of a particular decision or policy. One of the most important transformations in international politics in the late nineteenth century was the shifting relationship between European and world politics. The web of connections between global and European concerns became denser. The search for world power became a central foreign policy ambition for the great powers around the turn of the century. But this was a struggle in which German expansion was blocked, sometimes intentionally, but sometimes not, by Britain, France, and Russia. While the leaders of these powers saw Germany as an aggressive power, German leaders considered imperial expansion a legitimate interest, a necessary pre-condition for the maintenance of their great power status. The result of this tension was that the Triple Entente, formed by the three world powers, ended up encircling Germany, thwarting its expansion, and forcing it to conduct an increasingly desperate and reckless foreign policy. The international system in the early twentieth century faced two fundamentally incompatible choices – either Germany could advance to world power status, overthrowing the balance of power in Europe in the process; or the Triple Entente could block German expansion, but this was likely to provoke a war, as German leaders sought to escape the confines of Europe. Peace was fragile and the détentes and moments of cooperation only served to postpone war.[30]

[28] Stefan Schmidt, *Frankreichs Aussenpolitik in der Julikrise. Ein Beitrag zur Geschichte des Ausbruches des Ersten Weltkrieges* (Munich, 2009).

[29] Jack S. Levy and John A. Vasquez, eds, *The Outbreak of the First World War: Structure, Politics and Decision-Making* (Cambridge, 2014).

[30] Sonke Neitzel, *Weltmacht oder Untergang. Weltreichslehre im Zeitalter des Imperialismus* (Paderborn, 2000).

The dissolution of the Ottoman Empire, resulting from the predations of the European great powers and the ambitions of Balkan nations, marked the point where imperial and European politics intersected. From the British occupation of Egypt in 1882 to the Italian invasion of Libya in 1911, the great powers chipped away at the Ottoman Empire. While the great powers tried to manage its decline in Europe, the rise of Balkan nation-states, particularly in two Balkan Wars of 1912 and 1913, transformed European politics. In particular Austro-Hungarian leaders perceived the growth of Serbian power in these wars as an existential challenge to its vital interests.[31]

David Stevenson and David Herrmann have identified the arms race as a systemic threat to peace in the years before the First World War. They pay considerable attention to the domestic political impulses, the financial debates, and the technological aspects of the arms races between the European powers, but they stress the ways in which armaments increase in one great power, often for defensive purposes, provoked an increase in the size of the army and navy in another great power. The arms race, prompted initially by diplomatic and geopolitical factors, developed a dynamic of its own, which made European governments more willing to risk war in 1914. While the naval race between Britain and Germany had ended with clear British superiority by 1912, Dirk Bönker's comparison of naval elites and politics in the USA and Germany shows how 'navalism' contributed to escalating political and social tensions in the early twentieth century.

The challenges in the international system also reflected changes in how politics was conducted. Jan Rüger's and Dominik Geppert's examinations of public opinion in foreign policy move beyond previous accounts of the influence of popular nationalism on foreign policy, by showing how publics in two different countries (Britain and Germany in both cases) interacted. The results included press wars, mutual suspicion, and increasing pressures on the conduct of diplomacy. Both conclude that the expansion of the public sphere from the late nineteenth century was never adequately accommodated by the international system and the expert regulators of that system, the diplomats. Verena Steller's study, drawing on cultural history approaches, of Franco-German relations echoes these findings about the embattled position of diplomats. Crises were more difficult to control and expectations of war were more

---

[31] Dominik Geppert, William Mulligan, and, Andreas Rose, eds, *The Wars before the Great War: Conflict and International Politics before the Outbreak of the First World War* (Cambridge, 2015).

prevalent because the interaction between the different publics generated its own set of tensions.

One of the implications of recent studies – from both the advocates of an improbable war and those who argue that successive crises and changes in international politics created the conditions for, but did not pre-determine, the war – is a renewed emphasis on the July crisis. Christopher Clark's *The Sleepwalkers* and Thomas Otte's *The July Crisis* represent this emphasis on the July crisis and offer the most comprehensive accounts of the outbreak of the war in recent years. The text of both books comes in at well over five hundred pages each. At one level the two accounts differ sharply in their individual judgements of key moments and individuals. Otte is critical of the 'recklessness' of statesmen in Vienna, Berlin, and, to a lesser extent, St Petersburg. Leopold von Berchtold, the Habsburg Foreign Minister, and his fellow diplomats at the Ballhausplatz, Otte argues, suffered from 'tunnelvision', which reduced Austro-Hungarian foreign policy to *Balkanpolitik*. Otte frequently describes Berlin's crisis diplomacy as 'reckless', while the Chancellor, Theobald von Bethmann Hollweg, appears as 'marginal' in many key decisions. On the other hand, Sir Edward Grey, the foreign secretary, is a man of action, perspicacious, and committed to peace.[32] Clark offers different interpretations. Poincaré dissembled during the final days of peace. Grey, he argues, consistently prioritised the maintenance of the Triple Entente over the peaceful resolution of the crisis, which meant that his string of conference proposals in late July were half-baked, while he also completely failed to restrain Russian escalatory moves. The Russian decisions for partial and then full mobilization fuelled the crisis, while 'the Germans had remained, in military terms, an island of relative calm throughout the crisis.'[33]

Although these differences of interpretation relate to some of the most fundamental debates about the specific denouement of the July crisis and suggest a wide gulf between Clark and Otte, their overarching interpretations have much in common. First, they both emphasise the contingent character of the July crisis, how the cumulation of individual decisions led to outcomes often at odds with the intentions of the authors of those decisions. Both books, to use Clark's phrase, are 'saturated with agency.' Secondly, and perhaps paradoxically given the stress on individual decisions, they tend to view the crisis in systemic terms. While Otte warns historians against judging decisions against the norms of a given

[32] T. G. Otte, *The July Crisis: The World's Descent into War, 1914* (Cambridge, 2014), pp. 43, 169.
[33] Clark, *Sleepwalkers*, pp. 445–49, 493–506, 510.

international order – the great power order of the early twentieth century – his own careful analysis of how considerations of alliance, détente,
and relative military power shaped assumptions and led to disastrous
miscalculation is an instructive model of how to place individual decisions within a systemic context. Third, both express doubts about thinking about the July crisis in terms of national 'policies'. In Clark's view,
policy implies a coherence, which was impossible to achieve in the polycratic regimes and porous transnational connections of the era, while
Otte repeatedly notes the divisions between military and civilian leaders,
even within individual foreign ministries, that hampered the articulation
of clear strategies. Perhaps most fundamentally both agree that no single
belligerent or individual should shoulder the bulk of the responsibility for
the outbreak of war. Their differences are ones of emphasis and detail.

   This book is based, in large part, on these recent contributions to the
debate on the origins of the First World War. It is divided into four large
thematic chapters and one chapter on the July crisis. Chapter 2 assesses
the development of geopolitical competition amongst the great powers
between 1871 and 1914, giving more detailed attention to the period after
1900. It places particular emphasis on the development of the alliance
system, the impact of imperial rivalries, and the opportunities for cooperation as well as the moments of conflict between the great powers.
Geopolitical concerns shaped military plans, public opinion about international politics, and, to a lesser extent, the relationship between great
power rivalry and the international economy, which form the themes in
the subsequent chapters. Chapter 3 examines the role of the military in
international politics, considering the significance of the war plans, the
influence of the military on decision-making, the visions of the next war,
and the causes and consequences of the arms races. Chapter 4 looks at
the growing importance of public opinion in global politics, the efforts of
governments to control and manipulate public opinion, and its influence
on the atmosphere and conduct of foreign policy. Chapter 5 deals with
the relationship between economic issues and the international system.
It assesses the importance of economic power in great power politics,
trade relations, and financial relations. Chapter 6 examines the July crisis, asking why and how this crisis ended in a great power conflict when
so many previous crises had been resolved. Chapter 7 draws together
the main arguments and suggests that the history of the international
relations before 1914 can be read not just as a prelude to the First World
War, but as part of a longer history of the international system, reaching
back to the eighteenth century and continuing to the present.

   One of the central contentions of the book is that the history of international relations, even of great power politics before 1914, cannot be

reduced to a history of the origins of the First World War. If one starts at 1914 and asks what the origins of the war were, there are many answers. But this frames the history of international relations before 1914 in a teleology that robs the period of its contingency. Of course, there is a risk that contingency, if pursued to a radical conclusion, simply dashes historical narratives into tiny shards, making it impossible to understand the history of international relations in this period. This is why it is worth bearing in mind a longer chronological frame. From the eighteenth century to the present, the declining frequency of great power wars has been the most striking development in the history of international relations. As Paul Schroeder has suggested, this development requires an explanation, which cannot be provided if historians concentrate on the causes of war. So this book pays considerable attention to the factors that preserved peace for over forty years. Of course, one could argue that this is as equally teleological as accounts that take the war as the logical culmination of international relations in the early twentieth century. To try to answer why war broke out, the book suggests that the long peace since 1871 became increasingly frayed from 1911, as the Second Moroccan crisis triggered a series of wars in the Mediterranean and Balkans, which in turn prompted further crises, arms races, and press wars. By January 1914, a general war was a possibility, though not a probability. The book also leans more towards systemic explanations for the outbreak of war, rather than the intentionalist accounts. However, it argues that a series of decisions, favouring a more assertive approach to foreign policy, made from late 1912 in Vienna, St Petersburg, and Berlin set the course for the July crisis and the consequent war.

2   Security and Expansion: The Great Powers and Geopolitics, 1871–1914

Between 1871 and 1914, there were no wars between the acknowledged great powers. At first, this seems like an outrageous run of good fortune. After all, the international system had emerged from a series of wars in the 1850s and 1860s, there had been no general peace conference at which the great powers acknowledged the legitimacy of the system, the great powers embarked on aggressive expansionist policies by the early 1880s, and there were regular crises throughout the period. Yet peace was maintained for more than four decades, the longest period of peace between the great powers until the end of the Cold War. The maintenance of peace owed much to the development of the alliance system, the relative flexibility of great power alignments, the expansion of the great powers around the globe, and their willingness to expand at the expense of weaker states, including the 'dying nations', as the British prime minister, Lord Salisbury, called them, the Ottoman, Chinese, and Persian empires, rather than each other. Tensions were leavened by long-standing practices and norms in European politics, including great power congresses and compensation.

The disintegration of the Ottoman and Chinese empires, however, exacerbated great power tensions. Both were managed, just about, without war between the great powers, although Russia and Japan, the latter not being considered a great power, fought in the Far East in 1904–5. The disintegration of Ottoman power, partly the outcome of great power policies, partly due to the internal problems facing the empire, accelerated from 1908, and especially from 1911 onwards. Moreover, in 1912 and 1913, the great powers lost control over the collapse of the Ottoman Empire in Europe, as smaller Balkan states – Bulgaria, Greece, Montenegro, Romania, and Serbia – carved out their own foreign policy agendas. These wars also upset the already fragile norms that had underpinned great power since 1871. Austria-Hungary was the great power most affected by these developments, and by 1913, the stability of the international system rested on whether its perceived decline could be arrested or managed without a war.

25

The Development of the Alliance System, 1871–1894

Between 1854 and 1871, all the great powers had fought in a series of wars, which destroyed the remnants of the 1815 Vienna Settlement. The wars of Italian and German unification had forged two nation-states, which took their place alongside the other great powers, Britain, Russia, Austria, and France. Coupled with American reunification after the victory of the Union in the Civil War and the development of Japan after the Meiji Restoration in 1868 in the Far East, this period saw the emergence of the powers that were to dominate European and global politics until 1914, indeed, with the exception of Austria, until the Second World War. At the Congress of Vienna at the end of the Napoleonic Wars, diplomats had constructed the basis of the international system, which maintained peace in Europe until the 1850s. No such gathering took place after the Franco-Prussian War. Instead, the newly united German Reich imposed a peace settlement on the new French Third Republic. The ambassadorial conference, which met in London to revise the 1856 Treaty of Paris stipulations on the Black Sea – stipulations which particularly affected Russia, Turkey, and Britain – had a limited agenda, though the establishment of the principle that international agreements could not be changed without the consent of signatories had important implications in defining the scope of restraints on power politics. The new international system, its norms and structures, developed in an ad hoc fashion. From the perspective of the origins of the war, the period between 1871 and 1894 was significant for the creation of the core alliances which fought in 1914: Germany and Austria-Hungary on one hand, Russia and France on the other. The expansion of European powers in Central Asia and Africa in this period also showed the potential for imperial politics both to alleviate and to aggravate great power rivalries.

Was the new international system that emerged after 1871 inherently unstable? Did the expansion of great power rivalries in the imperial sphere alleviate tensions or intensify competition, which then rebounded on Europe to disastrous effect in the First World War? Had Bismarck run out of ideas by 1887, or did his resignation and the new course of German policy in the 1890s create instability? Was the alliance system, which emerged between the late 1870s and early 1890s, a force for stability, or did it mark the division of Europe into rigidly opposed armed camps? Historians have offered radically different answers to these questions. For some historians, Bismarck was an honest broker. His conception of the alliance system was defensive, corrupted by a subsequent generation which viewed international politics in the narrow terms of national security rather than in terms of the maintenance of peace. Others have suggested that by the late 1880s, Bismarck's policies creaked under the weight of their own contradictions, both at home and abroad. The maintenance of peace and stability in the 1870s and 1880s was temporary, an artifice, which only delayed the unrestrained rivalries before the First World War. A third group sees Bismarck as the practitioner par excellence of *Realpolitik*. This approach to international politics only served to sharpen tensions. His secret diplomacy and his willingness to foster and exploit rivalries between the other great powers ultimately sowed the seeds of the origins of the war. Historians' attention to Bismarck has also made 1890, the year of his resignation, into something of a potential turning point in European and world history.

Doubtless Bismarck would have considered the attention lavished upon him by historians as an appropriate tribute to his importance. Yet, although he was a towering figure, he was also aware that he conducted politics within a framework that was not of his own making. He recognised the limits of German power, the challenge of reconciling the international system to the new Reich, and the dangers of further expansion. The difficulties of concluding the war against France in 1870–71 led Bismarck to reject war as an instrument of policy. Moreover, the unification of Germany meant that Bismarck now favoured the preservation of the status quo. In terms of international politics, the radical of the 1860s had become a conservative. In 1875, the War in Sight crisis confirmed Bismarck's analysis that Germany had to work to preserve the peace in Europe. In early 1875, the publication of articles in the German press, threatening a preventive war against France, caused alarm in Paris and irritation in London and St Petersburg. Britain and Russia put aside their differences to make clear to Bismarck that they would not stand aside in any future conflict between Germany and France. The War in Sight crisis brought to an end the era of great power conflict, which had begun with the Crimean War in 1854. Britain and Russia effectively declared their recognition of the territorial status quo in western Europe, French security was enhanced, and Bismarck, who had not wanted war, accepted the outcome of the crisis.

Between 1871 and 1875, the international system had stabilised, particularly in western and central Europe. Austria had accepted the verdict of the wars of Italian and German unification, which had expelled the Habsburgs from Italy and Germany. The newcomers, Italy and Germany, were busy consolidating power. The two wing powers in Europe, Russia and Britain, regarded the new Reich with a certain amount of equanimity. After all, they were global powers, and while European affairs were a central preoccupation, they had a range of other interests. 'As powerful as the new German Reich is', commented the Russian paper *Russki Mir*, 'without the permission of Russia, neither it nor another state will make use of its power; in all the important questions, the last word remains with the Russian Tsar.'[1] The only power with a revisionist agenda was France, but most French leaders recognised that regaining Alsace and Lorraine was such a distant project that it did not shape the day-to-day preoccupations of diplomats and politicians. Occupied by German troops until 1873, isolated, and weak, France did not pose a threat to the stability of the international system. Otherwise none of the great powers had a claim on the territory of another great power. While there were potential flashpoints – in the Balkans, Central Asia, and North Africa – the great powers were competing for influence and territory in weaker states, not for each other's land. This marked a significant change in the stakes of international politics, and the absence of territorial confrontation contributed to the maintenance of peace and stability after 1871.

Despite Germany's apparent military advantages over the rest of her continental rivals, Bismarck was haunted by a sense of insecurity. This was partly related to his background. Prussia had been the least of the five great powers in the first half of the nineteenth century, overshadowed by the Tsarist colossus in the east, hemmed in by Austria in Germany, and periodically threatened by France in the Rhineland. Bismarck claimed that he suffered from 'the cauchemar des coalitions' – a nightmare that the three other continental powers would combine against the new Reich, a re-creation of the Kaunitz coalition of the mid-eighteenth century, when Frederick II, king of Prussia, only just succeeded in staving off the partition of his kingdom. To secure the Reich, Bismarck resorted to two devices – the building of alliances and the diversion of great power rivalries to the peripheries (from Germany's perspective) in the Balkans, North Africa, and Central Asia. The rivalries of great powers elsewhere ensured that they would not coalesce against Germany. The vagaries of alliance politics and imperial expansion were to dominate the international system until 1914.

Alliances were instruments of policy. They served the security of the Reich and the preservation of peace in Europe, two virtually indistinguishable goals in Bismarck's mind. Alliances never became an end in themselves in Bismarck's foreign policy. The first foray into alliance building was a loose arrangement, the League of the Three Emperors, a series of agreements between Franz Joseph, William I, and Alexander II concluded in 1873, emperors of Austria-Hungary, Germany, and Russia, respectively. It included a vague commitment to monarchical solidarity

---

[1] Cited in Klaus Hildebrand, *Das vergangene Reich. Deutsche Außenpolitik 1871–1945* (Stuttgart, 1995), p. 25.

and the preservation of peace in Europe. More importantly, it isolated France, eased Austro-Russian tensions in the Balkans, and enabled Russia to concentrate on expansion in Central Asia. Nonetheless, Russian policy during the War in Sight crisis made it clear that the League was not designed to cover further German aggression in Europe.

The League collapsed, however, during the Eastern crisis, which began with a revolt against Ottoman rule in the Balkans and escalated into a crisis about the future of the Ottoman Empire in Europe. This created tensions between Russia, Austria-Hungary, and Britain, each of which had ambitions and interests in the region. While the Ottoman Empire was peripheral in Bismarck's conception of the international system, its future was of immense importance to other European powers. Eastern crises, a regular feature of nineteenth-century European politics, always had the potential to cause a great power war. The decline of the Ottoman Empire, therefore, required careful diplomatic management if war was to be avoided. The diplomacy of the Eastern crisis was complex, with myriad options open to the different protagonists. In 1876 and 1877, Austria-Hungary was prepared to cooperate with Russia, leaving Disraeli's government isolated. In April 1877, Russia declared war on Turkey. By early 1878, Britain and Russia were on the brink of war, after Russia's advance took them past the stronghold of Plevna towards Constantinople. In the treaty of San Stefano, Russia imposed a peace settlement, which created a large Bulgarian state, effectively a satellite of Russia. Austria-Hungary, nervous about Russian ambitions in the Balkans, joined Britain's opposition to the treaty of San Stefano. The League of the Three Emperors had collapsed, and Bismarck stepped in, claiming to act as an honest broker. In summer 1878, the leaders of the great powers gathered in Berlin. Russia's gains at San Stefano were rolled back, while Austria-Hungary occupied Bosnia and Britain occupied Cyprus.

The Eastern crisis, pitting Russia and Britain against each other, but without ending in a general great power war, exemplified the diversion of great power rivalry to the periphery, which Bismarck sought to exploit. In the Kissingen Diktat of June 1877, he expressed a hope that if Russia could dominate the Black Sea and Britain take control of Egypt, then the two world powers would 'be in a position to content themselves with the preservation of the status quo for a long time to come and would nevertheless, as far as their wider interests are concerned, be plunged once more into a rivalry that makes them virtually incapable of participating in coalitions against us, quite apart from Britain's internal difficulties in that regard'.[2] In addition to Anglo-Russian rivalry, Bismarck also counted on

---

[2] Lothar Gall, *Bismarck: The White Revolutionary, 1871–1898* (London, 1986), 2:51–52.

Anglo-French rivalry in North Africa. He had described a system of balanced antagonisms, none of which was sufficiently serious to lead to war. It is important to note that he did not create these tensions but exploited and encouraged them. He was acting within a larger framework, in which the global interests of the great powers had begun to interact with the constellation of the powers within Europe (Map 1).

However, this approach carried risks for Bismarck and his desire to secure peace in Europe. The Russian Chancellor, Gorchakov, did not consider Bismarck an honest broker, instead blaming the German Chancellor for the setbacks Russia encountered during the Congress of Berlin. In addition to these political differences, trade disputes damaged Russo-German relations so that by late 1878, German leaders took seriously the prospect of a war against Russia. On 15 August 1879, Alexander II sent the famous 'clip around the ear' (*Ohrfeigenbrief*) letter to William I, in which he claimed Bismarck's foreign policy was motivated by his hatred of Russia and reminded the Kaiser that German unification took place with the blessing of the Tsarist regime. It was in this context of rising tensions between the two states that Bismarck chose to press for an alliance with Austria-Hungary. He hurried to Vienna in late September, but the treaty bore the imprint of Julius Andrassy, the Austro-Hungarian foreign minister. Whereas Bismarck wished for a permanent and general alliance, Andrassy had more limited aims. He had no interest in getting dragged into a Franco-German war. It was a defensive alliance to be renewed at regular intervals. The alliance would only apply if Russia attacked either Germany or Austria-Hungary.

The alliance with Austria-Hungary was to evolve into one of the cornerstones of international politics before the First World War. Yet in 1879, Andrassy and Bismarck considered it in more prosaic terms. Bismarck successfully used the treaty to bring Russia back into the fold, by reminding Gorchakov that Germany was not dependent on her eastern neighbour. In June 1881, Russia, Austria-Hungary, and Germany concluded a neutrality and consultation pact, which was renewed in 1884. The terms of the 1879 alliance between Austria-Hungary and Germany were clearly defensive and limited. Andrassy would only promise benevolent neutrality in the case of a Franco-German war. The alliance offered security to both parties, it encouraged restraint, and it maintained the balance of power in Europe. Bismarck widened his alliance system in May 1882, when Italy joined Austria-Hungary and Germany to form the Triple Alliance. Again, this was a largely defensive alliance; it meant that Austria-Hungary effectively recognised Italy's borders, and it further isolated France. French isolation was compounded in 1882 when Britain occupied Egypt, an area where France had traditionally exercised

Map 1. The Balkans in 1878. After Gildea, *Barricades and Borders*, 239.

considerable influence. This caused a division between the two liberal powers, which endured until the early twentieth century. Alliances, therefore, emerged as a defensive instrument, in which allies offered their partners a modicum of security but restrained them from taking offensive action. Alliances were also used to manage conflicts of interest between powers – between Austria-Hungary and Italy and between Austria-Hungary and Russia in the Balkans. The origins of the alliance system were cast in an atmosphere of defence and restraint, with a view to preserving peace.

European imperial expansion, which accelerated in the first half of the 1880s, caused some tensions, but it never seemed likely to spill over into a general war. As Bismarck had anticipated in the Kissingen Diktat, colonial interests were sufficiently important to fuel rivalries but were not considered sufficiently vital to fight over. The French occupation of Tunis in 1881, the British occupation of Egypt the following year, and the accelerated expansion of European powers into Africa in the mid-1880s triggered a series of crises, but ones which the great powers found relatively easy to contain. In 1884–85, the European powers met at Berlin for a conference, which regulated the division of Africa, partitioning the continent into spheres and setting out rules for governance. Great power expansion in Africa diverted tensions away from Europe, although this came at a heavy price for African states and societies. There was even a brief moment of Franco-German cooperation in the mid-1880s. French leaders, like Léon Gambetta and Jules Ferry, saw colonial expansion as marking the recovery of national prestige and a necessity in a world dominated by expanding great powers. In Britain, Gladstone's government between 1880 and 1885 was a reluctant, yet active, imperialist, while Bismarck's brief foray into colonial expansion ended in 1885. The diversion of conflict to the periphery and the creative use of alliances within Europe seemed to offer the combination of flexibility and stability, which preserved peace between the great powers.

A series of crises, starting in 1885, unravelled Bismarck's alliance system, divided Europe into two blocs, and showed the potential for peripheral conflict to escalate towards war. International politics between 1885 and 1887 was beset by multiple, related crises, which historians consider brought Europe closer to a general war than at any other time between 1871 and 1914. The influential journalist Konstantin Rößler commented that peace was 'on the knife's edge' in early 1887.[3] There

---

[3] Jost Dülffer, Martin Kröger, and Rolf-Harald Wippich, *Vermiedene Kriege. Deeskalation von Konflikten der Grossmächte zwischen Krimkrieg und Ersem Weltkrieg* (Munich, 1997), pp. 369, 391.

were five areas of tension. First, France and Italy had a serious trade war, which added to the tensions between the two states over colonial expansion in North Africa. Second, Britain and France remained at loggerheads over Egypt. Third, the brief flurry of revanchist sentiment in France in 1886 and 1887, with the emergence of General Boulanger, led to calls for a preventive war amongst German military and political leaders. Fourth, in Central Asia, Russian expansion seemed to threaten Indian security, causing a severe crisis with Britain. Finally, and most seriously, a crisis erupted in the Balkans when Prince Alexander of Bulgaria tried to unite Eastern Rumelia (returned to Ottoman rule in the treaty of Berlin) with the rest of Bulgaria and declared independence in September 1885. In the Balkans, Russia sought to regain influence but faced Austro-Hungarian and British opposition. Broadly speaking, the crises pitted Britain, Germany, Austria-Hungary, and Italy on one side and France and Russia on the other.

Politicians regularly hinted at war and generals actively called for war. The Austro-Hungarian foreign minister Kalnóky spoke against peace at any price in November 1886. After his appointment as Italian prime minister in August 1887, Francesco Crispi leaked war scares to the press. In Berlin, leading generals called for a preventive war against Russia. Yet, despite the pressures for war, governments managed to find a means of de-escalating the tensions and ending, if not fully resolving, the crises.

How and why was peace – with the exception of a brief clash between Serbia and Bulgaria – preserved? First, while there were numerous calls for war and threats of mobilisation, there were also strong figures who wanted to preserve the peace. General Giovanni Goiron, Crispi's military envoy to Berlin and Vienna, noted that 'around Count Kalnóky there exists a kind of sentimental and philanthropic love of peace'.[4] Kalnóky's forthright speech in November 1886 had been a form of sabre-rattling, a warning, rather than a declaration of intent. Bismarck was not averse to creating the odd shiver here and there amongst French politicians, as he warned of war, but his real aim was to frighten the French government into jettisoning General Boulanger, which they did, and to boost support for extra military spending at home. Second, the most powerful great powers worked to restrain the others. By January 1888, Crispi had concluded a military convention with Bismarck, but Bismarck and Lord Salisbury, prime minister and foreign secretary since 1886, ensured that it was not a prelude to an Italian war against France. In 1887, Salisbury concluded two Mediterranean agreements with Italy and

---

[4] Cited in Christopher Duggan, *Francesco Crispi: From Nation to Nationalism* (Oxford, 2002), p. 530.

Austria-Hungary, both of which aimed at the preservation of the status quo, not its revision. Bismarck also made it clear to Kalnóky that the Dual Alliance was a defensive agreement. He refused to support Austro-Hungarian ambitions in the Balkans, partly because he realised that Britain would back Austria-Hungary and therefore Germany did not need to place itself in opposition to Russia, and partly because he believed that Russian interests in the eastern Balkans were legitimate. Finally, the issues at stake were too diffuse for the powers to come together in two opposing blocs, at least in the short term. The preservation of alliances had not yet become an end in itself, a pillar of the national interest. Alliances remained an instrument, not an objective, of international politics. And the objective in most capitals remained peace.

One of the consequences of the Bulgarian crisis was the final collapse of the alliance between Russia, Germany, and Austria-Hungary. It was no longer possible to manage the antagonism between the Romanov and Habsburg empires within the framework of a single alliance. Russian leaders began to question the value of German support. In fact, Russian interests were blocked by Britain and Austria-Hungary, not by Germany. However, the lack of more active German support for Russian objectives in the Balkans and the Ottoman Empire grated in St Petersburg. Tensions in the Russo-German relationship increased with trade disputes, the blocking of Russian loans on the Berlin money market, and the persistent criticism of German policies by pan-Slavist opinion. It was in this context that a possible Franco-Russian alliance was first raised, though it remained a vague prospect. Giers, the Russian foreign minister, was irritated at French 'swindlers' who 'mistake every itinerant Russian for a confidential agent of the Emperor and erect a mountain of hopes and dreams on every phrase he utters'.[5] Instead, in June 1887, Russia and Germany concluded the Reinsurance Treaty.

The treaty reflected the restraint with which Bismarck conducted foreign policy. In January 1887, he rejected a proposal aired by the Russian diplomat Schuvalov for a bilateral pact, guaranteeing Russian neutrality in the case of a Franco-German war and German neutrality in the case of an Austro-Russian war. Instead, Bismarck warned Austria-Hungary, in a speech to the Reichstag, not to go to war over Bulgaria, while in December, he made clear his opposition to a preventive war against Russia, following a request from Beck, chief of the Austro-Hungarian General Staff. In June 1887, he revealed the terms of the Dual Alliance to Schuvalov, indicating that Germany would not stand by if Russia launched a

---

[5] Cited in George Kennan, *The Decline of Bismarck's European Order: Franco-Russian Relations, 1875–1890* (Princeton, 1979), p. 244.

war of aggression against Austria-Hungary. Bismarck used the alliance to restrain both Austria-Hungary and Russia from aggressive measures. On 18 June 1887, the Reinsurance Treaty was signed. The treaty stipulated that Russia and Germany would adopt a stance of benevolent neutrality if the other power were attacked, but if either party launched an aggressive war – Germany against France or Russia against Austria-Hungary – then the terms of the treaty would not apply. Germany also recognised Russian interests in Bulgaria, Eastern Rumelia, and the Black Sea. This served to divert Russia's interests to the south, not west into Austria-Hungary's sphere of influence in the western Balkans.

Historians have criticised Bismarck's foreign policy in his final years as Chancellor on a number of counts. First, the tangle of treaties and alliances were contradictory. While Bismarck maintained that the Reinsurance Treaty would not apply in the case of a Russian attack on Austria-Hungary, ascertaining who was the aggressor and who was the defender in a war was extremely difficult, as the events of 1870 had demonstrated. His encouragement of Russian expansion in the eastern Balkans and Ottoman Empire was at odds with the Mediterranean agreement between Britain, Italy, and Austria-Hungary, with which Germany was closely associated, for the maintenance of the status quo in the area. Second, the increasingly contorted treaty obligations were a reflection of the inflexibility of and tensions within the system. Conflicts in the periphery had sharpened the divisions between the great powers, which, in turn, threatened peace in Europe. It must, however, be taken into account that Bismarck's aim was to prevent the outbreak of war. He recognised that all bets were off once a great power war broke out. While statesmen considered the ambiguities of what constituted aggressive and defensive war, these ambiguities served as a restraint against a would-be aggressor – no government wanted to risk being cast in this role. According to his son, Herbert, the value of the Reinsurance Treaty in a war that France might start against Germany was not that it would ensure Russian neutrality but that it would delay Russian entry into the conflict. Taking the preservation of peace as his objective, Bismarck was successful, even if he had to thank others for their restraint. Moreover, the idea that the international system could achieve a form of permanent stability, based on a coherent treaty system, set the bar of achievement too high. Statesmen were concerned with resolving the problem at hand and perhaps setting an agenda for the foreseeable future. The unexpected event could upset calculations, but it could also offer fresh room for manoeuvre.

In March 1890, Bismarck resigned as Chancellor. This was not unexpected. Even had he not fallen out with William II, Kaiser since June 1888, age would have forced him out of office within a few years.

Historians have identified Bismarck's resignation as a significant turning point in European as well as German history, the moment the international system lost its manager and began to turn towards a more confrontational conception of alliances and a more unrestrained conduct of imperial expansion. In summer 1890, the Reinsurance Treaty was due for renewal. Moreover, Giers wanted to renew it – an indication that it remained a feasible option for regulating international politics. The new German Chancellor, Leo von Caprivi, and leading figures in the German Foreign Office, such as Friedrich von Holstein, opposed renewal. They considered Bismarck's system overly complex and duplicitous, liable to expose Germany to charges of double-dealing. They favoured a more logical alignment of German foreign policy and of the international system. The crises of 1885–87 had brought Britain closer to the Triple Alliance. Holstein favoured developing this relationship with Britain, leaving open the possibility of a Franco-Russian alliance. This would divide Europe into two blocs but offer Germany greater security.

Whereas Bismarck had sought security by preserving peace, the new generation of German leaders identified security more closely with the alliance system. This made the alliance with Austria-Hungary a much more important aspect of German policy. The Dual Alliance was no longer simply an instrument of policy – its maintenance had also become an objective of policy. This transformed Austro-Hungarian security and interests into a German concern. Security was also conceived in more narrowly military terms rather than in terms of diplomatic agreements and the stability of the international system. German military expenditure doubled between 1886 and 1893. Bismarck's army bill of 1887 was responsible for some of this, but Caprivi's 1893 bill was the largest expansion to date. Caprivi argued that war was inevitable in the long term and that therefore Germany had to prepare for it, by consolidating the alliance with Austria-Hungary and increasing military strength.

The failure to renew the Reinsurance Treaty opened the space for a Franco-Russian alliance. In the late 1880s, when the possibility was first mooted, opponents of an alliance in both countries offered cogent objections. The two countries had very different domestic political systems: France might drag Russia into a war against Germany, Russia might drag France into a war against Britain, France supported the status quo in the Ottoman Empire, Russia wished to overturn it, and neither side could offer effective military security to the other. There were strong counter-arguments in favour of an alliance. Since 1887, French loans to Russia meant an increasing economic interdependence. Britain was a common global rival, while Germany's abrupt termination of the Reinsurance Treaty and increase in military power posed a threat to Russia as well as to France. Finally, both states were isolated, without partners or allies of any kind.

The first steps towards an alliance took place in August 1890 at military manoeuvres, when General Raoul de Mouton de Boisdeffre discussed the benefits of mutual military assistance with General N. N. Obruchev, chief of the Russian General Staff. The two soldiers, acquaintances for a decade, played a central role in the formation of the alliance. By 1891, political leaders, including Giers; Alexandre Ribot, the French foreign minister; and Charles de Freycinet, the French premier, were discussing the political benefits of the alliance. The renewal of the Triple Alliance in May 1891, amidst rumours that Britain had joined, gave an impetus to Franco-Russian discussions. In August 1891, the two governments exchanged letters, agreeing to consult each other during international crises. French leaders pushed for a military convention. Because France's major potential enemy was Germany, and Russia's were Austria-Hungary and Britain, this proved more difficult. However, neither side believed that a future great power could be localised, as had happened in the 1850s and 1860s. Therefore, both governments agreed to a military convention in August 1892, which guaranteed mutual mobilisation. The visit of the Russian fleet to Toulon in October 1893 was a public staging of the new Franco-Russian alliance, which came into formal existence in January 1894.

The role of the military in forging this alliance suggests that it represented a further militarisation of European politics, in parallel with the changing nature of the Triple Alliance. However, political leaders in France and Russia considered the alliance to be a force for peace and stability, a reconstitution of the balance of power in Europe. 'The common action of the two allied powers', Ribot told a meeting at Bordeaux in May 1895, 'in whatever part of the globe it is exercised, is a guarantee of peace and the security of the nation.'[6] Giers, in 1891, before the conclusion of the alliance, noted that the 'entente cordiale' between Russia and France formed a 'certain counterweight to the influence of the Triplice ... At a time when the Triple Alliance is ruining itself in military preparations, the agreement between Russia and France, meaning as it does the gradual and natural development of their power and prosperity, genuinely guarantees the preservation of peace.'[7] In fact, the value of the alliance was limited in the 1890s. It enabled both France and Russia to devote more attention to imperial expansion in Africa and Asia,

[6] Pierre Guillen, *L'expansion, 1881–1898* (Paris, 1984), p. 269.
[7] George Kennan, *The Fateful Alliance: France, Russia, and the Coming of the First World War* (Manchester, 1984), p. 57.

while maintaining some security in Europe. Financial links between the two countries developed rapidly, as French bankers lent to fund Russian industrialisation and railway building projects.

The position of Britain, upon which Holstein and other German officials had placed so much of their calculations in 1890 and which acted as a spur to the conclusion of the Franco-Russian alliance, was transformed in the early 1890s. Salisbury had never intended an agreement with Germany over Heligoland and Zanzibar to be anything more than the resolution of a specific problem. Holstein misread the 1890 agreement as the prelude to a firmer commitment by Britain to the Triple Alliance. In fact, the change of Germany's policy towards Austria-Hungary began to ease Britain's position. Whereas Bismarck had relied on Britain and Austria-Hungary to support the status quo in the Balkans and Ottoman Empire, and thereby avoided antagonising Russia, Salisbury recognised that the greater commitment by Germany to the Dual Alliance meant Germany would begin to take on Britain's role in that part of the world. This, in turn, would drive a further wedge between the two most powerful states on the continent, Russia and Germany, easing Britain's position in Europe and elsewhere around the globe. Moreover, by remaining outside the alliance system, Britain became a potentially more valuable partner, could charge more for its support, and could avoid being dragged into unnecessary quarrels.

The formation of two alliance blocs had both modified and reflected a change in the assumptions of statesmen about security and the constellation of the great powers. In 1888, Paul Leroy-Beaulieu, the French economist, had made the counter-intuitive argument that a Franco-Russian alliance would not serve French interests, because Russia wished to destroy Austria-Hungary. Teasing out this argument, he suggested that Austria-Hungary was a vital element of the European balance of power and a counter-weight against her partner in the Dual Alliance, Germany. On this reading, French security was served by the preservation of a great power, Austria-Hungary, which was allied to Germany, the greatest threat to French security. Equally, in 1875, during the War in Sight crisis, Alexander II deemed the preservation of France's great power status a concern so great that he was willing to warn Germany, allied to Russia, against a preventive war. In the 1870s and 1880s, security was partly achieved through military power and alliances, but also through the common desire to preserve the international system and the great powers, which were the pillars of the system. The French economist and the Russian Emperor articulated what Bismarck had realised, namely that the maintenance of peace and the stability of the international system represented the best guarantee of national security. This did not mean that conflict and confrontation were banished from international politics, but it enabled the great powers to control these antagonisms. Alliances were simply an instrument to oil the cogs of the international system; expansion in the periphery, while generating crises, gave the system its flexibility.

By the early 1890s, the assumptions and structures of the alliance system had changed. The Bismarckian tangle of agreements had been replaced by two alliances, whose military commitments were directed against each other. The assumption underpinning the alliance system was that security could only be guaranteed through alliances and military power. The maintenance of alliances was being transformed into a vital interest. This increased the potential rigidity in the international system. The changing conceptions of the international system and their concrete manifestations in alliances and military conventions altered the structure and practices in the international system. The cause of this change requires further research. Generational change probably played some role, as men like Holstein, Crispi, and Caprivi came to the fore. Perhaps it was significant that British policy continued to eschew alliances and military commitments while Lord Salisbury, a member of the Bismarckian generation in political, if not chronological, terms, remained prime minister in the 1890s. It was younger men, like Joseph Chamberlain, who were the strongest advocates of alliances in British politics. A second impetus lay in what Bismarck considered peripheral crises in the Balkans, North Africa, and Central Asia. These were less peripheral, as far as other powers were concerned. The accumulation of these crises and the displacement of rivalries from central Europe ended up rebounding on the structures of European politics. It showed the limits of Bismarck's ability to manage the system, as the foreign policies of Austria-Hungary, Russia, Britain, France, and Italy were shaped by imperial crises. Germany began to play a more active role beyond its geopolitical heartland, as it embarked on a brief colonial policy. Bismarck was aware of the wider global tensions, particularly between Britain and Russia, but he could not prevent these tensions reshaping European politics.

The changes to the international system in the early 1890s had consequences for international politics up to the outbreak of the First World War, particularly the increased importance attached to alliances. Nonetheless, the alliances remained defensive, as a succession of politicians made clear. Alliances were supposed to preserve the peace by deterring attack, they were designed to offer security, and, because they were committed to military support, allies now had an added incentive to restrain their partner from pursuing a policy likely to end in war. Flexibility in the system was also maintained by Britain's independence from either alliance and the opportunities for imperial expansion, which were pursued with increasing vigour in the 1890s.

Great Power Politics as Global Politics, 1895–1904

The development of a global balance of power was the most fundamental change in great power politics in the final decade of the nineteenth century. Of course, ever since European expansion in the sixteenth and seventeenth centuries, great power politics had been played on a global scale. This global rivalry between the European powers took on a new quality in the 1880s and 1890s. Tensions heightened and rivalries were exacerbated as European powers started to scramble for territory in Africa and Asia. Already in the 1880s, imperial rivalries in North Africa and Central Asia shaped relationships amongst the great powers. This process intensified from the late 1880s onwards, as great power rivalries extended into eastern and southern Africa, Latin America, and East Asia. The USA and Japan became important players in world politics – and also in European politics, as great powers saw an interaction between global and regional alignments.

By the late nineteenth century, it was appropriate to speak of a global, rather than a European, balance of power. Disraeli famously spoke of the 'German revolution' in February 1871. This was no prophecy of future Anglo-German antagonism; rather it was a reference to the shift in the global balance of power following the collapse of French power and the emergence of a united Germany in the wake of the Franco-Prussian War, which had been fought the previous year. He claimed that Russia and the USA were the greatest beneficiaries of France's defeat. No longer could Britain and France combine to restrain Russian ambitions in the Near East. Britain, left alone to manage Russian expansion in Central Asia and the Near East, was in no position to offer any opposition to the advance of the USA. French politicians would surely have dissented from his assertion that Britain's geopolitical position had suffered most from the Franco-Prussian War. But what was significant about his speech – and has often been missed owing to the enduring appeal of the phrase 'the German revolution' – was his global perspective on European politics.

Other politicians and academics reiterated this sense of an emerging global balance of power. The Swedish geographer, Rudolf Kjellen, pointed to the development of a unitary global system before the First World War, in which decisions in one part of the globe spread well beyond a particular region. Gustav Schmoller, a German economist, and Friedrich Ratzel, a German political geographer, were amongst many to argue that the era of the small state had come to an end and that the twentieth century would belong to powers with extensive territory and economic resources. The former American president, Teddy Roosevelt, warned the German diplomat Hermann von Eckardstein in 1911 that should Germany overturn the balance of power in Europe, the USA would be obliged to intervene, as 'we ourselves are becoming, owing to our strength and geographical situation, more and more the balance of power of the whole globe'. In 1907 the Habsburg Foreign Minister, Alois von Aehrenthal, speculated about the impact Russia's relations with Japan and the USA would have on the projection of Russian power in the Balkans. British journalist Spenser Wilkinson noted 'that the great fact of today is that any movement which is made in one part of the world affects the international relations of the world'.[8] While each region had its own particular characteristics, they linked together to form a single international system. Events in the Far East, Central Asia, Africa, and the western hemisphere, interacted to provide policy makers in the leading powers with new horizons, challenges, and opportunities.

But what was the significance of the emerging global balance of power and great power imperialism? On one reading, imperial expansion corrupted and undermined the balance and restraints of nineteenth-century European politics. Expansion became the essence of great power politics, transforming the ambiguities, checks, and restraints of international politics into a clear-cut, zero-sum game of winners and losers. The stakes were high. Great powers faced the choice of attaining world power status or sinking to the deplorable depths of a Venice or a Dutch Republic, a fate that no self-respecting great power government could countenance. Time was of the essence, as states feared missing out on expansion in the present, a failing that could not be rectified at a later date. As Lord Rosebery, British prime minister and turf enthusiast, put it, it was necessary to 'peg out claims for the future'. This gave imperial politics a much greater urgency. Expansion exacerbated old rivalries, between Britain and Russia, for instance, and fuelled new ones, between Britain and Germany, for instance. As the great powers, including the USA and Japan, expanded, there was correspondingly less territory to be carved up and so compromise became less feasible.

---

[8] Magnus Brechtken, *Scharnierzeit 1895–1907. Persönlichkeiten und internationale Politik in den deutsch-britischen-amerikanischen Beziehungen vor dem Ersten Weltkrieg* (Mainz, 2006), p. 104; Sönke Neitzel, *Weltmacht oder Untergang. Weltreichslehre im Zeitalter des Imperialismus* (Paderborn, 2000), pp. 18–20, 88–90; Solomon Wank, ed., *Aus dem Nachlass Aehrenthal. Briefe und Dokumente zur österreichisch-ungarischen Innen- und Außenpolitik 1885–1912*: Part 2. *1907–1912* (Graz, 1994), pp. 448–52; Robin A. Butlin, 'The Pivot and Imperial Defence Policy', in Brian Blouet, ed., *Global Geostrategy: Mackinder and the Defence of the West* (Abingdon, 2005), p. 41.

Moreover, some historians have argued that there was a fundamental incompatibility between the European and global balance of power. Within Europe, Germany was the potential hegemon; on a global level, however, Germany was comparatively weak, dwarfed by Britain, Russia, and the USA. If Germany did not attain world power status, then the consequence would be the emasculation of its European position. On the other hand, if Germany did achieve world power status, this would transform it into the hegemonic European power, overturning the balance on the continent and hence threatening global stability. This structural weakness in the international system, the incompatibility of the European and global balance, led Britain, Russia, and France to block German imperial expansion, which in turn led the Kaiserreich to engage in ever more aggressive and risky policies initially aimed at winning a world power position and ultimately at defending its European position.

However, there is a very different interpretation of the consequences of imperial expansion for the international system. This interpretation starts from the position that none of the numerous imperial crises led to a general war. It was a series of European, not imperial, crises that shaped international politics in the years before the war. While the rhetorical stakes generated noise and bombast, the great power political stakes of imperialism were comparatively low. Setbacks in the imperial sphere could be made good. Territorial compensation could ease rivalries. Rivalries could be transformed into cooperation, as happened with the formation of ententes between Britain and France in 1904 and Britain and Russia in 1907. Minor agreements between the great powers on peripheral matters could improve the general state of relations and the atmosphere, in which diplomatic relations were conducted. Tensions within Europe could be managed by the diversion of great power ambitions beyond the continent. Of course, great power expansion came at an enormous cost, as thousands died in colonial wars, African and Asian societies were shattered by their encounters with European powers (and the USA and Japan), and states lost their independence. The corollary of peace and stability in Europe was upheaval around the globe.

The period between 1894 and 1905 was bounded by two wars in East Asia – between Japan and China in 1894/5 and Japan and Russia in 1904/5. Other wars also marked this decade, including the Ottoman-Greek War of 1896/7, the Spanish-American War of 1898, and the South African War of 1899–1902. It was a violent decade, but it was also one in which the wars were localised. Moreover the Spanish-American War, the South African War, and the Russo-Japanese War were followed by periods of peaceful stability in their respective regions. The historian must explain why so many conflicts occurred, but also why they did not escalate into general wars and how governments arrived at stable political settlements.

Before turning to consider the complexities of great power rivalry in East Asia, it is worth examining events in the western hemisphere and southern Africa. In the western hemisphere, the USA was clearly the hegemonic power. 'It is very sad', the ageing Lord Salisbury noted in 1902, 'but I am afraid America is bound to forge ahead and nothing can restore the equality between us.'[9] The French political economist, Paul Leroy-Beaulieu, argued in his 1904 book, *The United States in the Twentieth Century*, that Americans 'have inherited the role, which, until recently, Britain played in the world'. This, he stressed, was not necessarily a bad thing, as the USA would provide a market for European goods as well as competition to European manufacturers.[10] The resignation of the British prime minister and the qualified optimism of the French economist offer a clue to why American hegemony was established relatively peacefully. First, the USA was in such a strong position that it was difficult to oppose its ambitions with any hope of success. Spanish politicians and soldiers realised that the odds were heavily stacked against them in 1898, despite having a larger army in Cuba and in the Philippines than the USA had. Second, Britain accepted American hegemony in the western hemisphere as the best possible outcome of changing balances of power around the globe. For men like Joseph Chamberlain, married to an American, and Arthur Balfour, who counted many Americans amongst his close friends, war between the two countries would have been unnatural. This cultural affinity was bolstered by the Roosevelt corollary of 1904. Following an Anglo-German naval blockade in 1902/3 against Venezuela, whose government had failed to repay debts, the USA had intervened to mediate between the two sides and to uphold the Monroe Doctrine. However, Roosevelt acknowledged that the Monroe Doctrine could not be used to shield states, who refused to comply with the normal obligations of international politics. In 1904, he declared in his Annual Message that the USA would act against 'chronic wrong-doing or an impotence which results in a general loosening of the ties of civilized society'.[11] By acting as a benevolent hegemon (at least as far as most great powers were concerned), the USA secured the Monroe Doctrine and geopolitical stability in the Americas.

---

[9] Cited in John Gooch, 'The Weary Titan: Strategy and Policy in Great Britain, 1890–1914', in Williamson Murray, MacGregor Knox, and Alvin Bernstein, eds, *The Making of Strategy: Rulers, States, and War* (Cambridge, 1994), p. 289.

[10] Paul Leroy-Beaulieu, *Les États-Unis au XXe siècle* (Paris, 1904), pp. xxii, 416–23.

[11] Cited in Iestyn Adams, *Brothers across the Ocean: British Foreign Policy and the Origins of the Anglo-American Special Relationship, 1900–1905* (London, 2005), pp. 75–76.

In southern Africa, Britain was the leading power. The Cape of Good Hope remained an important point in the geopolitics of the British empire, even after the opening of the Suez Canal offered a quicker route between India and Britain. But Britain's primacy was challenged by what the *Spectator* and *Economist* called 'stockbreeders of the lowest type' and 'a rough mob of good marksmen', the Boers, who dominated the Transvaal Republic.[12] While Germany, which had established colonies in southern Africa, could irritate Britain, there was never any question that it would seek to overturn Britain's position. During the war, the German government maintained a policy of strict neutrality, despite coming under intense pressure from public opinion. Instead the Transvaal, strengthened by an economic boom fuelled by gold mining, threatened Britain's position. By the late 1890s, a series of geostrategic, economic, and political factors brought the Boers to the brink of conflict with the British empire. 'What is now at stake', Chamberlain argued in September 1899, 'is the position of Britain in South Africa and with it the estimate of our power and influence in our colonies and throughout the world.'[13] But what was striking was that once the war began – and it began disastrously for Britain – none of the other great powers sought to exploit Britain's entanglements in southern Africa. Boer leaders travelled to Europe, but got no material support. By 1902, the war was over. Although the expense, the concentration camps, and the scale of losses horrified liberal Victorians, Britain remained pre-eminent.

Hegemony, achieved through a combination of war, latent power, and presumed benevolence, had established stability in the western hemisphere and southern Africa. But in the Far East, as with the Ottoman Empire, there were too many great powers with interests in 'the dying nations' for a hegemonic settlement to be acceptable. Instead, compromise, restraint, ambiguity, and an awareness of other powers' vital interests were required to preserve the peace and manage the decline of Imperial China.

The most telling sign that the European states system had become a global one was the reaction of the great powers to the war fought between Japan and China in 1894/5. The immediate cause of the war was the invitation of the Korean government to the Chinese government to send troops to suppress anti-foreigner uprisings on the peninsula. For Japan, the Korean peninsula was a vital strategic interest. Japan sent her own troops, and by July 1894, these had occupied the Korean royal palace.

---

[12] Bill Nasson, *The South African War, 1899–1902* (London, 1999), p. 69.
[13] Cited in Peter Henshaw, 'The Origins of the Boer War', in Keith Wilson, ed., *The International Impact of the Boer War* (Chesham, 2001), p. 22.

A contest for imperial influence between two of Asia's leading powers ensued, but it was an unequal contest, owing to the modernisation of the Japanese fleet and that country's greater internal stability. By early 1895, Japan had imposed a treaty on China, which included the annexation of the Liaotung peninsula, the imposition of an indemnity on China, and the concession of commercial privileges to Japan on a par with those of the western powers.

The background to Japan's intervention in Korea lay not just in competition with China, but in the expansion of European states, especially Russia, into Asia. Since 1890, members of the Japanese military expressed concern that the construction of a railway across Siberia would enable Russia to exercise influence in Korea. In fact, Russian ambitions did not extend as far as dominating Korea. Amongst St Petersburg's francophone elites a joke was doing the rounds: 'la chiccorée m'intéresse plus que la Corée'. But policy makers quickly re-evaluated the significance of the war, once Japan had achieved a decisive military and political victory. It was no longer conceived as a localised conflict, but one with ramifications for the future of East Asia. The initial expectation that China would win was ill-founded. By early 1895, Russian diplomats both respected and feared Japan's ambitions in East Asia. Faced with the option of cooperating with Japan or checking her expansion, Sergei Witte, the Finance Minister and the leading architect of Russia's East Asian policy, chose to force Japan to roll back from some of its gains – without the use of military force. For much of the next decade, he warned that war was a dangerous instrument of policy against Japan, one which risked destabilising the Tsarist regime. He aimed at the establishment of Russian economic predominance in Manchuria in northern China by means of *pénétration pacifique*, commercial and political influence.

The impending collapse of China – the British Foreign Secretary, Lord Kimberley, dismissed China as 'rotten to the core' – complicated great power politics after 1895.[14] The powers variously sought to preserve Chinese territorial integrity, carve out spheres of influence, and instrumentalise the China question in alliance politics. Aims, interests, and tactical ploys both cut across and reinforced traditional rivalries and the alliance system, which had developed between 1879 and 1894. Russia, aware of its relative military weakness in the Far East, needed partners to check Japan. Russia's note demanding Japan's withdrawal from the Liaotung peninsula was supported by France and Germany. Germany's participation was partly motivated by a desire to cut a dash on the world

[14] T. G. Otte, *The China Question: Great Power Rivalry and British Isolation, 1894–1905* (Oxford, 2007), p. 52.

stage, but also by the need to ease the pressure in Europe, where the conclusion of the Franco-Russian alliance had hemmed in the Kaiserreich. German leaders failed to loosen the ties between the Third Republic and the Romanov empire, but for the next decade, its policy pivoted on Russia's entanglement in East Asia.

One of the outcomes of Russia's interest in East Asia was the lessening of tensions in the Balkans and the Ottoman Empire. Events, which could have given rise to great power crises, passed without a major flare-up. The Armenian massacres of 1895/6 and the Ottoman-Greek War of 1897 did elicit great power consultations, but nothing that matched the dramas of the late 1870s and 1880s. The rivalry between Austria-Hungary and Russia abated, as the former felt that Germany did not take Vienna's interests into account and the latter sought to secure its western flank. In early 1897, Austria-Hungary and Russia concluded an entente, which sought to preserve the status quo in the Balkans. At Mürzsteg in October 1903 Russia and Austria-Hungary agreed to recognise the new Serbian king, who had come to the throne after the murder of the previous pro-Habsburg occupant. German policy towards Russia became increasingly friendly throughout the 1890s and early twentieth century, particularly after Bernhard von Bülow became Secretary of State in 1897 and Chancellor in 1900. Self-confident and an excellent speaker, Bülow set out to promote Germany as a world power, chiming with the ambitions of his master, William II. In order to free Germany from the risks of a two-front war against the Dual Alliance, Bülow set out to develop better relations with Russia.

But as rivalries eased in Europe, the conflicts of interest between the great powers at a global level increased. The crumbling Chinese empire provided the stage for the most significant dramas in great power politics in the late nineteenth and early twentieth century. In 1897, following the murder of two German missionaries in China, William II ordered the occupation of the port of Kiaochou. The unilateral action and the fact that the port was in the Russian sphere of influence in China sparked an international crisis. Russia followed with the seizure of Port Arthur and Britain took compensation, seizing the port of Wei-hai-wei. The growing influence of the western great powers sparked resistance within China. In the summer of 1900, the anti-foreigner Boxer rebellion began, threatening westerners and their commercial interests in China. The great powers scrambled for a solution. As with the Ottoman Empire, the great powers recognised the advantages of cooperation, which would allow them to suppress a common threat and manage each other's avaricious appetites. An international force, under the German general Alfred von Waldersee crushed the Boxer rebellion and imposed a harsh settlement on the

Chinese imperial government. However, it was less easy for the great powers to return to the status quo ante of their own positions.

In this context, the variety of options for the realignment of great power relations was highly complex. Within each great power there were advocates of several different approaches. The outcomes depended on high political machinations as well as geopolitical interests. For instance, proposals for an Anglo-German alliance in 1898 and 1901 were scuppered by the opposition of Salisbury, who doubted the value and feared the costs of an alliance with Germany, and by Bülow, for whom good relations with Russia, rather than Britain, were the alpha and omega of German world policy. Japanese leaders, such as Ito and Yamagata, seriously considered an alliance with Russia, yet in January 1902, Britain and Japan concluded a defensive alliance pact. In response, Russia concluded an agreement with France in March 1902, pledged to defend the status quo in China. This extended the reorientation of the Dual Alliance against Britain, which had begun in 1900 and 1901, when Delcassé and Lamsdorff exchanged plans for combined action against Britain. Germany stood to one side, but it was clear from its decision not to oppose Russian ambitions in Manchuria in 1901 that it leaned towards its eastern neighbour.

Whether these agreements would lead to restraint or war was an open question. Within France, Britain, Japan, and Russia, there were many advocates of compromise. In particular, Delcassé sought to restrain Russia throughout 1903. In fact, French and Russian interests in China (and the Ottoman Empire) were often at odds, as French politicians and investors wanted the preservation of Chinese territorial integrity and the repayment of debts. For British leaders, the alliance with Japan fulfilled several purposes. It balanced, or was supposed to, French and Russian naval forces in the Far East, it prevented the emergence of a dangerous Russo-Japanese alliance, it checked Russia's advance in China, and it enabled London to exercise some control over Japanese policy. It was conceived as an instrument for the maintenance of peace. Since the 1890s, Russian policy had been predicated on a policy of *penétration pacifique*, not war. Following a tour of the Far East in 1902, Witte and General Kuropatkin were resolved to maintain Russian influence in Manchuria, but they also warned that a war against Japan would have disastrous implications. In Japan, the foreign minister, Ito, remained conciliatory towards Russia.

But in 1903, these bonds of peace fell apart. The Russo-Japanese War was far from inevitable; indeed, Witte considered it the outcome of poor judgement, telling his fellow dove, Kuropatkin in December 1903: 'Imagine that I invited some friends to the Aquarium [a nightclub in

St Petersburg] and they all proceeded to get drunk. Then going on to a brothel, they ended up starting a fight there. Would I be responsible? I only took them to the Aquarium.'[15] A responsible Far Eastern policy, respecting Japan's interests, could have been conducted peacefully. The outstanding issue, between Russia and Japan, was the delineation of their respective spheres of influence in Manchuria and Korea. Both had concerns since the 1890s that the other would seek to expand beyond these zones. Until the middle of 1903, war had been avoided due to the actions of other great powers and the predominance of the peace parties in Tokyo and St Petersburg. But these restraints were pushed aside in 1903. In Tokyo, there was growing frustration that Russia had not come to an agreement on Korea. At a meeting of the leading Japanese decision-makers on 21 April 1903, Yamagata, Katsura, Ito, and Komura agreed that Japan could never give up Korea, a position that appeared to be under threat as Russia expanded its sphere of influence in China. Within the Russian leadership, more expansionist arguments were gaining ground. Nicholas II sacked Witte in August 1903 and established a new Vice-Royalty of the Far East under General Alekseev. Although the Tsar instructed Alekseev to 'take all measures so that there is no war', the general and his advisers refused to make any concessions to Japan. Russian policy was also damaged by chaotic structures and blurred lines of command, so that Japan's final proposals in January 1904 were never properly considered.

The other great powers refused, or were too weak, to mediate effectively. In fact, some considered a localised war in a positive light. In Britain, the cerebral prime minister, Balfour believed that war would weaken a financially brittle Russia, even if she emerged victorious. Lansdowne's concerns that Russia might crush Britain's ally, Japan, were brushed aside. Bülow had always argued that Russian expansion in the Far East would benefit Germany. War between Russia and Japan was the next best thing to an Anglo-Russian conflict; perhaps Britain might end up embroiled in the conflict. Delcassé was in the most difficult position, but his fear that France and Britain might get dragged into the war by their allies proved unfounded. Instead, the Russo-Japanese War provided extra impetus to London and Paris to resolve their differences in North Africa.

On the night of 8–9 February 1904, Admiral Togo Heiachiro's fleet attacked and sank the Russian fleet at Port Arthur, starting the war before it had even been declared. The war was a disaster for Russia, which lost

---

[15] David Schimmelpenninck van der Oye, *Towards the Rising Sun: Russian Ideologies of Empire and the Path to War with Japan* (De Kalb, 2001), p. 81.

two fleets, underwent a revolution, and effectively ceased playing an active role in great power politics for several years. Yet before examining the repercussions of the war – especially Russia's unexpected defeat – it is worth noting that it did not escalate into a general war. The successful localisation of the conflict demonstrated the inherent restraints in the imperial politics of the great powers. After all, there was potential for escalation. Russia and Japan were members of two opposing alliance blocs, China had been the scene of great power rivalry and serious crises for a decade, and comparatively minor incidents, such as the sinking of British fishing ships at Dogger Bank by the Russian navy, had the potential to develop into a serious diplomatic crisis. If imperial expansion amongst the great powers was likely to cause a general war, then the Russo-Japanese War of 1904/5 provided as good an opportunity as any.

How and why was a general war avoided? First, none of the other powers had vital national interests at stake in the Far East. The powers had been willing to advance their interests with all means, short of war against another great power. Loans, railway concessions, the seizure of ports from an ailing China, and diplomatic pressure were all considered legitimate means of furthering the national interest. In imperial politics, great power war was not deemed a continuation of politics, but a negation of it. Second, the alliance system did not have primacy in the considerations of statesmen, at least as far as East Asian politics was concerned. Alliances were a means to an end, so that their preservation did not become a vital interest. Neither France nor Britain was under any obligation to their respective allies, Russia and Japan. Significantly, both countries moved quickly to ensure that they would not find themselves at war with each other. The defeat of Russia had profound implications for French security, but they were consequences that Delcassé hoped to manage and never felt the need to forestall by entering the lists on Russia's side (Map 2).

By 1905, both sides were exhausted. The outbreak of revolution and the sinking of a second Russian fleet, the Baltic fleet, in the straits of Tsushima in May 1905, led Nicholas II to decide against the continuation of the war. In late April, the Japanese government decided to ask Roosevelt to mediate, though on condition that Japan retain its position in Korea and Russia evacuate troops from Manchuria. Roosevelt was concerned about the growth of Japan's power in East Asia, but there was little he could do to moderate Japanese demands. The treaty was negotiated at Portsmouth, a coastal town north of Boston. The treaty recognised Japan's dominance in Korea and ceded Russia's lease of the Liaotung peninsula to Japan. There was no indemnity, and in Tokyo, the terms were greeted by riots because popular expectations had not been

Map 2. Great power rivalries in the Far East and the end of the Russo-Japanese War. After Gildea, *Barricades and Borders*, 349.

met. Although general war was avoided, the Russo-Japanese War had profound consequences for international politics. These consequences were worked out during what the French diplomat Maurice Paléologue called 'the great turning point', between 1904 and 1907.

The Great Turning Point, 1904–1907

The years between the outbreak of the Russo-Japanese War in 1904 and the conclusion of the Anglo-Russian entente in 1907 witnessed a revolution in international politics. There were two fundamental revolutionary possibilities – either the creation of a close relationship between Britain and Russia, with the potential to dominate world politics, or the formation of a continental league, under German leadership, which would dominate European politics, and probably world politics. At the centre of this revolutionary situation were, first, the collapse of Russian power, and, second, Britain's entente policy, starting with the entente cordiale with France in 1904 and culminating with the Anglo-Russian entente in 1907, which undermined one of the central assumptions of nineteenth-century international politics – that Britain and Russia could never cooperate, owing to their global rivalry. At the same time, Bülow tried to forge a German diplomatic revolution, by engineering an alliance with Russia, making France dependent on the Reich, and isolating Britain in European and global politics. The collapse of Russian power in 1904/5 created such a vacuum in world politics that a radical reshaping of international politics was always likely. The sharpening of Anglo-German antagonism shaped the policy options for other states, in particular for Austria-Hungary, which traditionally had enjoyed good relations with both Britain and Germany. The implications of this revolution in international affairs were teased out after 1907.

The collapse of Russian power had several consequences for the international system. Within Europe, the Franco-Russian alliance had formed one pillar of the balance of power since 1894. The alliance was largely passive, owing to European expansion around the globe, but the security the alliance provided for France and Russia gave a safe European basis for imperial expansion. Russia's defeat meant that the alliance no longer fulfilled this balancing function. The major beneficiary from Russia's defeat, within Europe, was Germany. Its relative power had increased, giving it potentially more leverage over France and Russia. It was liberated from the fear of war on two fronts, which created opportunities for a more aggressive policy. Apart from Russia, France was the main loser of the war, its security undermined by the defeat of its ally. Austria-Hungary also seemed like a beneficiary, though in the long term it was likely that Russia would turn its attention to the Balkans, placing pressure on the Habsburg position. At a global level, Britain benefited most from the collapse of Russian power, as it alleviated security concerns about India. The imponderable question in all capitals, including St Petersburg, remained the reaction of Russia to defeat. Concentration on internal consolidation required securing Russia's foreign policy position as much as possible. Options included an alliance with Germany, maintaining the entente with Austria-Hungary in the Balkans, upholding the alliance with France, and developing better relations with Britain. The international system, therefore, was in a state of considerable flux.

At the same time as Russia's predicament opened up new possibilities in international politics, Anglo-German antagonism was hardening. German *Weltpolitik* was the fundamental cause of this antagonism. On 18 January 1896, the twenty-fifth anniversary of the founding of the Kaiserreich, William II declared that Germany was to become a world empire. To achieve William II's ambition Germany required naval bases, colonies, and the promotion of commercial interests around the globe. Though vague in its detail, this conception of *Weltpolitik* was directed against Britain, considered an obstacle to the pursuit of legitimate German colonial and commercial ambitions. By 1897, William II had promoted two of the principal architects of *Weltpolitik*, Bülow and Tirpitz, to the position of foreign secretary and Secretary for the Navy, respectively. Bülow considered that German *Weltpolitik* could take advantage of Anglo-Russian rivalry, but that Germany must also secure its position in Europe by improving relations with Russia. Tirpitz's naval programme was also directed against Britain, which he saw as Germany's primary economic rival. In order to achieve the vague ambitions set out by the Kaiser in 1896, Bülow and Tirpitz developed a policy that aimed to challenge Britain's position as the leading world power. The pre-conditions were a sufficiently strong fleet to deter a British attack and closer relations with Russia. Both men also hoped to disguise the challenge to Britain, fearing that the Royal Navy might launch a preventive strike against the German fleet.

Weltpolitik combined various strands of German foreign policy – naval, geopolitical, colonial, and commercial – but its actual achievements were extremely limited. Agreements with Britain over the future of the Portuguese empire in 1898 and over the control of the Samoan islands in 1899 were small beer compared with the prizes secured by Britain in Egypt and South Africa, Russia in the Far East, France in West and North Africa, and the USA in the Caribbean and Pacific. Moreover, the British public and government had begun to suspect German ambitions. The press wars during the South African War created tensions between the two countries. Apart from the strained atmosphere, which the press wars engendered in Anglo-German relations, politicians, admirals, and diplomats identified a series of German threats to British interests. Lord Lansdowne was less alarmed by German policy than his successor, Edward Grey. In early 1902, Lord Selborne, the First Lord of the Admiralty, claimed that the German fleet building programme constituted a threat to British security, but Lansdowne and Balfour expressed doubts. The foreign secretary believed that the bitter Anglophobia in Germany would soon pass, while Germany could not afford to 'let us go under before a great European coalition', as the Reich would then face Russia and France without the prospect of British assistance. 'Broadly speaking', Balfour claimed, 'her interests and ours are identical.'[16]

Others disagreed with this favourable view of Anglo-German relations. According to Francis Bertie, assistant under-secretary at the Foreign Office and a future ambassador to Paris, the 'Germans' aim is to push us into the water and steal our clothes', referring to German support for Russia in China.[17] In the view of the rising generation of Foreign Office officials, Germany repeatedly blackmailed Britain, exploiting British differences with France and Russia. In January 1903, Grey claimed Germany was 'our worst enemy and our greatest threat'. The future Liberal foreign secretary identified Germany's naval programme and imperial expansion as central elements of the threat. Added to these direct threats to British security, Grey was concerned at the prospect of an alliance between Russia and Germany. This would have amounted to a revolution in world politics. It would have left France with a choice between isolation in Europe or dependency on Germany, it would have given Russia a free hand to challenge Britain in Central Asia and the Far East, and it would have provided the basis for German dominance in central and western Europe and expansion overseas. The maintenance of the balance of power in Europe was the pre-condition of Britain's imperial position as well as the basis of British security in Europe. Grey saw the development of better relations between Britain and Russia as the best means of foiling a Russo-German alliance. Yet he failed to recognise the worrying implications of an Anglo-Russian rapprochement on the position of Germany and Austria-Hungary.

The origins of Anglo-German antagonism pre-dated the Russo-Japanese War, but it did not become a determinant of British foreign

---

16 William Mulligan, 'From Case to Narrative: The Marquess of Lansdowne, Sir Edward Grey, and the Threat from Germany, 1900–1906', *International History Review*, 30, 2 (2008): 281.

17 Zara Steiner, *The Foreign Office and Foreign Policy, 1898–1914* (Cambridge, 1969), p. 62.

policy until 1905 and 1906, partly because Lansdowne, who remained in office until late 1905, did not attach much significance to the German challenge until the Moroccan crisis and partly because the war in the Far East dominated international affairs from 1903 to 1905. Concerns about Germany, therefore, played only a minor role in the creation of the Anglo-French entente. Instead, the wider global concerns of both powers shaped the entente. From the British perspective, this was an imperial bargain, in which Britain secured its position in Egypt and was freed from the constraints of French rivalry; in return, Britain recognised France's paramount position in Morocco. Lord Cromer, the British consul in Cairo and a dominant figure in imperial politics, pressed for the conclusion of the entente. The British government was also slightly concerned that Britain and France might get dragged into a general conflict by their respective allies, Japan and Russia, an eventuality which the entente effectively rendered impossible. Indeed, Balfour and Lansdowne saw the entente with France as a means of improving relations with Russia over the longer term. One of the benefits for British diplomacy was that Germany could no longer exploit Anglo-French differences, but this was not so much a case of British policy checking Germany, as Britain gaining extra room for manoeuvre.

Amongst French politicians, the prospect of improving relations between their ally, Russia, and their new entente partner, Britain, was enticing. 'The Russian alliance, without a doubt, must remain the operating basis of our foreign policy', wrote Clemenceau, a Radical Republican and premier between 1906 and 1909. 'But it is not a matter of indifference to enlarge it with an entente with Italy and with England. And if, through us, a rapprochement could be achieved between this power and Russia, everyone would see that the global balance would thereby be changed.'[18] The foreign minister, Théophile Delcassé, was a relatively late convert to the idea of an entente with Britain. In 1900 and 1901, Russia and France developed plans for joint military action against Britain, while Delcassé led efforts to intervene in the South African War with the purpose of putting pressure on Britain in North Africa. But the realities of Britain's dominant position in Egypt and Delcassé's growing suspicion of German ambitions in the Mediterranean basin converted him into a supporter of entente by 1903. Primacy in Morocco was the price France placed on accepting Britain's dominance in Egypt. In February 1903, Paul Cambon, the ambassador to London, placed an article in *The Times*, raising the idea of Egyptian–Moroccan barter. Cromer took up the article, pressing the Foreign Office to come to an agreement with

---

[18] Cited in Jean-Baptiste Duroselle, *Clemenceau* (Paris, 1988), p. 489.

France. Delcassé opened talks with Britain during his visit to London in July 1903, laying the groundwork for the entente concluded in April 1904.

German reaction was ambivalent. Bülow instructed the press to treat the entente as a sign of the 'peaceful arrangement of world politics'. William II had little interest in Morocco and cared little about the terms of the entente, but in private Bülow and the Foreign Office were concerned. The agreement represented a setback to *Weltpolitik*; after all, Britain and France had effectively partitioned North Africa, without the involvement of the other great powers, who had interests in the region, albeit relatively minor ones. Nonetheless, from the German perspective, the Anglo-French entente did not look quite like the logical distribution of spheres of interests, but more like a means of blocking German expansion. Further, Anglo-French cooperation in North Africa meant that Germany had lost the 'Egyptian lever', which, since the 1880s, had enabled Bismarck and his successors to exploit divisions between Britain and France. The permanence of tensions in imperial politics between the other great powers had been one of the basic assumptions of German foreign policy. The Anglo-French entente shook this assumption. Moreover, it showed that diplomatic combinations arising from global interests had consequences for the constellation of great power politics in Europe.

The First Moroccan crisis confirmed the European implications of the entente. In Morocco itself, events moved quickly, as the Sultan's authority was undermined by a series of revolts, financial problems, and the entente, which prevented him from playing off Britain and France. In France, Delcassé came under increasing pressure to seize the initiative in Morocco. In June 1904, the French government had organised a loan for Morocco, in return for control of 65 per cent of Moroccan customs receipts for a thirty-five-year period. This provided the wedge for France to present to the Sultan in January 1905 a programme of reforms, giving it a dominant position in Morocco. This prompted a declaration of support for the Sultan's sovereignty by William II, when he landed at Tangiers during a cruise in March 1905, which, in turn, triggered the First Moroccan crisis.

The crisis was much more than a contest for influence in a failing state; it was a contest between two different visions of the international system – a German-led continental league and a global entente between Britain, France, and Russia. The collapse of Russian power was the larger context for the crisis, in which Germany sought not only to snap the newly formed Anglo-French entente, but more significantly attempted to forge an alliance with Russia and to make France dependent on the

Reich. In the second half of 1904, as Russia endured a series of setbacks, the German shipping company, HAPAG, supplied the Russian fleet on its way from the Baltic Sea to the Far East with coaling facilities. The incident at Dogger Bank, when the Russian fleet sank a British fishing vessel, exacerbated already poor Anglo-Russian relations. It gave Bülow the opportunity to suggest that Germany, rather than France, offered Russia the most effective alliance against Britain. In late October, Holstein and William II floated the idea of an alliance with Nicholas II and his ambassador to Berlin. On 31 October, Bülow, Holstein, Schlieffen, and Tirpitz, amongst others, discussed the benefits and problems of a Russian alliance. Although Tirpitz feared it would provoke Britain into a pre-emptive strike against the German fleet, Bülow pressed ahead with his plans, sending a draft text to St Petersburg and warning the French government of the possibility of war. On 3 December, William II, Tirpitz, and Schlieffen discussed plans for a general war. But Nicholas II refused to accept the alliance without consulting Delcassé, who in turn informed Britain of Germany's intentions and moved quickly to prevent the escalation of tensions between Britain and Russia over the Dogger Bank incident. He also promised French support for the Russian fleet.

Bülow's first attempt to reorder the international system on the basis of a Russo-German alliance had failed, but in 1905, Germany sought to demonstrate to France that Russia was a broken reed, not a reliable ally, and that the Anglo-French entente was of limited significance in continental power politics. Morocco was to be the test case, where Germany refused to accept French pre-eminence. 'Whilst in the act of ravishing Morocco', noted the Grand Vizir of Morocco, 'France has received a tremendous kick in the behind from the Emperor William.'[19] French actions and the Anglo-French entente challenged multilateral practices by ignoring the rights of other powers who had signed up in 1880 to the convention of Madrid that determined the rights and interests of the powers in Morocco. 'In international relations', Holstein complained, without a sense of irony, 'right and wrong are without meaning, if the culprit is strong enough to flout everything.'[20] Yet both Germany and France were prepared for a trial of strength, if not for war. Confident of British support, Delcassé refused to negotiate with Germany. The weakness of the French army, the destruction of the Russian fleet in May 1905 at Tsushima, his growing unpopularity in the Chamber and cabinet, and the doubts of Paul Rouvier, the premier, that Britain could offer effective

---

[19] Christopher Andrew, *Théophile Delcassé and the Making of the Entente Cordiale: A Reappraisal of French Foreign Policy, 1898–1905* (London, 1968), pp. 273–74.
[20] Holstein to Neven-Dumont, 20 April 1905, in Norman Rich, M. H. Fisher, eds, *Die Geheimen Papiere Friedrich von Holstein*, vol. 4 (Göttingen, 1963), p. 304.

military support in a Franco-German war conspired against Delcassé. By the end of May 1905, Bülow pressed Rouvier to dismiss Delcassé. On 6 June, Delcassé resigned, paving the way for a conference, which would meet in Algeciras in 1906 to resolve the Moroccan crisis. The resignation of the French foreign minister was a stunning triumph for German diplomacy. It signalled Germany's complete dominance of continental politics.

Germany's position seemed even more secure when, just over a month later, William II met Nicholas II on a yacht at Björko. On 11 July, the two emperors signed a treaty, guaranteeing that each power would help the other if it was attacked by another European power. This contravened the Franco-Russian alliance and Nicholas II seems to have been so embarrassed that he covered part of the text of the treaty when he asked Admiral Birilev to counter-sign the document. Had this treaty stuck, it would have created a very different basis for the international system than the one that emerged by 1907. A continental bloc, under German leadership, would have emerged in all likelihood. Britain, isolated in Europe, would have formed a looser bloc with Japan and the USA. In 1905, Britain and Japan had renewed their alliance and extended it, so that Japan would offer Britain military aid in India and Britain would guarantee Japan's position in Korea. Anglo-American relations had improved as Britain ceded control of the western hemisphere to the USA and both countries were suspicious of German ambitions. However, an Anglo-American alliance or even a formal diplomatic arrangement was almost certainly out of the question.[21] Whether such an alignment of the great powers would have represented a more stable global balance of power than the one that emerged in the form of the Triple Entente is a hypothetical question.

This scenario never came to pass. Bülow was critical of the treaty, as it applied only to Europe. As a defensive treaty, it had significant benefits, but it would not help Germany shove Britain off her perch as the world's leading power. Bülow wanted Russia to exert pressure on Britain in Central Asia in the case of an Anglo-German war, but this treaty excluded that possibility. However, it was the opposition of Nicholas II's ministers that proved decisive. When Nicholas II showed the treaty to Witte and Lamsdorff, they immediately identified the disadvantages for Russian policy. It ratified Germany's hegemony in Europe, making Russia dependent on the Reich and ending the mainstay of Russia's European security for the past decade, the alliance with France. Moreover, Russia needed a loan from France, which would certainly not be forthcoming if the treaty of Björko stood. The summer of 1905 marked the highpoint of

---

[21] Adams, *Brothers across the Ocean.*

German influence in Europe before the First World War, an alternative to the entente system, which began to take root in the second half of 1905, as British support for France in Morocco increased. German leaders knew that this was an alternative. 'The situation begins to compare with that of the Seven Years' War', noted William II in November 1904. When Bülow fainted in the Reichstag in April 1906, it symbolised the demise of his concept of *Weltpolitik*. Even more seriously for Germany, a sense of encirclement developed in these years.

After Delcassé's resignation and the meeting at Björko, Lansdowne began to take more decisive steps to block German policy, by mending the entente with France and adopting a conciliatory tone towards Russia. He indicated to Lamsdorff that Britain was willing to come to an agreement, which would apply to Europe as well as Asia, while he assured the Russian foreign minister that the renewed treaty with Japan was defensive. In late June, the Admiralty prepared plans to support France in a war against Germany. By autumn 1905, however, Lansdowne and his fellow Conservatives were facing electoral defeat. Attention turned to the foreign policy of the Liberal party, which some commentators suspected would reorientate British policy towards Germany. Grey, one of the leading contenders for the post of foreign secretary in the new cabinet, made clear his policy in a speech in October, aimed at a foreign audience as much as at his own electorate. He emphasised his support for the pillars of British foreign policy – the alliance with Japan, the entente with France, and friendly relations with the USA. Significantly, he held out the hand of friendship to Russia: 'if Russia accepts . . . our intention to preserve the peaceable possession of our Asiatic possessions, then I am quite sure that no government in this country will make it its business to thwart or obstruct Russia's policy in Europe. On the contrary, it is urgently desirable that Russia's position and influence should be re-established in the councils of Europe.'[22] An Anglo-Russian agreement would serve two objectives, in Grey's view, namely the restoration of the balance of power in Europe and the prevention of a Russo-German alliance.

From the latter half of 1905, the French, British, and Russian governments worked to repair the Franco-Russian alliance and the Anglo-French entente. The Franco-Russian alliance had been knitted together by a series of loans in the 1880s and 1890s. In March 1905, French bankers broke off loan negotiations with the Russian government, as soon as news of Russia's defeat at the battle of Mukden was heard in Paris. Desperate for money, Witte and Kokovtsov turned to an international consortium, including German banks. The failure of the French

[22] Cited in Mulligan, 'From Case to Narrative', p. 299.

government to cajole its banks into lending to the Tsarist regime damaged the alliance. In July 1905, Witte met Rouvier in Paris and raised the issue of a further loan to shore up Russia's finances. Peace with Japan and support in Morocco were the two conditions Rouvier attached to a French loan. The support of the French government was vital, as banks were still reluctant to lend. In order to ensure Russian support at the Algeciras conference, France only advanced 100 million rubles, before giving the rest of the loan after the resolution of the Moroccan crisis. Moreover, whereas Bülow blocked further Russian loans on the German money market in late 1905, the British bank, Baring Brothers, supported the loan, in anticipation of better Anglo-Russian relations. 'On this occasion', Poincaré noted, 'Russia has as much need of us as we do of her.'[23] Diplomatic support in return for financial support marked the restoration of the Franco-Russian alliance as a functioning part of the international system.

After Delcassé's resignation, Lansdowne offered firmer support to France over Morocco. While this stopped well short of a commitment to military action, the tone of British diplomacy changed. Grey was not prepared to sanction military support, though conversations between British and French officers began under his watch, signifying the consolidation of the entente. Grey was determined to give France full diplomatic support, arguing that advancing French interests in Morocco 'will be a great success for the Anglo-French entente; if she fails, the prestige of the entente will suffer and its vitality will be diminished'.[24] Grey used the entente to deter Germany from attacking France, by hinting that Britain would support France, while also encouraging France to compromise on some issues, by suggesting that Britain would not support France if the latter provoked a war against Germany. Privately, Grey was deeply concerned at the prospect of war and was prepared to suggest to France that some 'great sacrifice should in our opinion be made to avoid war'.[25] But Germany was not prepared to go to war over Morocco and Grey's diplomacy succeeded. He established a pattern for his entente diplomacy in future crises – deterrence of Germany and restraint of Britain's entente partners. In 1906, it worked. At the conference at Algeciras, only Austria-Hungary supported Germany. France was able to secure its

[23] René Girault, *Emprunts russes et investissements français en Russie 1887–1914* (Paris, 1973), pp. 412–22, 441; Howard Mehlinger and John Thompson, *Count Witte and the Tsarist Government in the 1905 Revolution* (Bloomington, 1972), pp. 213–24; Jennifer Siegel, *For Peace and Money: French and British Finance in the Service of the Tsars and the Commissars* (Oxford, 2014).
[24] Grey to Nicolson, 21 December 1905, *BD*, vol. 3, p. 162.
[25] Memorandum by Grey, 20 February 1906, in ibid., p. 267.

political interests in Morocco; in return, Germany secured its economic interests with recognition of an Open Door policy. French success gave the entente with Britain greater currency in the international system. The Morocco crisis also damaged the status of multilateral agreements, while all sides used the conference as an offensive diplomatic instrument, rather than a forum for compromise.[26]

During the Moroccan crisis, Grey also gave some thought to the future development of British policy. He argued that a grouping of Britain, France, and Russia could secure peace in Europe. Compared to the Anglo-French entente, there was a much stronger European dimension in the conception of the Anglo-Russian entente, but the influence of British concerns about Indian security was also important. The Russian threat to the empire in India was a persistent theme in nineteenth-century British foreign policy. British policy makers saw defeat in 1905 as a temporary setback for Russia. It was possible that Russia might seek consolation in Central Asia for the loss of influence in the Far East. While Russia had a massive army, the main instrument of Britain's power, the Royal Navy, was ineffective in Central Asia. Further, the Liberal government wanted to reduce military expenditure and was unwilling to countenance the demands for large increases in the Indian army. The solution lay in an agreement with Russia, dividing Central Asia into spheres of influence. An entente with Russia would secure British interests in Asia and restore the balance of power in Europe.

Amongst Russian officials and ministers there was considerable debate about the merits of an agreement with Britain. In 1906, Witte hoped that German banks would participate in the loan. 'A loan made with the aid of France, England, and other countries', he wrote to the German banker, Ernst Mendelssohn-Bartholdy, 'but without Germany will mean for the whole world a rapprochement of Russia with a political grouping, which does not correspond to the interests of Russia or Germany.'[27] Russian conservatives feared the liberal orientation of foreign policy would bolster liberal forces in domestic politics. The possibility of getting dragged into an Anglo-German war alarmed some, as Russia, not Britain, would bear the brunt of Germany's military power. Finally, there were others who argued that Russia was giving up too much in Central Asia. By the spring of 1906, Russian conservatives had lost ground to reformist ministers. P. A. Stolypin and A. P. Izvolski replaced Witte and Lamsdorff. The new foreign minister, Izvolski, wanted to free Russia from potential

---

[26] Verena Steller, *Diplomatie von Angesicht zu Angesicht. Diplomatische Handlungsformen in den deutsch-französischen Beziehungen 1870–1919* (Paderborn, 2011), pp. 336, 359.

[27] Cited in Mehlinger and Thompson, *Witte*, p. 224.

points of confrontation around the globe. Russia improved relations with Japan by coming to a secret agreement in 1907 guaranteeing Japanese interests in Korea and Russian interests in Outer Mongolia. 'Russia must be assured of peace from Kamatchka to Gibraltar for ten years', Izvolski said in August 1907.[28] Yet his conception of the Anglo-Russian entente went beyond stability. He wanted to concentrate on Russian interests in the Ottoman Empire and Balkans. Access to the Eastern Mediterranean, which required a revision of the Straits agreements by all the great powers, was an important aim of Izvolski's foreign policy. He favoured cooperation with Britain, and even with Austria-Hungary, the two powers most interested in the Straits and Balkans.

The Anglo-Russian entente was concluded in August 1907. Its terms included the partition of Persia into two spheres, with British influence predominant in the south and Russian in the north. Britain could not annex Afghanistan, but Russia was not allowed to interfere in Afghan politics and Izvolski also gave up Russia's minimal interests in Tibet. In part the entente was aimed at Germany. Russia and Britain aimed to block German expansion in the Ottoman Empire and Persia. Britain had already refused to support the German-backed Baghdad railway project in 1903. Russian diplomats considered Germany a potentially formidable rival in the contest for influence in Central Asia. The Anglo-Russian entente blocked yet another avenue of *Weltpolitik*, though Germany would remain the dominant power at Constantinople until the end of the First World War. On a global level, Britain and her entente partners were blocking German expansion. World empire theory suggested that those states that did not or could not expand were doomed to become second-rate powers. To a certain extent, men like Bülow and Tirpitz shared this assumption, though imperial expansion was never raised into a vital interest. Therefore, Britain's ability to block expansion was a serious limitation on Germany's room for manoeuvre in global politics, though by no means was it a fatal blow to German security nor indeed was the stifling of German expansion complete. By negotiating on areas of mutual interest in the Baltics and on the Baghdad railway, Izvolski made clear to Germany that Russian policy had not taken a turn against Berlin. The entente, as far as Grey was concerned, also aimed to restore the balance of power in Europe, checking German ambitions to assume leadership of a continental bloc. In this respect, the entente was a defensive instrument, aimed at preserving stability in the international system.

---

[28] David McClaren McDonald, *United Government and Foreign Policy in Russia, 1900–1914* (Cambridge, MA, 1992), p. 109.

Paul Schroeder has suggested that Austria-Hungary suffered most from the Anglo-Russian entente. In the 1870s and 1880s, Austria-Hungary and Britain had cooperated to check Russia's ambitions in the Balkans and the Ottoman Empire. Since the 1890s, British and Austro-Hungarian interests had drifted apart. The entente meant Austria-Hungary could no longer rely on British support against Russia in the Near East. Indeed, even before the conclusion of the entente, Grey and Aehrenthal were in dispute over a reform programme for Macedonia, which the Austro-Hungarian foreign minister was blocking. Aehrenthal considered British reform projects as destabilising. Macedonia was the cockpit of Balkan politics, as Serbia, Bulgaria, and Greece staked claims to its territory on religious and ethnic grounds, the Ottoman Empire sought to uphold its sovereignty, and Austria-Hungary and Russia tried to manage the various antagonisms, while remaining suspicious of each other. Izvolski hoped to continue cooperating with Austria-Hungary. In September 1907, he met Aehrenthal to discuss Austro-Hungarian interests in the Balkans, especially Bosnia, which was under Habsburg occupation, and the Russian aim of revising the Straits settlement.

If anything, the state that suffered most from the entente was the Ottoman Empire, rather than Austria-Hungary or Germany. The great powers hatched various reform projects for Macedonia, the revision of the Straits settlement would affect Ottoman security, and Bosnia, although occupied by Austria-Hungary, remained formally part of the Ottoman Empire. Moreover, Anglo-Russian antagonism, which Ottoman diplomacy had exploited for decades, had diminished. Grey, Aehrenthal, and Izvolski were all prepared to countenance measures that would further impair Ottoman prestige and security. It was no surprise, therefore, that the first crisis, the Bosnian crisis, to pit the two alliance blocs against each other started with a revolt by Turkish army officers in Macedonia.

Before examining the Bosnian crisis, it is worth reviewing the argument that the period between 1904 and 1907 was 'the essential starting point for the diplomatic origins of the First World War'.[29] Stevenson pointed to the formation of two opposing groupings while A. J. P. Taylor argued that the Moroccan crisis 'gave a first hint of things to come and foreshadowed the world war . . . it was a "true" crisis, a turning point in European history', which put war between France and Germany back onto the international agenda for the first time since the War in Sight crisis of 1875.[30] First, Britain's entente policy created a more rigid bloc system. This made it difficult for Britain to act as a disinterested

[29] David Stevenson, *Armaments and the Coming of War: Europe, 1904–1914* (Oxford, 1996), p. 64.
[30] A. J. P. Taylor, *The Struggle for Mastery in Europe, 1848–1918* (Oxford, 1954), p. 441.

mediator or honest broker, as Bismarck might have put it. Upholding the ententes became an objective of British policy, just as the maintenance of alliances was an objective for the other great powers. For Germany, the alliance with Austria-Hungary had much greater significance after 1905 than it had had during the previous decade. Bülow reorientated German policy away from *Weltpolitik* towards a consolidation of Germany's position in central Europe. Unfortunately, however, Austria-Hungary was a weak ally, making it even more important for Germany to support the Habsburgs. German leaders were the authors of their own dilemma, however, as their policy in Morocco turned the Anglo-French entente against Germany and their efforts to forge a continental bloc in 1904 and 1905 fuelled suspicions of their aims in other capitals. Second, the focus of great power politics returned to Europe. The global ambitions of the great powers had always been linked to the European balance, but the Moroccan crisis, Björko, and the reorientation of Russian policy under Izvolski to the Balkans marked an important change in the theatre of international politics. Crises in Europe, North Africa, and the Ottoman Empire, weakened by the reorientation of great power politics, were likely to generate more severe tensions, because vital interests were at stake.

Nonetheless, the path from the end of the Russo-Japanese to the First World War was far from clear. Already in 1906, Grey's diplomacy showed how the ententes and alliances might be used as a means of managing international crises, encouraging restraint, and deterring aggression. Grey was not prepared to go to war to support French advances in Morocco; but he was prepared to support France if Germany attacked her in an effort to overthrow the balance of power in Europe. Austria-Hungary's support for Germany at Algeciras was lukewarm. The Habsburgs had no interest in getting dragged into a war over their ally's putative interests in North Africa. Alliances could act as restraints on the dangerous ambitions of great powers. Izvolski had a flexible attitude towards the groupings of powers. Although Russia was clearly associated with Britain and France, the Russian foreign minister was prepared to cooperate with Austria-Hungary and Germany on specific matters of mutual interest. Membership of a grouping did not automatically translate into antagonism towards powers in the other bloc. Alliances provided security for the great powers, while remaining a flexible instrument in international politics. They were both a means and an end, an instrument and an objective of great power politics.

From Bosnia to Morocco, 1908–1911

In early July 1908, a group of officers in the Turkish Third Army launched a revolt against the Sultan, calling for the restoration of the constitution of 1876. The Sultan's attempt to crush the revolt, in which officers combined with civilian members of the Committee of Unity and Progress (CUP), withered. The general, whom he sent to deal with the rebels, Semsi Pasha, was assassinated in Monastir on 7 July. By mid-July, the CUP controlled the whole of Macedonia. On 24 July 1908, the Sultan accepted the restoration of the constitution. The events of July entered history as the revolt of the Young Turks. The Young Turks aimed to preserve the Ottoman Empire from internal decay and foreign encroachment by reintroducing the constitution of 1876. The power of the Sultan was curbed, elections called, and basic freedoms recognised.

The dismemberment of the Ottoman Empire had fuelled this movement amongst a new generation of officers. The timing of the revolt was prompted by concerns about the intentions of Britain, Russia, and Austria-Hungary towards the Ottoman Empire and particularly towards the international plans for reforms in Macedonia, which, in turn, was the site of a complex struggle between Turkey, Greece, Serbia, and Bulgaria. In Macedonia a series of religious and ethnic divisions criss-crossed each other. The Balkan states used a variety of instruments to advance their influence in the province. Bulgaria and Serbia funded schools, while the Greek Orthodox and the Bulgarian Exarchate competed for the religious loyalties of the population. The Ottoman Empire played these groups off against each other, using Serbia as a balance against their more serious rivals, Greece and Bulgaria. By the late 1890s, Bulgaria had supported irregular forces and sent arms across the border. A Bulgarian-sponsored revolt in 1902 was easily crushed by Ottoman forces, but it provoked a renewal of international interest in the region. The usual spate of reform plans followed, while violence continued. In May 1908, the CUP had issued a declaration, demanding that the great powers abandon their reform plans and respect Ottoman sovereignty. The meeting of Edward VII and Nicholas II at Reval in June 1908, when the two entente partners agreed a set of reforms for Macedonia, was perceived as a threat to the Ottoman Empire and it triggered the revolt.

The crisis in Ottoman politics, in turn, led to the declaration of Bulgarian independence on 5 October 1908 and the annexation of Bosnia by Austria-Hungary the following day. These events, especially the latter, triggered one of the most severe crises, the Bosnian crisis, before the First World War. Historians have argued that the Bosnian crisis marked one, if not the most, important staging post on the way to war in 1914, as it signalled the renewal of confrontation within Europe, shattered the détente between Russia and Austria-Hungary, sparked antagonism between Germany and Russia, saw the first direct confrontation between the two blocs, and was only resolved by the threatened use of military force. For Williamson, the occupation of Bosnia by Austria-Hungary in 1878, its annexation thirty years later, and the assassination of the Archduke at Sarajevo 'though separated by decades are inextricably linked'.[31] Between the Bosnian and Second Moroccan crises, Schöllgen claimed a series of events destabilised international peace. The crisis rewarded 'a new, almost reckless style of diplomacy', contends John Charmley, 'the success of which inculcated lessons, which would be remembered in 1914'.[32] The Bosnian crisis is significant, argues Schroeder, not only because it 'started Europe's descent into the maelstrom, but even more because it involved the last serious attempt to turn European politics around by reviving its previous spirit and ethos'.[33] The crisis marked a further departure from the norms and practices that had sustained the great power peace. The Austro-Hungarian move unilaterally shredded the treaty of Berlin and Aehrenthal's justification of the annexation as for the benefit of the local population opened the space for Balkan states to claim that ethnic minorities in the Ottoman and Habsburg empire would enjoy greater freedoms within nation-states rather than multi-ethnic empires.

Schroeder notes that the crisis arose, somewhat bizarrely, from an attempt to renew Austro-Russian cooperation in the Balkans. But cooperation was purchased at the expense of the Ottoman Empire. The CUP was correct to identify the increasing external pressure on the empire from 1906 onwards, resulting from changes in British, Austrian, and Russian foreign policy. In 1906, Aehrenthal became Austro-Hungarian foreign minister. While he took up his post in the Ballhausplatz, Conrad became Chief of the General Staff and Archduke Franz Ferdinand began to press for a more activist foreign policy. Since the bloody coup of 1903 in Serbia, relations between the new Karadjordjevic dynasty and the Habsburgs had worsened, culminating in the Pig War of 1906, when Hungary closed its borders to Serbian agricultural imports. Previously a client of Austria-Hungary, Serbia now reorientated its policy towards St Petersburg. Aehrenthal decided that Austria-Hungary needed to bolster its position in the Balkans by using one of the more modern instruments of exerting great power influence – building a railway – and one of the more traditional methods – annexing territory. The proposed

[31] Samuel Williamson, *Austria-Hungary and the Origins of the First World War* (London, 1991), p. 59.

[32] John Charmley, *Splendid Isolation? Britain and the Balance of Power, 1870–1914* (London, 1999), p. 353.

[33] Paul Schroeder, 'Stealing Horses to Great Applause: Austria-Hungary's Decision in 1914 in Systemic Perspective', in Holger Afflerbach and David Stevenson, eds, *An Improbable War? The Outbreak of World War I and European Political Culture before 1914* (Oxford, 2007), p. 40.

railway line was to pass through the Sanjak Novi Pazar, a sliver of territory that ran between Serbia and Montenegro and linked Bosnia to the
rest of the Ottoman Empire.[34] A railway line offered commercial advantages and hemmed in Serbia. Aehrenthal's announcement of the plans
for the railway on 27 January 1908 met with opposition in London and
St Petersburg, effectively extending the 1907 entente to Europe. Coupled
with Anglo-Russian cooperation over the Macedonian reforms, Austria-
Hungary's room for manoeuvre was extremely limited in the Balkans.

On 21 January 1908, less than a week before Aehrenthal made public
the plans for the Sanjak railway, the Russian Council of Ministers had
met. Izvolski argued that Russian policy was being stifled in the Balkans,
alleging that Austro-Hungarian policy had departed from the spirit of the
Mürzsteg agreement. Izvolski urged the pursuit of a more active policy to
restore Russia's prestige. He identified the 1907 agreements with Japan
and Britain as the prelude to his policy initiatives in the Balkans and the
Ottoman Empire. Kokovtsov, Stolypin, and the military leaders opposed
him. 'Any policy other than a purely defensive one', argued Stolypin,
'would be at present the delirium of an abnormal government and would
bring with it danger for the Dynasty.'[35] In April, Izvolski, in a speech to
the Duma, reiterated Russia's mission in the Balkans, as protector of the
Balkan Christians and leader of the pan-Slavic movement. The speech
was a response to public outcry about Austria-Hungary's railway plans
and expansion in the Balkans, but in reality, Izvolski was more interested
in the Straits than in the fate of the 'little brothers'.

The breakdown of the Mürzsteg entente between Austria-Hungary
and Russia and their mutual need to bolster their great power positions
by pursuing a revisionist policy in the Near East was the basis for the deal,
struck in the summer of 1908 between Aehrenthal and Izvolski, two men
who harboured a deep dislike of each other. The Young Turk revolt
accelerated the talks between the two protagonists. As far as Russia was
concerned, the strengthening of the Ottoman Empire, through a reform
programme, pushed back the day when the agreement over the Straits
might be revised, while the planned elections throughout the Ottoman
Empire had the potential to undermine the Austro-Hungarian occupation of Bosnia, a territory still under Ottoman sovereignty. At Buchlau,
in September 1908, the deal was struck – Russia would not stand in the
way of Austro-Hungarian annexation of Bosnia, while Austria-Hungary
would support the Russian demands for the revisions of the Straits

[34] Tamara Scheer, *"Minimale Kosten, absolut kein Blut"*. *Österreich-Ungarns Präsenz im
     Sandžak Novipazar* (1878–1908) (Frankfurt, 2013).
[35] Cited in McDonald, *United Government*, p. 117.

agreement, which currently prevented Russian warships from accessing the Eastern Mediterranean. But Izvolski's task, securing the revision of the Straits, required the agreement of all the great powers. Although he had hints of support from Germany and Britain, he needed time to prepare his coup. Austro-Hungarian troops had occupied Bosnia since 1878, so the annexation was a much easier task and arguably a less significant change in the map of Europe than a revision of the Straits agreement, which might enable the extension of Russian naval power into the Mediterranean. It was however a violation of the treaty of Berlin. In the weeks before the annexation, the Council of Ministers in Vienna had discussed the public justification for the move. By basing their justification primarily on the grounds that absorption into the Habsburg empire would benefit the local population, Aehrenthal abandoned the multilateral treaty of Berlin. 'The treaty of Berlin is completely torn up', argued the liberal *Berliner Tageblatt*, 'and the solution of the confusing Balkan problems is made more difficult by the fact that one of the signatory powers, not just a disloyal vassal of the Sultan [Prince Ferdinand of Bulgaria], has broken it.'[36]

On 5 October, Bulgaria, still nominally under Ottoman sovereignty, declared independence. Immediately following Bulgaria's declaration, Austria-Hungary announced its annexation of Bosnia. The Buchlau agreement unravelled and, to the great embarrassment of Izvolski, the Austro-Hungarian Foreign Office published the text. His willingness to abandon Balkan Slavs (almost half the population of Bosnia was Serbian) for the Straits called forth widespread public criticism. Any possibility of revising the Straits agreement evaporated. In some ways, the crisis would show that in the Near East, Britain, France, and Germany shared a common interest in upholding the Ottoman Empire, while Austria and Russia were revisionist powers in the region. Regional interests cut across the alliance system. The crisis escalated as Serbia and Turkey sought compensation for Bulgarian independence and the annexation of Bosnia. Serbia's demands were predicated on Russian support, as Izvolski scurried around the capitals of Europe, trying to rebuild his diplomatic position and secure some compensation.

The crisis provided the first serious test of the alliance system since the conclusion of the Anglo-Russian entente. Grey refused to support any revision to the Straits agreement, but did support Russian proposals for compensation for Serbia and a conference to ratify the annexation. Grey was not prepared to back his diplomatic promises with military or naval power. British policy has come in for some trenchant criticism, for

---

[36] 'Oesterreich-Bosnien', *Berliner Tageblatt*, 8 October 1908, nr 513, p. 1.

allegedly giving Russia a blank cheque, adhering rigidly to bloc politics, and weakening Austria-Hungary. The most important cause of restraint in the crisis was Russia's lack of readiness for war, but her partners in the Triple Entente reinforced this restraint. In March 1909, as Serbia's refusal to accept the annexation made war in the Balkans a strong possibility, Grey put pressure on Belgrade to back down. Further, the demands for a conference and compensation for Serbia were not extreme. Grey saw the conference as a matter of form, as indeed these types of conference generally were – as Germany had found to its cost in 1906. Compensation was a means of ending crises, building golden bridges for overstretched power to retreat over, and balancing the international system. Granted, compensation for a small state like Serbia would have been an unusual step, but it would also have been a proxy compensation for her great power sponsor, Russia.

During the Bosnian crisis, Germany gave full diplomatic and military support to Austria-Hungary, tightening the bonds of an alliance that had been a shadow presence in the international system for over a decade. It confirmed what Bülow had told William II in May 1906, following Germany's defeat at Algeciras: 'our relations with Austria-Hungary are now more important than ever because the imperial state is our one truly reliable ally'.[37] In early 1909, the two chiefs of the General Staff, Moltke and Conrad, began talks on common military action. German and Austro-Hungarian military leaders realised that Russia was not in a position to fight, so when Germany delivered an ultimatum to St Petersburg in March 1909 to recognise the annexation, they were confident that the crisis would not end in war. This awareness of Russia's crippling military weakness affected diplomacy on both sides. In fact, it made the Bosnian crisis very different to the July crisis, when there was no such certainty about the military intentions and capabilities of the great powers. On 18 March 1909, the German ambassador told Franz Joseph, the Habsburg Emperor, that William II would 'stand faithfully by his side'. Others in German leadership circles were less enamoured with Austro-Hungarian policy. Germany's position in Turkey was undermined, relations with Russia damaged, and dependency on Austria-Hungary increased.

The Bosnian crisis was not the only issue creating tensions between Britain and Germany in 1908 and 1909. The notorious *Daily Telegraph* interview, in which William II claimed that the majority of the German people had wanted a war against Britain and were only held back by the Kaiser, came to symbolise the poor relations between the two countries.

---

[37] Jürgen Angelow, *Kalkül and Prestige. Der Zweibund am Vorabend des Ersten Weltkrieges* (Cologne, 2000), p. 190.

The gap between British and German interests remained wide, despite Bülow's willingness to abandon *Weltpolitik*. For one thing, Tirpitz's naval building programme caused a major scare in Britain in 1909, when it seemed that German dreadnought construction rates might surpass those of the Royal Navy. The British response was decisive. Lloyd George, initially sceptical of proposed increases in naval expenditure, supplied the extra money for naval and welfare expenditure in the 1909 People's Budget. Britain's financial strength proved to be a decisive advantage in the naval race with Germany. By the summer of 1909, the naval scare had died down in Britain and Bethmann Hollweg had replaced Bülow, who had fallen into disfavour after the *Daily Telegraph* interview. Bethmann Hollweg hinted at the possibility of a neutrality pact, according to which Britain would remain neutral if either France or Russia attacked Germany. In return, Germany would accept a smaller fleet. To British eyes, this was simply another trap, designed to split the entente and establish a German-dominated bloc on the continent. Before the First World War, Britain consistently refused such a deal. As Lahme has suggested, British policy became more and more like that of the continental great powers, focusing on the preservation of its entente partnerships and the building up of its naval and military power.

At the same time as Germany prepared to deliver an ultimatum at St Petersburg and Britain was in the throes of a naval scare, relations between France and Germany were improving. Blocs had not become completely rigid; cooperation across the divisions between the Triple Entente and Triple Alliance remained possible until 1914. The degree to which this represented an alternative, more peaceful and stabilising vision of the international system has been a contentious debate amongst historians in recent years.

Between the Bosnian crisis and the Moroccan crisis, there were important examples of cooperation between great powers across the divisions of the alliance system. In February 1909, France and Germany agreed to cooperate on commercial projects in Morocco. Since the end of the First Moroccan crisis, a warmer tone had entered Franco-German relations. Leading political figures spoke of a common civilising mission and the advantages of an economic détente. But it was the Bosnian crisis that gave the decisive impetus to negotiations. The negotiations drove a wedge between France and Russia, secured Germany's position on the continent, and promised to tie down French military resources in Morocco, which Bülow called a 'wasps' nest'. French diplomats were uncertain how to interpret the agreement. Jules Cambon, the ambassador to Berlin, was a persistent advocate of limited cooperation with Germany. He argued that German expansion, driven by her commercial strength and political power, could provide a safety valve for European politics. He pushed for cooperation on the Baghdad railway and Morocco. Others were more sceptical. Pichon told Jules Cambon's brother, Paul, the ambassador to London, that the agreement with Germany meant 'absolutely nothing'. At most it was a temporary expedient, in his view, to signal French unwillingness to support Russia in the Bosnian crisis. Pichon wanted to maintain the status quo in the Near East, whereas Izvolski's intrigues contributed to undermining the stability of the Ottoman Empire.

Alliance politics continued to be extremely fluid in 1909 and 1910. The great powers sought to divide their rivals, remind their allies of their worth, and gain local advantages. Arguably, this flexibility owed much to the absence of a major international crisis. In October 1909, Italy and Russia came to a secret agreement, in which they agreed to support the status quo in the Balkans, and if the status quo was undermined, to support any settlement based on the nationality principle. It was an agreement aimed at Italy's ally, Austria-Hungary. It was also the product of the tearing up of the treaty of Berlin. The nationality principle as the basis of political and social order in the Balkans replaced the assumptions of the treaty of Berlin, which had prioritised the interests of the great powers and stability guaranteed by treaty law. The following year, in November 1910, in a much more surprising turn of events, Germany and Russia came to an agreement. Both states agreed to support the status quo in the Balkans, against any further Austro-Hungarian advances. In August 1911, Germany and Russia agreed to stop blocking each other's respective railway projects: the Berlin–Baghdad railway and Russia's plans for a railway in northern Persia.

The significance of these agreements is tangled in a web of different motives, interests, and reactions. First, the manoeuvres created uncertainty about the reliability of the alliance systems. For Austro-Hungarian diplomats, Potsdam, the meeting place of William II and Nicholas II in 1910, became a by-word for German disloyalty to the Dual Alliance. Grey was concerned that Russia was drifting away from the entente, as differences between Russia and Britain over the future constitutional structure of Persia coincided with the agreements between Russia and Germany over the Balkans, Persia, and Baghdad railway. The rumours generated by these meetings and agreements indicated the high levels of distrust that characterised European diplomacy before the First World War. Second, the possibility of driving a wedge in the opposing bloc appealed to the great powers. This was destabilising because the alliance system had become a bulwark of each state's security policy. A more insecure great power was not necessarily a more restrained great power.

On the other hand, there is strong evidence to suggest that none of the powers intended to defect from their bloc. Bethmann Hollweg's first aim in 1910 was to repair relations with Russia and to signal Germany's willingness to restrain Austria-Hungary in the Balkans, a promise the German government kept during the Balkan Wars. Kiderlen hoped for 'more intimate and closer relations between Russia and Germany than between any two of the other powers, who belong to the two different groups, which have formed in Europe recently'.[38] Equally, while Sazonov assured Bethmann Hollweg in 1910 that Britain would not find support in Russia for a policy aimed against Germany, his real goal was to balance Russia between the two blocs. Sazonov defined the Triple Entente as a defensive grouping, conforming to the policy of his brotherin-law, Stolypin, who argued that war 'during the next few years would be fatal for Russia and for the dynasty'.[39] Bethmann Hollweg's proposed naval/neutrality pact with Britain was too radical to be accommodated within the existing alliance system, but Kiderlen suggested that specific agreements on secondary issues, including colonies and the Baghdad railway, would improve relations between the two countries. Nothing came of this suggestion in the short term, but Kiderlen anticipated the direction of Anglo-German relations after the Second Moroccan crisis.

These agreements in 1909 and 1910 did not alter the alliance system, but they were not designed to do so. Instead, they repaired fractured relations and enabled great powers to pursue specific interests. Austria-Hungary was hemmed in by the agreements between Russia and Italy and between Germany and Russia, but the annexation of Bosnia required consolidation and the Habsburg empire had become a status quo power after the crisis of 1908/9. Writing over the period between the onset of the Bosnian crisis and the spring of 1910, André Tardieu argued that the Triple Entente and Triple Alliance had achieved a balance of power in Europe, providing stability in international politics and the basis for 'a peace, which is equitable for all'.[40]

In early 1911, one of these agreements, between Germany and France over Morocco, collapsed. The collapse of the agreement was prompted by a dispute over commercial rights between a German company and a Franco-German mining consortium and French designs to exploit continued trouble in Morocco to establish a protectorate. As in 1905, France's aggressive policy in Morocco sparked an international crisis. In

---

[38] Ralf Forsbach, *Alfred von Kiderlen-Wächter (1852–1912)* (Göttingen, 1997), vol. 1, p. 400.
[39] McDonald, *United Government*, p. 159.
[40] André Tardieu, *La France et les alliances. La lutte pour l'équilibre, 1871–1910* (Paris, 1910), p. 416.

2. European sovereigns gather for the funeral of HM King Edward VII at
Windsor Castle in Britain (IWM Q 81794). Left to right, standing: King
Haakon VII of Norway, King Ferdinand of Bulgaria, King Manoel of Portugal,
Kaiser William II of Germany, King George I of Greece, King Albert of
Belgium. Seated: King Alfonso XIII of Spain, HM King George V, and King
Frederick VII of Denmark. Monarchs continued to play a role in diplomacy up
to the First World War, in terms of both their actual interventions in day-to-day
diplomacy and their symbolic role as representatives of states. This photograph
displays the 'monarchical international' (Paulmann), though the deceased king,
Edward VII, disliked Kaiser William II intensely.

Germany, public opinion was outraged at French actions. Kiderlen, the
guiding hand of German policy in the crisis, also saw Morocco as an
opportunity to force French concessions to Germany in central Africa. If
French policy triggered the crisis, Kiderlen's reaction turned it into a full-
blown war scare. On 17 May 1911, French troops began their march on
Fez. William II was reluctant to take any action, but on 26 June, Kiderlen
and Bethmann Hollweg convinced him to send a gunboat, SMS *Panther*,
to the Moroccan port of Agadir. In early July, Cambon and Joseph Caillaux, the French premier, hinted at some territorial compensation in

central Africa, but baulked when Kiderlen demanded the whole of the French Congo. As the crisis escalated, Lloyd George made a speech at the Mansion House on 21 July 1911, where he signalled British support for France. This setback to German ambitions was followed by an outflow of French capital from the Berlin money market in early September. Diplomatically isolated, cornered by the expectations of radical nationalist opinion, and unprepared for war, Germany began to retreat. Negotiations between France and Germany recommenced on 18 September and concluded on 4 November 1911. In return for recognising a French protectorate over Morocco, Germany received some territories from the French Congo.

How did the Moroccan crisis reflect the strength and weaknesses of the international system and what were the consequences? First, international crises continued to arise over contests for influence in weak states and volatile regions. The great powers were responsible for this, as they partitioned countries, even continents, and carved out spheres of influence. Significantly, the revolution in China in 1911 – coinciding with the Moroccan crisis – did not spark a parallel crisis in the Far East, as would have been the case a decade earlier. States such as Morocco and the Ottoman Empire found that the shifting constellation of the great powers came at their expense. Although Bismarck might have considered that the Balkans were not worth the bones of the unfortunate Pomeranian musketeer and that tussles between the great powers in North Africa were a diversion of tensions to the periphery, his map of Europe was too restricted. The Balkans, the Mediterranean, and North Africa had been part of the European balance of power throughout the nineteenth century. Crises in these regions had always been much more serious than the spats over colonies in Africa or the contest for influence in the Far East. Changes in the balance of influence in North Africa and the Balkans caused stresses and strains amongst the great powers.

French actions marked a further devaluation of international agreements. Although German claims that they were defending principles of international law rang hollow, the easy dismissal these claims was a further blow to the great power peace. The importance of public justifications of foreign policy moves – such as the annexation of Bosnia in 1908 and French expansion in Morocco – is that they provided a guide to the norms that underpinned expectations of great power politics. By devaluing these norms, such as the non-violability of international agreements without the consent of all signatories and the principles of international law, the restraints on great power action were removed. Before the First World War, new norms – notably the nationality principle – were emerging as an alternative basis for the European and international order. But the principle of nationality was difficult to reconcile with the system of great power politics. With the exception of France and Italy, all of the great powers were multi-national empires. British, Russian, and Austro-Hungarian politics faced serious challenges from national minorities on the eve of the war. In the case of Austria-Hungary, this challenge was compounded by the success of Balkan states, who claimed that their co-nationals were trapped in a Habsburg prison. The prospect of national unifications was incompatible with Austria-Hungary's continued existence as a great power.

But did these tensions encourage thoughts of resolving tensions by means of a general European conflict? The answer by 1911 seemed to be no. Caillaux favoured negotiations with Germany, rather than escalating the crisis with military measures. He preferred to pressure the German government by withdrawing French capital from the Reich. William II was resolutely opposed to war and Kiderlen never seriously considered war as an option during the crisis. He was prepared to adopt a policy of brinkmanship. 'Whoever declares in advance', he told Bethmann Hollweg, 'that he will not fight will achieve nothing in politics.' He continued, however: 'I do not think that the French will pick up the gauntlet; but they must feel that we are decided on extreme measures.'[41] Kiderlen's policy failed because the British countered with their own policy of brinkmanship. Lloyd George's Mansion House speech, signalling British support for France and turning the Moroccan crisis into an issue of national prestige, was designed as a warning to Germany. The famous meeting of the Committee of Imperial Defence (CID) on 23 August, at which the War Office's strategy of sending the British Expeditionary Force (BEF) to the continent, if a general war broke out, triumphed over the Admiralty's preference for a naval blockade, indicated that British war planning had stepped up a notch. However, it did not mark a commitment to fight alongside France – the prime minister, Asquith, was concerned that British military backing might make France more intransigent.

Finally, the Moroccan crisis sheds further light on the alliance system. Alliances were defensive, encouraged restraint, and provided security. In October 1911, William II and Nicholas II staged a high-profile meeting. Nothing could have more effectively displayed the refusal of Russia to support France over Morocco. In August 1911, Izvolski, now ambassador to Paris, told Caillaux that the alliance was defensive. Russia had her own interests, notably the maintenance of peace and domestic political recovery, but it was also a snub to France, following that country's agreement with Germany over Morocco at the height of the Bosnian

[41] Cited in Forsbach, *Kiderlen*, vol. II, pp. 471–73.

crisis. In short, the Franco-Russian alliance retained its defensive orientation, to the extent that Sukhomlinov's 1910 war plan concentrated
forces so deep within Russia that they would be unable to offer France
any effective aid in case of a Franco-German war. Initially, the British
cabinet refused to give full support to its entente partner, holding France
largely responsible for the crisis. Germany's excessive demands and the
show of force at Agadir transformed British policy. In other words, the
entente only became a determinant of British policy late in the crisis. In
Vienna, Aehrenthal noted that 'there were certain limits' to the alliance
with Germany and those limits did not extend to North Africa. Austria's
unwillingness to support German policy over Morocco was not the most
significant restraint, but it contributed to the maintenance of peace in
1911.

The Moroccan crisis is prominent in the long list of turning points in
international politics before 1914. Some features of the crisis indicated
the increasing fragility of peace. First, a growing number of politicians,
soldiers, and members of the public considered a general great power
conflict as a possibility. Despite the general desire to avoid war, governments feared that crisis management might break down. The conduct of
diplomacy had also been transformed into a dangerous 'who blinks first'
game. Bluff, threat, and inflexibility characterised the diplomatic postur-
ing of Germany, France, and Britain at certain stages during the crisis.
Kiderlen's argument that Morocco was a question of prestige was a desperate miscalculation of Germany's national interest and was a viewpoint
fortunately not shared by William II. Second, the crisis led to a general
arms race. Reeling from its diplomatic isolation, Germany took the lead,
planning massive increases in military spending in late 1911. By 1913, the
great powers were engaged in a spiralling arms race. This contributed to
the militarisation of diplomacy. Third, the impact on the alliance system
was less clear. The entente between Britain and France was strengthened. However, Britain had been reluctant to support France in the first
part of the crisis and allies in both camps stressed their defensive, not
offensive, responsibilities.

As the crisis began to ease in early September, Grey wrote to Lloyd
George: 'Unless Germany really intends war at this moment, which I
do not believe, there will be no war, but after this crisis is over the
whole question of future developments of foreign policy will have to
be considered very carefully and coolly in the light of recent events.'[42]
There were some potential benefits from the crisis. Statesmen, having

---

[42] Grey to Lloyd George, 5 September 1911, Lloyd George Papers, Houses of Parliament
Archive, C/4/14, fol. 5.

come close to war, now devoted more attention to strengthening the bonds of peace. Of course, each great power had different views on how to achieve this. The conflict between alternative conceptions of a stable international system rumbled on after 1911. What was significant was the general desire to improve crisis management and to ease the tensions that had built up since the formation of the blocs.

The most important immediate consequence, and the one which damaged the international system the most, was the Italian decision to invade Tripoli in September 1911. It triggered two further wars in the Balkans in 1912 and 1913, which eroded the foundations of peace. Bismarck's diversion of conflicts to the periphery was about to rebound along the North African coast of the Mediterranean around to the Balkans and back to the heart of Europe.

From Morocco to Bosnia, 1911–1914

Between the Moroccan crisis and the assassination of Archduke Franz Ferdinand at Sarajevo, governments sought to preserve their national security and maintain peace by building up military power as a deterrent against attack, consolidating alliances, cooperating across the divisions of the two blocs, and reviving the practices of the Concert of Europe. Peace between the great powers was maintained through a series of crises and wars – the Moroccan crisis, the Italo-Turkish War, the two Balkan Wars of 1912/13, and the Liman von Sanders crisis in 1913/14. By early 1914, many informed experts believed that the international system had weathered its most severe test and could look forward to a more stable future. In April 1914, Gottlieb von Jagow, the German Secretary of State, suggested that great power rivalry in the Ottoman Empire could be directed into 'peaceful channels'.[43] The resolution of a succession of crises, the maintenance of peace between the great powers, and the comments of perceptive contemporaries suggest that war was certainly not the inevitable or indeed likely outcome of developments in international politics after the Moroccan crisis. However, the bonds of peace frayed over the course of the Balkan Wars. The region became the fulcrum on which European politics turned, a site where the security interests of two powers, Austria-Hungary and Russia, confronted each other, where the value of alliances were tested, and where new norms and practices, such as the nationality principle, challenged the logic of great power politics.

[43] Klaus Wilsberg, *Terrible ami – aimable ennemi. Kooperation und Konflikt in den deutsch-französischen Beziehungen 1911–1914* (Bonn, 1998), p. 164; Friedrich Kießling, *Gegen den großen Krieg? Entspannung in den internationalen Beziehungen 1911–1914* (Munich, 2002), pp. 301–4.

In the aftermath of these wars, decisions in Vienna, St Petersburg, and Berlin, made between October 1913 and June 1914, provided the context for the decisions of these powers in the July crisis.

The main instigator of the consolidation of the alliance system was Raymond Poincaré. Elected as President of the Council (premier), in January 1912, he told the Chamber of Deputies that 'we intend to remain faithful to our alliances and our friendships'.[44] Alliances were fundamental to French national security, but also to the maintenance of peace. Poincaré offered a vision of Franco-German relations in which the two neighbours lived side by side, in a 'sincerely pacific spirit', based on 'mutual respect of interests and dignity'.

During his first year in office, he worked to restore the alliance with Russia and to develop the entente with Britain into a more precise agreement. He replaced the ageing ambassador to St Petersburg, Georges Louis, with Théophile Delcassé, the former foreign minister, who favoured closer relations. French and Russian General Staff officers met to discuss military strategy. In August, Poincaré visited St Petersburg to discuss the common interests of the two allies. The extent of his commitment to the alliance is a controversial subject, particularly the question of French support for Russian policy in the Ottoman Empire and the Balkans. French and Russian interests in this area were at odds, as France had large investments in the Ottoman Empire and wanted to preserve it, while Russia pushed, yet again, for revision of the Straits settlement. By April 1912, French diplomats were aware of the Serbo-Bulgarian agreement, backed by Russia. This grouping was a potential threat to the status quo in the area. Keiger argues that Poincaré opposed the Balkan League on the grounds that it threatened stability in the Near East. Girault, on the other hand, notes that even after Poincaré knew about the Balkan League, he made little effort to restrain Russia. Effectively, Schmidt argues, he had prioritised the alliance over peace in the Balkans. Poincaré assured Russian leaders on several occasions that in the case of a general European war starting in the Balkans, France would support Russia. The scenario – the 'Balkans inception scenario' as Clark has termed it – played out in the following sequence: if Austria-Hungary attacked Serbia, Russia would attack Austria-Hungary, Germany would attack Russia in accordance its alliance with Austria-Hungary, and then France would mobilise against Germany. Poincaré hoped that this clear offer of support would prevent any Russia defection from the Triple Entente and deter Germany from underwriting an Austro-Hungarian attack on Serbia. But in defining the *casus belli* under the terms of the

<hr>

[44] Wilsberg, *Terrible ami*, p. 58.

Franco-Russian alliance so clearly, he had also diminished the French capacity to restrain its ally.[45]

Anglo-French relations were strengthened in November 1912, when Grey and Cambon exchanged letters, agreeing to non-binding consultations between the two entente partners during international crises. This followed the withdrawal of the British fleet from the Mediterranean and the stationing of the French fleet at Toulon, effectively dividing the naval burden between the two powers. There was no formally binding agreement, but the French government placed great value on the consolidation of the entente.

Poincaré's commitment to the alliance system went so far that he desisted from trying to upset the Triple Alliance or forge a détente with Germany. He believed that détente with Germany was a trap, which would leave France isolated from Russia, as she had been in 1911. When the French ambassador to Vienna, Philippe Crozier, tried to lure Austria-Hungary towards the Triple Entente, he was sacked, while Poincaré's forceful condemnation of Italian policy in the Italo-Turkish War damaged relations with Rome. 'The penetration of the alliances', wrote St Aulaire, 'in fact, corrupts and dissolves them. By upsetting the balance and by obscuring the clarity of the situation, in reality, it leads to ambiguity and instability. In doing so, it eventually weakens the guarantees of peace, while claiming to increase them by the chimera of universal harmony.'[46]

Alliances were threatened by internal differences, as well as external temptations. The Anglo-Russian entente in Central Asia was coming under pressure. In Persia, there was continued friction, as Russia supported the deposed Shah against constitutional parties, which looked to Britain for backing. The spheres of influence in the north and south, carved out in 1907, looked increasingly unstable. At a meeting at Balmoral on 24 and 25 September, Grey and Sazonov managed to agree on the restoration of stability in Persia, but this agreement covered a multitude of differences over the extension of their spheres of influence and the financial future of the country. Tensions in Central Asia continued to afflict the Anglo-Russian entente until the outbreak of the war. Nonetheless, while there was pressure for a new agreement, neither Grey nor Sazonov was prepared to abandon the framework of the entente.

By the end of 1911, the Triple Alliance was in a sorry state. Neither Italy nor Austria-Hungary was prepared to support German claims in

---

[45] Clark, *Sleepwalkers*, p. 242.
[46] Cited in John Keiger, *France and the Origins of the First World War* (London, 1983), p. 85.

Morocco, while Italy's war against Turkey was condemned as a dangerous adventure. Aehrenthal feared that the war would spread into the Balkans. The war placed Germany in an awkward position, caught between support for its Italian ally and its own interests in the Ottoman Empire. Kiderlen prioritised the alliance, while the Italian foreign minister, San Giuliano, concerned at the exposure of Italy's northern border to a sudden attack by Austria-Hungary, agreed to renew the Triple Alliance earlier than necessary. The Triple Alliance was renewed in December 1912. In return for Italian gains in North Africa, Austria-Hungary would receive a port on the Adriatic and both countries would support the creation of an Albanian state. Doubts about Italy's commitment to the Triple Alliance were common in Berlin and Vienna. The alliance was as much an instrument to control Austro-Italian tensions as to deter attack by other great powers. Relations between Austria-Hungary and Germany were also tetchy in 1911 and 1912. Within the German Foreign Office, dependence on Austria-Hungary was considered a weakness of German foreign policy. In Vienna, officials at the Ballhausplatz regularly complained that Germany did not support Austria-Hungary's interests. 'In the guise of a friend', wrote the new Austro-Hungarian foreign minister, Leopold von Berchtold of Tschirschky, the German ambassador, 'he appeared to me today as a bird of prey, not to mention a vulture.'[47]

The consolidation of alliances was one response to Morocco; a second was the promotion of détente between antagonistic powers, notably Britain and Germany. A policy of détente before the First World War aimed at improving the atmosphere in bilateral relations between two powers in separate blocs, without undermining the blocs. 'One does not make new friendships worth having', Grey told the House of Commons, 'by deserting old ones. New friendships by all means let us have, but not at the expense of the ones we have.'[48] The difficulty at the heart of détente was the fear amongst other great powers that rapprochement was the prelude to defection from the bloc. In other words, détente could generate suspicions and tensions within the international system, as well as contribute to the strengthening of great power peace.

The détente between Britain and Germany was one of the most important developments in the international system after 1911. It enabled the two powers to play the leading role in maintaining peace during the Balkan crises in 1912 and 1913. Its significance has been challenged by

---

[47] Angelow, *Kalkül und Prestige*, pp. 268–69; Franz-Josef Kos, *Die politischen und wirtschaftlichen Interessen Österreich-Ungarns und Deutschland in Südosteuropa 1912/13* (Vienna, 1996), pp. 35–43.
[48] Cited in Kießling, *Gegen den großen Krieg?*, p. 71.

historians, who contend that because détente was based on issues of secondary importance in the Anglo-German relationship – the future of the Portuguese colonies, the Balkans, and the Baghdad railway – it was 'hollow'. The failure of the German and British governments to resolve the major differences over naval policy and the balance of power in Europe showed the limits of détente. However, the primary aim of détente policy for both governments was the improvement of bilateral relations and the maintenance of peace, not a major change in the alignment of the great powers. Détente also provided the basis for the operation of the Concert of Europe in late 1912. On this reading, détente was an important contribution to the maintenance of peace after the Moroccan crisis.

German efforts to improve relations with Britain were deliberately based around issues of secondary importance. Leading architects of Germany's policy towards Britain, such as Kiderlen and Richard Kühlmann, the chargé d'affaires in the London embassy, argued that a rapprochement based on small steps would have a better chance of success. The first attempt to improve relations after the Moroccan crisis, the mission to Berlin in February 1912 of Lord Richard Haldane, the Lord Chancellor, renowned for his admiration of German culture, was almost a complete failure because it concentrated on the major differences between the two powers. Haldane failed to get any concessions on German navy policy, while Bethmann Hollweg's efforts to promote a neutrality pact aroused suspicion. The mission also caused concern in Paris, where Poincaré viewed détente as destabilising. Bethmann Hollweg was not discouraged by the Haldane mission. The publication of the German naval programme by Tirpitz, while Haldane was in Berlin, was embarrassing, but Bethmann Hollweg was able to out-manoeuvre Tirpitz over the following year, so that the naval race effectively came to a halt in 1912. German proponents of détente with Britain had always identified naval issues as the major obstacle to better relations with Britain and so it proved.

In the spring of 1912, Kühlmann opened negotiations with the Colonial Secretary, Lewis Harcourt, on the future of the Portuguese empire. This had already been the subject of an agreement between the two powers in 1898, but Britain's treaty with Portugal the following year contradicted the Anglo-German agreement. The two sides reached a second agreement in October 1913, though it was never ratified. At one level, the negotiations over the Portuguese empire seemed like a damp squib; at another, they served the purpose of improving relations between Britain and Germany. This was also the case with negotiations about the Baghdad railway, which were successfully concluded just before the July crisis. Most importantly, the gradual improvement in Anglo-German relations throughout 1912 laid the basis for cooperation during the First Balkan

War. While Poincaré's policy of consolidating the blocs gave stability to the international system, détente offered flexibility. The Crisis management did not degenerate into confrontation between two rigid blocs; at the same time, the Triple Entente and Triple Alliance provided a basic minimum of security.

At this point, it is necessary to return to the narrative of events since the Moroccan crisis to ask whether the shifts in the international system since the Moroccan crisis – the consolidation of the alliances and the promotion of détente – were capable of withstanding the pressures generated by a succession of crises. When Italy declared war against the Ottoman Empire in September 1911, Giolitti saw it as a means of preserving Italy's position in North Africa, bolstering prestige, and winning plaudits at home. The escalation of Italian war aims to include the annexation of Tripoli, rather than the establishment of a protectorate, meant that the Ottoman Empire offered stiff resistance. Instead of localising the war, Italian generals extended the war to the Eastern Mediterranean. The war destabilised both liberal Italy and the Ottoman Empire with disastrous repercussions for the international system, most immediately in the Balkans, where the Bulgarian and Serbian governments saw an opportunity to increase their territory at the expense of the Ottoman Empire.

On 13 February 1912, Bulgaria and Serbia signed an agreement, forming the core of the Balkan League. In May, Greece joined them. It was widely assumed that Russia had sponsored the League and could control the small states. 'The Balkan dogs will not bite, as long as the great, white Papa in St Petersburg doesn't want them to; they will only yap', remarked Kiderlen in 1910.[49] Russian aspirations to direct the Balkan League were an illusion. Russia saw the Balkan League as a check against Austro-Hungarian expansion in the Balkans; in other words, it had a defensive function. However, the Russian envoy in Belgrade, N. V. Hartvig, encouraged the Balkan League to direct its energies against the decaying Ottoman Empire. Bulgaria and Greece had long-standing territorial goals against the Ottoman Empire, while Serbia was interested in Albania and all three wanted to extend their territory to parts of Macedonia. In the initial treaty, Serbia was assigned northern Albania and Bulgaria the port of Salonika.

As the prospect of a war between the Balkan League and the Ottoman Empire became likely, the great powers scrambled to prevent it, or failing that, to localise it. Russia's claims to protect the Balkan states and to act as the dominant power in the region were undermined by her lack of capacity to control her allegedly client states. Nicholas II never issued a

---

[49] Forsbach, *Kiderlen*, vol. II, p. 683.

Russian version of the Roosevelt corollary. Because Russia's great power prestige was bound up with its role in the Balkans, the gap between its claims and its power and willingness to enforce those claims in the interests of stability in the international system undermined peace and stability in the region, and therefore in Europe. As Russia lost control of the Balkan League, it briefly turned to cooperate with Austria-Hungary. In August 1912, Berchtold had circulated a note to the other great powers, arguing that the maintenance of peace in the Balkans was linked to the maintenance of peace in Europe, but the great powers failed to develop a coherent response. On 8 October 1912, Austria-Hungary and Russia issued a démarche to the Balkan states. The basis for the Austro-Russian agreement was the maintenance of the status quo, but this lacked the juridical strength of a justification based on the treaty of Berlin, itself demolished by the annexation crisis in 1908. The war went against expectations as the Balkan League easily defeated Turkish forces. The great powers had now lost control of events; indeed, the policies of Austria-Hungary and Russia were shaped by their reactions to what had happened on the battlefield.

Serbia's claim to a port on the Adriatic became the focal point of tensions between Austria-Hungary and Russia. Both powers resorted to armed diplomacy, mobilising units in late 1912. For Russia, the promotion of Serbian claims was a test of her great power status. Austria-Hungary pursued its by now usual policy of seeking to hem Serbia in, by establishing a large Albanian state and denying Serbia access to a port. Behind these geopolitical calculations lay the fear that a greater Serbia, especially an economically independent one, would prove a great attraction to the minorities in the Habsburg empire. Therefore, vital interests were at stake for Austria-Hungary. By late 1912, well-informed diplomats considered war inevitable. As the crisis between Russia and Austria-Hungary escalated, the war continued. However, tensions between the Balkan states rose. Greece had seized Salonika, which had been assigned to Bulgaria. Bulgaria was closing in on Constantinople, much to the concern of Russian diplomats, who feared that the prize might be snatched by one of the little brothers.

War was avoided because of the restraint of key figures in Vienna and St Petersburg and the intervention of Britain, Germany, and, to a lesser extent, France. These three powers restrained their allies and established the diplomatic basis for the London conference, which marked the final revival of the Concert of Europe before the First World War. Poincaré had raised the idea of a European conference on the Balkans on 10 October 1912, but cooperation between London and Berlin was the foundation of the Concert. Neither Britain, Germany, nor France wanted war and all three shared similar interests in preserving the Ottoman Empire from complete collapse. Between October and early December, Britain, supported by Germany and France, took the lead in establishing the Concert. On 17 December 1912, the ambassadors of the five continental great powers and Grey opened the London ambassadors' conference. Grey calculated that once the conference met, it would make it more difficult for any of the great powers to abandon the process, as it would leave them isolated and open to charges of aggression. 'Diplomatically we have passed the biggest rocks', noted Grey with satisfaction on 21 December 1912.[50] The practices of the Concert became an important stabilising factor in European politics in late 1912 and early 1913. Initially the powers reached multi-lateral decisions and issued joint declarations to the warring states in the Balkans.

Britain and Germany also acted to restrain their partners. In Germany, there was some confusion over the nature of the threat the Balkan states, particularly Serbia, posed to Austria-Hungary. William II told Kiderlen in early November that the establishment of a Serbian port on the Adriatic was neither a danger nor a matter of prestige to Austria-Hungary. A few days later, he had changed his mind. On 25 November 1912, an officially inspired article in the *Norddeutsche Allgemeine Zeitung* poured 'cold water' on the suggestion that Austria-Hungary would issue an ultimatum to Serbia. Just over a week later in the Reichstag Bethmann Hollweg reaffirmed Germany's support for Austria-Hungary. German policy offered some security to Austria-Hungary, but it refused to underwrite an aggressive policy. At a meeting at the palace of Schönbrunn, just outside Vienna, on 11 December, Austria-Hungary's leaders decided against war as a policy option. Equally, Grey's attempt to act as an honest broker at the London ambassadorial conference meant that British support for Russian and Serbian claims in the Balkans was limited. On the other hand, Poincaré urged Russian leaders to strengthen the military measures directed against Austria-Hungary in December 1912. The self-restraint in St Petersburg and Vienna was a vital element of successful crisis management.

The success of the Concert depended on the capability and willingness of the great powers to enforce their decisions. The rights of the great powers 'should not be rudely challenged', Grey had warned the Serbian government in November 1912. But the Balkan states were not in a mood to kowtow to the great powers. In March 1913, Bulgaria violated a ceasefire to seize Adrianople from the Ottoman Empire. More seriously, on 23 March 1913 Serbia and Montenegro seized the port of Scutari on the

---

[50] Dülffer, Kröger, and Wippich, *Vermiedene Kriege*, p. 654.

Adriatic coast. This represented a challenge to Austria-Hungary, which wanted the port to form part of the Albanian buffer state against Serbian expansion. The occupation of Scutari was the first significant test of the Concert's willingness to support its claims with military force. Crucially, Russia had agreed that Serbia would not get Scutari in any peace settlement, in return for adjustments to the Serbo-Albanian border. Tensions between Russia and Austria-Hungary eased further in March 1913, when Franz Joseph sent a special envoy to Nicholas II to agree on demobilising military measures taken the previous year. The great powers decided to enforce their demand that Serbian and Montenegrin troops leave Scutari with a joint naval demonstration. Russia did not participate, but it did succeed in getting the Serbians to withdraw. When Montenegro failed to follow the Serbian example, Austria-Hungary started military preparations. On 4 May, Montenegrin soldiers evacuated the town, which was occupied by troops from the great powers, mostly Italian and Austrian, under a British commander.

On 30 May, the treaty of London was signed, ending the First Balkan War. The Ottoman Empire ceded all of its European territory, including the island of Crete. Several issues remained unresolved, including the future of Macedonia, the Albanian border, and some islands in the Aegean. Nonetheless, the evacuation of Scutari and the treaty of London seemed a triumph for Concert diplomacy. Common great power action had apparently reasserted control over the Balkan states, stabilised the international system, and, through the practices of the Concert, improved relations between the great powers. The two blocs remained, but they provided security for their members without preventing the necessary cooperation across blocs. For almost a decade, a series of crises had tested peace between the great powers. The resolution of these crises suggests that war was not inevitable. The restraint of individual statesmen was an important guarantee of peace. The structures and processes of the international system – alliances, détentes, and the Concert amongst others – also provided a basis for the continued peace between the powers.

However these bonds of peace and restraints on war were slowly, even unconsciously, eroded. As the remnants of the Ottoman Empire collapsed during the First Balkan War, the great powers and Balkan states sought new principles to underpin the regional order. The nationality principle became the primary reference point in debates about the peace settlement in the Balkans. Implementing this principle was accompanied by ethnic cleansing, forced conversions, and other forms of violence. Nor did the principle lend itself to establishment of neatly demarcated borders – as peacemakers discovered again after the end of the First World War. Nonetheless the victorious expansion of the Balkan states marked

what Gabriel Hanotaux, the former French foreign minister, called the
establishment of the 'Balkans for the Balkan peoples.'[51] The nationality principle had several implications for the great power peace. First, it
challenged the primacy of the great powers. Indeed, the Balkan states in
1912 and 1913 proved capable of escaping the dictates of the great powers. When the Balkan states submitted in the face of ultimatums, it often
caused serious divisions within the Concert. In other words, the logic of
the nationality principle operated at cross purposes with that of the Concert. Second, the nationality principle also transformed the normative
environment within Europe, even what 'Europe' came to mean. If the
nationality principle legitimised the European order, then 'Europe' was
departing from its moorings in the concert of the great powers. Europe
recast in this way presented a challenge to the ontological security of the
multi-national great power, Austria-Hungary. As Krobatin, the Minister
of War, complained, 'Europe has shown that it wants to hold us back',
while on another occasion, István Tisza, the Hungarian prime minister,
lamented that 'all Europe' supported Serbia.[52] The primacy of the great
powers and their customary right to dictate any changes on the European map no longer provided sufficient justification for political action.
Instead, change was couched in the language of the nationality principle –
even Austro-Hungarian diplomats employed this language to justify the
establishment of Albania, with a view to blocking the national pretensions
of Serbia. Finally, the logic of the nationality principle posed an existential threat to Austria-Hungary. It was losing the ideological resources,
with which it could justify its existence. This does not mean that the
other powers wanted the dissolution of the empire, but rather that when
Austria-Hungary faced challenges from nation-states, especially Serbia,
it proved difficult to articulate an effective Habsburg case within the
European public sphere.

The peace concluded in May in the Balkans was short-lived. In late
June 1913, Bulgaria attacked its former allies in a bid to gain further
territory, especially in Macedonia, which it had been denied in the treaty
of London. The war went disastrously for Bulgaria, which ended in ced-
ing territory to Serbia, Greece, and the Ottoman Empire. The outcome
of the Second Balkan War was ratified by the treaty of Bucharest, with
Romania playing a leading role in the settlement. The success of the great
powers in the first half of 1913 had proved an illusion. The final meeting
of the London ambassadors' conference took place on 11 August 1913,

---

[51] 'Les Balkans aux balkaniques', 22 November 1912, in Gabriel Hanotaux, *La guerre des
Balkans et l'Europe, 1912–1913* (Paris, 1914), pp. 165–71.
[52] Anatol Schmied-Kowarzik, *Die Protokolle des Gemeinsamen Rates der österreichisch-
ungarischen Monarchie, 1908–1914* (Budapest, 2011), pp. 581–83, 609.

but the Concert had lost its raison d'être, the enforcement of the will of the great powers against smaller states. Elements of the Concert survived, such as the principle of multi-lateral discussions before significant action was taken and the international commission on the Albanian border continued its painstaking work, but to all intents and purposes, the Concert was finished as an effective mechanism for resolving international crises.

Austria-Hungary was the great power most affected by the Second Balkan War. The doubling of Serbia's territory and the increase in her population from 2.9 million to 4.4 million as a result of the two Balkan Wars and the loss of Bulgaria as a counter-weight to Serbian power shifted the balance of power both in the Balkans and in Europe. The relative diminution of Austro-Hungarian power also weakened Germany, which became increasingly reliant on its détente with Britain as a means of avoiding isolation. In October 1913, Berchtold's foreign policy became more aggressive. Serbian troops had occupied parts of northern Albania in contravention of the terms of the treaty of London. On 3 October, on the same day as the visit of the Serbian prime minister, Pašič, to Vienna, a meeting of the Ministerial Council recognised that a war against Serbia was inevitable. On 18 October, Berchtold issued an ultimatum to Serbia demanding the withdrawal of Serbian troops. Austro-Hungarian demands were based on the treaty of London, but there had been no prior discussions with the other powers, a clear violation of the practices of the Concert. Two days later, Pašič withdrew Serbian troops. While the performance of the Serbian army and the increase in her power during the Balkan Wars impressed contemporaries, Pašič was concerned at the weakness of his position. The country had been exhausted by two wars and was surrounded by potential enemies, such as Austria-Hungary and Bulgaria.

Serbia's retreat emboldened Austria-Hungary. The conversion of Berchtold to the view that war with Serbia was inevitable and his willingness to issue ultimatums backed by armed force marked the first step in the capitals of the great powers towards a general war. Austro-Hungarian leaders had not made a decision in favour of European war, but this was the implication of the shift in their policy. Their concentration on the Serbian challenge, while ignoring the strong possibility of Russian support for Serbia, showed that their conception of the international system had contracted dangerously. Austria-Hungary ignored the important question of maintaining the international system because leaders in Vienna were almost unanimous in their belief that the system had failed Austria-Hungary. The failure of the Concert to uphold the treaty of London and to control the Balkan powers prompted this shift in Austro-Hungarian policy. For Austria-Hungary, the rewards of unilateral action became clear in October 1913.

There were also signs that Germany was no longer willing to restrain Austria-Hungary, though it hoped that Britain would restrain Russia (and France). Just before Austria-Hungary had issued the ultimatum, Arthur von Zimmermann asked Britain to press Serbia to withdraw. While there was some annoyance in German diplomatic circles about the lack of more detailed consultations about the ultimatum, William II told the Austrian ambassador: 'Now or never! Order and peace must be established.'[53] On a host of outstanding questions, including the establishment of Albania, the future of the Dodecanese islands, and relations between Greece and Turkey, the great powers refused to take united action, instead retreating into their blocs.

In late 1913, relations between Russia and Germany took a turn for the worse. Since the 1880s, Germany had supplied the Ottoman Empire with military expertise and weaponry. In late 1913, General Liman von Sanders was appointed to a new military mission to help reorganise the Ottoman forces after the Balkan Wars. What made his appointment slightly different to previous ones was that he commanded troop units in Constantinople. The Ottomans and Germans argued that the command was essential to facilitating reforms, but to Russia, always sensitive about the influence of other powers at Constantinople, it would give Germany a decisive influence over Ottoman politics. Given the unstable condition of Ottoman politics since 1908, there was much to be said for the Russian analysis. Moreover, setbacks in the Balkans had been accepted in early 1913, but this merely made Constantinople more of a neuralgic point in Russian foreign policy. Sazonov's demands for a change in Sanders's status prompted a major crisis, which was only resolved when Germany and Turkey made some concessions in January 1914 by removing Liman from his command post, but leaving him in charge of training (Map 3).

The crisis marked a serious escalation in tensions between Russia and Germany. Previously, confrontations between these two powers resulted from the differences between Austria-Hungary and Russia in the Balkans. Germany's ambitions in the Ottoman Empire and Central Asia were viewed with concern in St Petersburg, but agreements in 1910 and 1911 showed that it had been possible to manage their differing interests. During the Liman von Sanders crisis, Sazonov had sought support from Grey and Pichon, the French foreign minister. Both were lukewarm. Grey noted that the appointment of a German general to a command

---

[53] Cited in Angelow, *Kalkül und Prestige*, p. 424; R. J. Crampton, *The Hollow Détente: Anglo-German Relations in the Balkans, 1911–1914* (London, 1980), pp. 113–18.

Map 3. The Balkans in 1914. After Gildea, *Barricades and Borders*, 424.

post in Constantinople 'though sufficiently disagreeable to all the other powers, is a matter of more intimate concern to Russia than to any of us. It is therefore not a question in which we can be more Russian than the Russians, and the German government are much more likely to be influenced by their apprehensions of how far Russian remonstrances are likely to be carried than by fear of British actions.'[54] Without French or British backing, though, Russia was not in a position to take any serious measures against Germany. During the Liman von Sanders crisis, British and French restraint of Russia was an important means of resolving the affair. The interests of the great powers in the Ottoman Empire cut across the blocs. By late 1913 Germany, France, and Britain were close to coming to terms over issues such as the Baghdad railway and the division of the Ottoman Empire into spheres of economic dominance and political influence.

In St Petersburg, the Liman von Sanders crisis triggered a change in policy. Since 1905, Russia had suffered repeated setbacks in international affairs. These, rather than the growth in their military power, preoccupied leading Russian statesmen. In the Balkans and the Ottoman Empire, Russian influence had declined. Bosnia, the Balkan Wars, and the Liman von Sanders crisis constituted a long list of woe. France and Britain conspired to deny Russia a seat on the Ottoman Debt Council. Only in Persia was Russian influence advancing. One of Russia's fundamental problems, exposed during the Liman von Sanders crisis, was its lack of alternatives to military power. It did not have large reserves of capital to use as a financial lever in foreign policy. Few states, even the Balkan ones, looked to Russia as a model of constitutional stability. Whereas French, German, British, and American military, naval, and financial experts were in demand in (or sometimes pushed on) smaller modernising states, Russia could not offer any significant technical aid. In short, Russia lacked the 'soft power' that had become increasingly important in the exertion of influence in regions such as the Near East. Finally, Sazonov took the failure of Britain and France to back Russian demands during the Liman von Sanders crisis as evidence that the Triple Entente lacked the cohesion that would make it an effective diplomatic instrument.

In February 1914, Nicholas II, emerging once again as a more forceful figure in Russian politics, and Sazonov adopted a more assertive foreign policy. Within the Russian leadership, the principle of 'peace at any price' came under attack. Kokovtsov, the leading proponent of this view, was

---

[54] Cited in William Mulligan, 'We Can't Be More Russian Than the Russians: British Policy in the Liman von Sanders Crisis, 1913–14', *Diplomacy and Statecraft*, 17, 2 (2006): 267.

3. The battlecruiser SMS *Goeben* in the Mediterranean, 1913 (IWM Q 65787).
By 1913, tensions across the Mediterranean had increased owing to a series of
diplomatic crises and wars, triggered by the Moroccan crisis. The struggle for
dominance in the Mediterranean was important to all the great powers, even
Germany, which sent the SMS *Goeben* to the area. In 1914, at the outbreak of
war, SMS *Goeben* eluded an Allied chase to reach Constantinople, a prelude to
the entry of the Ottoman Empire into the war on Germany's side.

removed as Minister for Finance in early 1914. The maintenance of Russia's great power status required a more active foreign policy. 'We will do
everything for Serbia', the Tsar told Pasič on 2 February. In fact, Russia
remained more interested in the Black Sea and the Straits. At a meeting
on 21 February 1914, Sazonov warned military and political leaders that
the status of the Straits could change without warning. Russia, he argued,
needed to develop a plan to seize control of the Straits. He also pointed
to the growing naval power of Turkey, a threat to the Crimean coast.
One of the decisions of the conference was to build up Russian naval
power in the Black Sea.[55] The final component of Sazonov's new course
in foreign policy was to consolidate the Triple Entente. The lack of unity,

[55] Journal einer Sonderkonferenz, 21 February 1914, in Otto Hoetzsch, ed., *Die internationalen Beziehungen im Zeitalter des Imperialismus*, 1st Series, vol. I (Berlin, 1931), pp.
283–96.

epitomised by Britain's failure to commit to an alliance, squandered the diplomatic resources of the entente, giving the Triple Alliance a powerful advantage. Like Grey in early 1906, Sazonov believed that the consolidation of the Triple Entente would act as a force for peace and a deterrent to German military and diplomatic aggression. Sazonov did not plan for war in 1914; indeed, he remained committed to peace, but on the condition that Russia did not consistently suffer setbacks in the international arena. This condition reversed the relationship between prestige and peace. The maintenance of Russia's great power status, linked to its geopolitical interests and its prestige, took priority over the reserved, cautious, and peaceful policy that had dominated Russian foreign policy since 1905.

Sazonov repeatedly pressed Britain for a more substantial commitment to the entente. French leaders also worked to strengthen the entente, fearing that otherwise Russia would turn to Germany. The proposal, which French and Russian diplomats advanced, was for an Anglo-Russian naval convention. Given the difficulties of offering any effective naval aid, such a convention would have been a largely symbolic affirmation of the entente. In April 1914, during a visit to Paris, Grey agreed to the principle of a convention, a decision which was confirmed by the cabinet in May. In fact, no concrete discussions between the admiralties in Britain and Russia took place before the outbreak of war. Why did Grey agree to the convention, given that he had doubts about its practical purpose and feared the repercussions for Anglo-German relations, if news of the plans leaked out? Distracted from foreign policy by the continuing crisis over Irish Home Rule, Grey was more amenable than usual to advice from officials in the Foreign Office. Nicolson wanted a full alliance with Russia, but knew this was impossible from the domestic political point of view. He argued that peace was now secure and Grey tended to agree with him. Given that the Anglo-German détente had served the immediate purpose of maintaining peace in 1912 and 1913, it was now time for Britain to restore relations with Russia, which were bruised by events in Central Asia, as well as the lack of support during the Balkan Wars and the Liman von Sanders crisis. The Triple Entente consolidated would help maintain peace and secure the national interests of each member.

As Grey feared, German leaders found out about the naval conversations from a Baltic German, Benno von Siebert, who worked in the Russian embassy in London. It had a devastating impact on Bethmann Hollweg's foreign policy, bringing about an important shift in German thinking about the international system. Historians have criticised the entente powers for ignoring German concerns about encirclement. The death of Bethmann Hollweg's wife had already depressed the German

Chancellor, when news of the conversations reached him in May. For the past two years, his policy had relied on Anglo-German détente. The détente ensured that Britain restrained Germany's most dangerous enemy, Russia, provided a ballast to the Reich's alliance with a shaky Habsburg empire, and maintained peace and stability in Europe. Bethmann Hollweg had accepted that Germany could not challenge Britain's global pre-eminence. Instead, he pursued a policy of *Weltpolitik ohne Krieg*, world policy without war, effectively as a junior partner to Britain. In April 1914, he told Wangenheim that Germany required another decade of peace, during which its commercial power could secure its political supremacy within Europe. He saw war as a possibility, but he did not want to provoke one to secure Germany's European position. Of course, William II's outburst to the Belgian king, Albert, in November 1913 that Germany would attack France within a year suggested a very different attitude towards war as an instrument of policy. Nonetheless, William II had ceded considerable control of foreign policy to his Chancellor since the *Daily Telegraph* interview. In short, German leaders had prepared for the possibility of a general war with the army bills of 1912 and 1913, they were nervous that public opinion in France or Russia might provoke a war, and they had concerns about the crumbling Habsburg empire and the growth of military power. But détente constituted an important restraint on German foreign policy until the news reached Berlin of the Anglo-Russian naval convention.

Undoubtedly, Bethmann Hollweg overreacted to the Anglo-Russian naval convention. Just four days before the assassination of the Archduke, Grey held out the prospect of continued cooperation in the Balkans. The proposed naval convention was largely symbolic, one of the nods, to paraphrase Churchill, which propped up the international system. The convention would hardly have adjusted, let alone overturned the international system. After all, the members of the Triple Alliance were busy discussing naval and military cooperation in 1913. By 1913 Italy was more firmly attached to the Triple Alliance than had been the case for several years, as her interests in North Africa clashed with those of Britain and France. The tightening of the bonds of the Anglo-French entente in November 1912 had not elicited such a strong reaction from Germany. Bethmann Hollweg's perception of the importance of the convention led him to reorientate German policy. He believed that it marked the end of détente and of cooperation on specific issues, especially in the Balkans. His faith in Britain's ability to restrain Russia and France, to act as the leader of the Triple Entente, was shaken. Finally, it weakened the Chancellor's position against his rivals for influence with the Kaiser, particularly the generals and Tirpitz.

Bethmann Hollweg considered the alliance with Austria-Hungary to be more important than ever. Germany's détente with Britain had strained the alliance with Austria-Hungary. Berchtold felt that Germany tried to assuage British concerns at Vienna's expense. Repairing relations with Vienna would require Germany to offer more substantial support in a future crisis. Bethmann Hollweg also doubted whether Grey would really act as an honest broker in a future crisis, the British Foreign Secretary's credibility being further undermined by the ambivalent replies he gave to German inquiries about the proposed naval convention. The German Chancellor in June 1914 regarded cooperation with Britain as offering few rewards.

By the eve of the assassination of the Archduke, the structures, assumptions, and practices that had underpinned peace for the previous three years were undermined. Berchtold, Sazonov, and Bethmann Hollweg now favoured a more assertive foreign policy. They did not want war, but their changing assumptions suggested that they were more willing to risk one than in early 1913. The changes in their policy came about for different reasons, but significantly each power saw itself as getting progressively weaker. The consolidation of alliances, the shattering of détente, and the failure of the Concert to manage effectively the international system contributed to the changes in policy. There were too many changes in the policies and structures of the international system before 1914 to argue that the shift that took place from the second half of 1913 would be a permanent or even long-term feature of great power politics. It was the coincidence of the July crisis with the adoption of more assertive policies in Vienna, St Petersburg, and Berlin from October 1913 onwards, which caused the outbreak of war.

The maintenance of peace between the great powers between 1871 and 1914 was a striking achievement, the second longest period of peace between the great powers since the modern international system emerged in the mid-seventeenth century. This achievement requires as much explanation as the origins of the war. Historians have their own particular favourite turning point, the moment when war became the likely outcome of crises within the international system. The years 1871, 1879, 1890, 1894, 1905, 1908, and 1911 make up the list of usual suspects, with most historians opting for the latter three. Strong cases for viewing these dates as turning points can be made. Each date privileges a certain aspect of the international system, such as alliances, imperial expansion, reckless diplomacy, the triumph of power politics, and so on. This chapter has argued that alliances, imperial expansion, détente, limited cooperation on secondary issues, ententes, and the Concert were important foundations of peace. Arguably, the most important reason for the preservation of peace between 1871 and 1914 was that, in most crises, vital interests were not at stake. The most significant problem in the international system after 1911, and particularly from 1913 onwards, was that vital interests – as defined by the great powers – *were* at stake. Sheer survival, prestige, and the maintenance of an ally were the respective vital interests of Austria-Hungary, Russia, and Germany. By June 1914, the leading statesmen of three powers had decided that they needed to adopt a more assertive approach in defence of their vital interests. The defence of these vital interests was incompatible with peace between the great powers. This was the fundamental weakness of the international system on 28 June 1914.

3   The Military, War, and International Politics

'The consequence of the recent war', the Austro-Hungarian foreign minister, Julius Andrassy told Emperor Franz Joseph in February 1872, 'is that power trumps justice.'[1] Historians have identified the militarisation of great power politics as one of the major consequences of the wars between 1854 and 1871. The unification of Germany consecrated Bismarck's open embrace of power politics as the form of diplomacy to which other states should aspire. Doering-Manteuffel labelled the period between 1871 and 1945 as the era of the *Machtstaat*. According to Conze, the validation of the idea of the *Machtstaat* in the Franco-Prussian War undermined restraints within the international system and contributed to the militarisation of international political conduct. On this reading the wars of the mid-nineteenth century marked a decisive rupture with the more restrained norms that had emerged in the Congress of Vienna in 1814/15. The alternatives to power politics, such as the free trade system espoused by Britain in the 1860s, were marginalised in the new Bismarckian dispensation.

At the risk of being too reductionist, the implication of these arguments is that the likelihood of another general war between the great powers was high after 1871. In this narrative, centred on power politics, the military are said to have played a key role. They planned for offensive wars, they pressed for increases in naval and military spending, they sparked and fuelled arms races, they influenced important decisions in domestic and foreign policy, they saw war as a creative, positive force in the history of mankind, and, in general, they pushed Europe towards a general war. However, as we shall see, there were powerful restraints on war as an instrument of politics in the early twentieth century. War plans certainly made it likely that any war between two great powers would soon escalate into a general war, but this made the prospect of war so drastic that states would only choose war in the last resort. Statesmen were well aware of

---

[1] Cited in Johannes Paulmann, *Pomp und Politik. Monarchbegegnungen in Europa zwischen Ancien Régime und Erstem Weltkrieg* (Paderborn, 2000), p. 152.

the potentially catastrophic consequences of a great power conflict and sought to restrain the influence of their generals on foreign policy. The militarisation of the international system and the arms race before 1914 was the result of civilian decisions and geopolitical developments rather than the impulse of the military elites.

War Planning before 1914

Planning for war was the task of the general staffs of the European powers. Drafting war plans is not the same as seeking to bring about a war. After all, planning for war began as soon as the Franco-Prussian War came to an end, but peace between the great powers lasted for another forty-three years. However, the war plans demonstrate some of the stresses and strains of international politics. The war plans reflected the security dilemmas facing the great powers, the shifts in the balance of power, and the changes in the constellations of great power alignments.

At the centre of European military politics stood Germany, at once a model for and a threat to its neighbours. Its military system – based on conscription and the General Staff – was placed on a pedestal at home and abroad after victory in 1870/1. Helmuth von Moltke, the Chief of the General Staff and the architect of Prussia's military campaigns in 1866 and 1870, was as aware of the dangers facing the newly united state as he was proud of the victories of the previous years. By early 1871, he was concerned about the prospect of a two-front war against a revived France and Russia. Exposed in central Europe and surrounded by potentially hostile powers, German military planners faced a major dilemma – how to win a war simultaneously against Russia and France. This problem, which became a much more significant threat after the conclusion of the Franco-Russian alliance in 1894, remained at the centre of military considerations until the outbreak of war. Moltke himself toyed with two ideas. Germany could attack in the west against France and stand on the defensive in the east against Russia – or vice versa. In any case, a choice had to be made about where to allocate the mass of the German army. These options remained the two principal choices facing German military strategists for four decades.

Alfred von Schlieffen, who became Chief of the General Staff in 1891, made the crucial decision to focus on the west, lending his name to the most famous war plan of this era. He had drawn up a war plan, the fruits of his long experience, during his last days in office in 1905 and bequeathed it to his successor, Helmuth von Moltke, the nephew of the victor of Sedan. This plan aimed to defeat France within a six-week period. To achieve this ambitious goal, the mass of the German army

4. The Kaiser greeting his staff during the manoeuvres of 1905 (IWM HU 68475). On the right is the Chief of the German General Staff, Moltke. Military manoeuvres took place regularly before the First World War. They were an opportunity to test military effectiveness, but they were also displays of military theatre and a social ritual.

would wheel through the Low Countries, strike into French territory, encircle the French army, and annihilate it. Victory secured in the west, the German armies would turn around and travel east, where they would meet the Russians, who mobilised more slowly than their French allies and therefore posed less of an immediate threat. Terence Zuber has challenged this view, suggesting that Schlieffen had much more flexible ideas about German war plans, was not necessarily committed to an offensive in the west, and foresaw a decisive battle between French and German forces in Lorraine, not in eastern France.

The broad thrust of Zuber's argument has not been widely accepted, but the variations in German war planning, and in particular their reflection of changing geopolitical circumstances, deserve consideration. When Schlieffen put together his memorandum in December 1905, Russia was racked by defeat and revolution, enabling Germany to concentrate its forces in the west without fear of being attacked in the east. Ageing and out of favour after he had pressed unsuccessfully for a preventive war against France, Schlieffen resigned as Chief of the General Staff in

December 1905. His memorandum became the starting point for his successor, Moltke's war planning. Moltke stuck with the principle that Germany should concentrate its forces against France, but, from 1908, he changed several other aspects of Schlieffen's prescription for victory. Worried by the prospect of France invading southern Germany, he decided to bolster the left wing of the German army. Instead of invading both Belgium and the Netherlands, Moltke planned to leave the Netherlands alone and pass through Belgium. A neutral Netherlands could 'be the windpipe that enables us to breathe'.[2] Significantly, Moltke believed that the next war would last for several years, meaning Germany would have to import vast amounts of material to continue the struggle. A neutral Netherlands provided an ideal entrepôt for the German war effort. In April 1913, Moltke abandoned the alternative plan for an offensive strategy in the east and a defensive stance in the west. This potentially reduced the military options open to Germany. In July 1914, when Grey dangled the vague possibility of neutrality in return for peace in western Europe, German military strategy prevented the government from exploring this option. But, it must be said that the possibility of fighting a war against Russia alone was highly unlikely.

By 1913, Germany had a single war plan, predicated on the assumption of a two-front war against Russia and France and a war that would last years, not months. In fact, to say that Germany (or any other power for that matter) had a war plan, is to confuse the plans for the initial operations, with a plan to win the war outright. Military leaders only gave fleeting thought to how Germany might win such a lengthy contest against foes with larger material resources. The capture of key industrial areas in Belgium and northern France and access to productive agricultural regions in eastern Europe would boost German resources, but these resources were on a continental scale, while Britain and France had access to resources on a global scale. But the memory of rapid victory in 1870, which obscured the continuation of the war into 1871 against irregular French forces, made it difficult for the German officer corps to admit to themselves and the civilian leaders that a general war would be an extremely risky venture. Planning a two-front war was based on the assumption that the next war would be a general European one. While this was a realistic assessment, there was also an element of the self-fulfilling prophecy in German war planning. The plans drawn up by Moltke, Schlieffen, and Moltke the Younger compounded the potential for escalation into a general war, evident in joint French and Russian

---

[2] Annika Mombauer, *Helmuth von Moltke and the Origins of the First World War* (Cambridge, 2001), p. 94.

planning from the early 1890s. The German plans made a localised, limited war between great powers on the European continent virtually impossible.

Germany and her allies, Austria-Hungary and Italy, coordinated their war plans far less effectively than the members of the Triple Entente. In Berlin, it was widely felt that the fate of the Habsburg empire would be settled on the Seine. From the Bosnian crisis of 1908, Moltke and his Austrian counterpart, Conrad, exchanged views on war planning. As far as Germany was concerned, Austria-Hungary's role was to hold up Russia, while Germany dealt with France at the outset of the war, before transferring troops back east. But Austria-Hungary had an even greater range of threats to cover – against Serbia in the south-east, against Russia, and against her alliance partner, Italy. Austrian war planning was undermined by indecision and soldiers began to take an increasingly narrow view of the international system. In February 1872, military planners had identified Russia as the only potential enemy. By the end of the Balkan Wars in 1913, the focus of Austro-Hungarian military planning was on Serbia, with Conrad hoping that Germany would allocate more of its troops to deal with Russia.

The dominant figure in Austro-Hungarian military planning was Franz Conrad von Hötzendorf, appointed as Chief of the General Staff in 1906, after his unfortunate predecessor, Friedrich von Beck, had fallen from his horse during the autumn manoeuvres. Initially, Conrad saw Italy as the major threat to the Habsburg empire. Russia was weakened after the revolution of 1905, and Serbia was a nuisance factor in the Balkans but not a serious military threat. The Bosnian crisis in 1908/9 exacerbated tensions between Austria-Hungary and Serbia, backed by Russia. Conrad's deployment plan to deal with the various threats had the virtues and vices of flexibility. He divided Austro-Hungarian forces into three groups – a Minimum Group Balkans, of ten divisions, which would take the offensive against Serbia; Formation A (A-Staffel) of thirty divisions, which would defend against a Russian attack in Galicia; and a reserve group, Formation B, of twelve divisions, which could be sent to the Balkans if Russia remained neutral, and to Galicia if Russia entered the war. The problem was that it would be difficult to transfer Formation B from the Balkans to Galicia if Russia entered the war after a short period of neutrality. In December 1908, with the knowledge and approval of the civilian leaders, Conrad and Moltke began to exchange information. While they promised each other support, the prospects of their fulfilling these promises were extremely limited. The significance of the exchanges is that they enabled Austria-Hungary to place more emphasis on war against Serbia. The Germans fondly imagined that the Austro-Hungarian reserves would join battle against the Russians, whereas it was always more likely that they would be deployed against the Serbians.

Conrad's military planning took account of political factors, but it also avoided hard choices. Conrad adjusted his plans to meet the changing threats facing Austria-Hungary before 1914. What he failed to do was to develop a military strategy that matched means and ends. The focus on Serbia also betrayed the waning power of Austria-Hungary, whose military strategy grew more obsessed with the Serbian threat. Austria-Hungary had begun to act like a Balkan power, not a great power in the years before 1914. Austro-Hungarian leaders recognised that war against Serbia would almost certainly see Russia enter the lists on the side of Belgrade. However, they looked to Germany to deal with the Russian threat, and therefore, it became a secondary consideration. Defeating Serbia had primacy in the thinking of Austria-Hungary's military and political elites, but this primacy ignored the wider international system. More Austro-Hungarian divisions were concentrated in Galicia, but in relative terms, the attention devoted to winning the war against Serbia was disproportionate. Austro-Hungarian war planning was predicated on the assumption that the next war would likely be a general, not local, war, but, at the same time, there was a gap between policy aims and means. Only by ignoring this gap could leaders in Vienna risk a war.

Like Germany and Austria-Hungary, Russia was surrounded by potential foes. General Danilov, one of the key Russian military strategists before 1914, sketched a scenario in which Russia faced a coalition of forces in Asia and Europe, including Germany, Austria-Hungary, Sweden, Turkey, China, and Japan. This geopolitical vulnerability was central to Russian thinking on war plans. Two other factors heavily influenced the debates amongst Russian officers. The vast geographical expanse of Russia presented both opportunities and dangers. Russian forces could give up territory at its frontiers in Poland and the Ukraine, concentrate its armies in the interior, and slowly wear down the enemy. Concentration at the frontier was risky because of the length of time it took to mobilise the army. While railway construction gathered pace in the 1890s and in the years before the outbreak of the war, mobilisation times were far slower than those of Germany and Austria-Hungary. On the other hand, the French alliance forced Russian strategy to place emphasis on time, not space. French security required that Russia take the offensive in the east against Germany, drawing German troops away from the western front. Although French planners acknowledged that Germany would concentrate on its western front in the initial weeks of the war, the more quickly Russia mobilised and invaded Eastern Prussia, the less time Germany could concentrate on the western front. The choice between time and space dominated Russian military planning between the Russo-Japanese War and 1914. It was an unpalatable choice, made even more difficult by the underlying weaknesses of Russia – its financial weakness, its relative technological backwardness, and the political fragility of the Tsarist regime.

Historian William Fuller has described the 'strategic pessimism' which afflicted military planning, but also led the General Staff to take refuge in what he called 'magical strategies'.[3] After the Russo-Japanese War, planning concentrated on the threat from Germany, though there were residual concerns about a renewal of war against Japan in East Asia, despite the improvement of diplomatic relations with Japan. By 1910, planners had drawn up Schedule 18, the first significant plan since 1905. It was really a plan for the concentration of Russian forces, but it had crucial implications for how Russia would fight a future war. It was a defensive plan, which placed a screening force on Russia's north-west frontier and an army on the border with Austria-Hungary and Turkey. The bulk of forces were to be concentrated in the interior. The Minister of War, Sukhomlinov, was prepared to cede territory in the west. It was too expensive to upgrade the fortresses at the western frontier, and it also meant that, should Japan attack in the east, Russian forces could be transferred more rapidly. Danilov, who was an ultra-pessimist, and General Vitner, who distrusted France, exercised considerable influence on the plan. The concentration plan also fitted with the reorganisation of the army, which Sukhomlinov had pressed through since 1908.

This plan soon came under attack. The influential commander of the Kiev military district, General Alekseev, considered Schedule 18 too passive and argued, partly because of the role units from the Kiev military district would play in a war, that Austria-Hungary should be the focus of a Russian offensive. In early 1912, Alekseev circulated a fresh plan. At the same time, Danilov was reconsidering Russia's options in the light of changed political circumstances and a review of the alliance system. The French were worried that Schedule 18 would leave them to deal with the German army. Danilov had revised his pessimistic view of Russia's isolation in the international system. By 1912, he was more confident of French aid. He also believed that Britain would enter a general European war, while Sweden would remain neutral. Danilov argued that an early offensive was essential to help the French and ultimately to defend Russia. After all, if Germany defeated France and then turned to the east, Russia would be left fighting the combined German and Austro-Hungarian forces alone. At a meeting of General Staff officers and the

---

[3] William C. Fuller, *Strategy and Power in Russia, 1600–1914* (New York, 1992), p. xx.

commanders of military districts in St Petersburg on 21 February 1912, a compromise emerged, which became known as Schedule 19. There were two variations, 'A' and 'G'. 'A' assumed German weakness in the east and allowed for more concentration on Austria-Hungary. 'G' would come into operation if Germany attacked in strength in the east. In that case, Russia would redeploy forces to the north. Russia would launch an offensive on two fronts, in the north against Germany and in the south against Austria. But this meant that it would have too few troops in both theatres to deliver victory. In April 1914, a war game, based on Schedule 19, omitted logistics and rail transport from its test so as not to complicate matters!

Like their counterparts in Germany and Austria-Hungary, Russian officers were aware of the vast difficulties a general war would cause. Similarly, they never re-evaluated their assumptions that war was a viable instrument of policy, despite the experiences of the Russo-Turkish War of 1877/8 and the Russo-Japanese War. Based on the range of threats they faced (including the growth of the Turkish navy in the Black Sea in the years just before the outbreak of war) and the inherent weaknesses of Russian power, the logical response would have been to urge a foreign policy of caution and restraint. Arguably, Schedule 18 mirrored Sazonov's policy of retrenchment in foreign affairs, pursued between 1910 and 1912. But it was soon abandoned. The French alliance and the rise of Anglo-German antagonism gave Russian officers renewed hope that the Triple Entente could triumph in a general war. Schedule 19 was far more confident and aggressive than its predecessor. It reflected a change in Russian foreign policy, which set aside the caution of the post-1905 years in favour of the assertion of the national interest in the Balkans and the Near East and the consolidation of the Triple Entente. Russian war planning, therefore, reinforced the tendency of other war plans towards a general war.

French military plans concentrated overwhelmingly on the threat from Germany. Until the early twentieth century, France had also faced the risk of war against Italy and Britain. Agreements with Italy in 1902 and the Anglo-French entente of 1904 allowed French General Staff officers to focus their planning on the eastern front against Germany. Completed in May 1914, Plan 17 – the previous sixteen plans had been largely defensive – was essentially a deployment plan, which concentrated almost half of French forces along the Franco-German border in preparation for an offensive. Just under a quarter of the French army, five corps, were based on the Franco-Belgium border, while another six corps were held in reserve, ready to be deployed to the north or to the east, depending on circumstances. It was a flexible plan, which sought to thwart a

German offensive through Belgium and prepare for an offensive into Lorraine.

French military plans were shaped by a mix of contradictory factors. Joseph Joffre, appointed Chief of the General Staff during the middle of the Moroccan crisis in July 1911, was one of the foremost advocates of the cult of the offensive. 'Battles are moral contests', Joffre declared and the offensive was held to suit the moral fibre of the French soldier. French observers of the wars in the East Asia and the Balkans in the decade before 1914 saw confirmation of the value of the offensive spirit.[4] Joffre and the officers of the Troisième Bureau, notably Colonel Grandmaison, dominated French military thinking in the years before the outbreak of the war, with their ideology of the offensive.

However, Joffre's offensive inclinations were limited by diplomatic and political restraints. French planners were well aware that Germany would attack through Belgium. Joffre's predecessor, General Victor Constant Michel, had suggested placing two-thirds of the French army on the Belgian border and making that area the main theatre of the war. His demise marked the end of that plan. Belgian military weakness and perceived unwillingness to defend against a German attack led to occasional threats against Belgian neutrality. 'If you cannot prevent your neighbours from the east from passing through', the French president, Raymond Poincaré, informed Brussels in October 1912, 'I cannot give you the guarantee that we will await our enemy behind your frontier.'[5] Yet this outburst, and others like it, was designed to encourage greater Belgian readiness. French politicians and soldiers knew that British support might evaporate if France invaded Belgium. At a meeting of the Supreme National Council of Defence (CSDN) on 11 September 1911, Joffre's discussion of an invasion of Belgium made no progress. The securing of British aid had priority over the purely military plans for an offensive.

The Franco-Russian alliance and the Anglo-French entente framed French military planning before 1914. French leaders recognised that they could only defeat Germany by means of a general war. In short, France's relative weakness against Germany compelled her leaders to plan for a general war. Since the Moroccan crisis of 1905/6, French and British military and naval planners had exchanged information and

---

[4] Robert Doughty, 'French War Plans', in Richard Hamilton and Holger Herwig, eds, *War Planning 1914* (Cambridge, 2009); Olivier Cosson, *Préparer la grande guerre. L'armée française et la guerre russo-japonaise, 1899–1914* (Paris, 2013), pp. 195–203, 260–73; Adrian Wettstein, 'The French Military Mind and the Wars before the War', in Geppert, Mulligan, Rose, eds, *Wars*, pp. 176–89.

[5] Cited in Marie-Thérèse Bitsch, *La Belgique entre la France et l'Allemagne, 1905–1914* (Paris, 1994), p. 458.

prepared war plans, though this did not translate into a formal alliance. Indeed, Grey kept the talks a secret from the British cabinet, as he worried about radical opposition to the French entente. Only in 1911 were the talks discussed at cabinet level for the first time. In terms of French military planning, the talks had more importance at a political, than at a military, level. Sending the BEF to northern France made good the difference in size between the French and German armies, but it would also tie Britain into a continental war. Similarly, the agreement in 1912 that France would station its fleet in the Mediterranean and Britain would draw its dreadnoughts back to the North Sea distributed the defence burden between the two entente partners. In a Franco-German war, the burden of defending France's northern coast against the German fleet would fall to Britain. None of this, it should be reiterated, translated into an automatic commitment to a wartime alliance between France and Britain, but it made it a practical and likely option.

Soldiers such as Obruchev and Boisdeffre had played an important role in forging the Franco-Russian alliance in the early 1890s. Although military talks had taken place in 1901, it was only after the Moroccan crisis of 1911 that the military aspects of the alliance came to the fore. At a meeting in the summer of 1912, French officers urged the Russians to mobilise more quickly and to take the offensive to Germany. In return the French had to show that they were willing to take the offensive as well. Whereas the Anglo-French entente favoured restraint, the Franco-Russian alliance implied simultaneous mobilisations and offensives against Germany. The requirements of the alliance were one of the factors that led France to adopt the Three Year Law in 1913. This meant that troops would serve for three, not two years, as had been the case since 1905. The objective was to strengthen the front-line army and make it a more effective offensive force, though mobilisation concentrated French troops behind the border.

France's entente partner, Britain, had a wide range of military and naval commitments around the globe. The extent to which the German naval challenge and threat to the balance of power in Europe shaped British strategy before the First World War has been a contentious issue. The concentration of the fleet in home waters, the creation of the BEF, and the military and naval talks with France indicated that British strategy before 1914 shifted from an imperial to a European focus. From the 1980s, a host of studies on naval policy and foreign policy have challenged these assumptions. Jon Sumida's work on the Royal Navy has pointed to financial restraints and technological developments as the determinants of policy. But the revisionists have been revised in recent years, as studies show that, without disregarding financial and technological considerations, the German threat was the starting point for British policy makers. The recent work of Nicholas Lambert shows how the revisionist emphasis on the technological and financial dimensions of naval warfare can be accommodated within an account that shows that Germany was the primary target of naval planning. Since the elevation of Admiral Alfred von Tirpitz to the position of Secretary of State for the Admiralty, German naval planning and construction had been aimed at Britain. Whether Tirpitz intended his fleet to act as a deterrent, to make Germany more attractive as an alliance partner, or to challenge Britain's world power status continues to be a matter of debate. In any case, by 1902, senior British politicians were becoming worried about the German naval threat. These fears would grow over the next decade.

British policy makers had a number of options in responding to the German challenge. As long as the German threat was defined as a naval and imperial challenge, then the question revolved around the Royal Navy's mastery of the North Sea. The obvious solution was to build better ships, and more of them. But naval technology became increasingly complex in the early twentieth century, as the submarine and torpedo were developed. Sumida and Lambert have shown that naval strategy did not simply concentrate on building dreadnoughts, but involved complex debates over the use of submarines and destroyers to defend the British Isles against a German invasion. But could the Royal Navy preserve Britain's interests in continental Europe? The Admiralty's response was that a naval blockade would cut off Germany from her supplies of raw material and food and force her to sue for peace. In 1903 a Royal Commission had concluded that Britain was vulnerable to a blockade, as food supplies were dependent on imports. The same, naval planners quickly realised, applied to Germany. As the Director of Naval Intelligence, Charles Ottley, told Reginald McKenna, the First Lord of the Admiralty, 'grass would sooner or later grow in the streets of Hamburg'.[6] But if Germany defeated France and Russia, then she would have access to the raw materials and agricultural produce of the continent, making a blockade a far less effective strategic tool. The blockade was also an instrument of economic warfare. By bringing a halt to German trade and by denying German firms access to British banking and insurance facilities, Royal Navy planners aimed to bring about a credit crunch in Germany, causing the economy to seize up. This was also a long war strategy. The naval blockade – either as a form of economic warfare or an attack on enemy civilians through starvation – was predicated on a

---

[6] Cited in Avner Offer, *The First World War: An Agrarian Interpretation* (Oxford, 1989), p. 232.

catastrophic vision of war, which sought to disrupt the political, social, and economic order of the enemy.

The British army was keen to push for a continental commitment. During the Moroccan crisis, as war loomed, an important meeting of the CID took place. The CID had been established in 1904 to coordinate strategy, and it included the prime minister, the foreign secretary, the Chancellor, and generals and admirals. At a meeting on 23 August 1911, in the midst of the Moroccan crisis, Arthur Wilson, the First Sea Lord, and Colonel Henry Wilson, the Director of Military Operations, put forward two different strategic options. The admiral made a poor fist of what was always a weak argument – that a blockade could bring Germany to its knees. Henry Wilson, an Irishman with a deep fondness for France, argued that Britain should send its expeditionary force to northern France. It would make up the difference in size between the German and French forces, demonstrate a clear commitment to France, and prevent German forces from defeating France and establishing a hegemonic position on the continent. The prime minister and other ministers accepted Wilson's plan. This did not translate into a specific political commitment to support France against a German invasion, but it was now likely that in the case of a general European war, Britain would send a military force to the continent.

Although Italy was a member of the Triple Alliance, a neutrality agreement concluded with France in 1902 made it likely that Italy would not enter a general war at the very outset. However, the Italian Chief of the General Staff between 1908 and 1914, Pollio, was unaware of this agreement. He died of a heart attack on the same day as the assassinations at Sarajevo, but in the years before the war, he had based his war plans on the assumption that the Triple Alliance would fight together. Amongst Italian officers, suspicions of Austro-Hungarian intentions waned in 1912 and 1913, as the Habsburgs concentrated on the Balkans and Italian relations with France deteriorated. In January 1913, negotiations for a military convention between the Triple Alliance began. Italy's role in the Triple Alliance war plans was two-fold. The Italian and Austrian navies were supposed to interrupt the transport of French troops from North Africa across the Mediterranean. Three Italian army corps were to be transported through Austria to fight alongside German troops on the Rhine. This agreement was only concluded in April 1914, too late to be included in the mobilisation plans for that year. Gooch and Palumbo argue that these plans represented a substantial addition to the military power of the Triple Alliance in the initial weeks of the war. Italian neutrality was a major, if widely expected, blow to Germany's hopes of defeating France.

To what extent were these war plans a cause of war? At one level, the plans made a general war extremely likely. Few military planners thought in terms of a localised conflict between two of the great powers. This reflected an alliance system created by civilian leaders. War planners took political constellations into account and adapted their plans to suit changing circumstances. Moreover, war plans took account of the worst-case scenario. The general staffs may have had a narrow reading of the political possibilities, but anything else would have been a neglect of professional duty. Indeed, it could be argued that the prospect of general conflagration, bolstered by the war plans, made war seem a more extreme option and therefore made it less likely. Military planners failed to make clear the limitations and inadequacies of military and naval power as an instrument of policy. To have done so might have involved generals and admirals talking themselves out of a job.

The Expectations and Realities of War, 1871–1914

The war plans of the great powers were really plans for the mobilisation, concentration, and perhaps initial operations of their forces. What vision of warfare did soldiers and politicians entertain? The Russian diplomat Andrew Kalmykov, looking back on pre-revolutionary Russia from exile in the USA, gave a succinct description of the rupture that the First World War caused in Europe:

The twentieth century was ushered in as an era of progress, peace, and prosperity. Europe was guided by far-sighted statesmen of conservative tendencies; socialists were branded as unpractical dreamers and unpatriotic pacifists. Preparedness for war was supposed to be the best guarantee of peace. But the champagne youth I saw in Paris and London were doomed to die on the fields of battle, torn to pieces by explosives, riddled by machine gun bullets, asphyxiated by poisonous gases. So much for peace and progress.

He laid the blame for the war, as far as Russia's responsibility was concerned, squarely on the military caste. He criticised the generals for their lack of experience, suggesting that many of them had only fought in small wars against tribes in Central Asia, conflicts that were 'often costly in men and money'.[7] Although the period between 1871 and 1914 was one of peace between the great powers, warfare between the great powers and others remained common. The Russo-Turkish War of 1877/8, the Abyssinian-Italian War of 1896, the Spanish-American War of 1898, the South African War of 1899/1902, the Russo-Japanese War of 1904/5,

[7] Andrew D. Kalmykov, *Memoirs of a Russian Diplomat: Outposts of the Empire, 1893–1917* (New Haven, CT, 1971), pp. 146–48.

5. Hiram Maxim sits with the first portable, fully automatic machine gun, which he invented, and a Dundonald gun carriage (IWM Q 81725). Developments in firearms and artillery technology, such as the machine gun, would transform the battlefield and tactics during the First World War. Some military thinkers before the First World War predicted the emergence of trench warfare in response to these technological developments, but others adhered to the doctrine that attacks by well-disciplined and highly motivated troops would deliver victory.

and the Turkish-Italian War of 1911/12 provided ample evidence of the difficulty of winning decisive victories against apparently inferior foes. Generals also re-evaluated the significance of Sedan, the decisive battle of the last great power conflict in Europe, between the North German Confederation and her allies against France. These wars demonstrated that short conflicts, costing little in terms of blood and money, were rare.

Underestimating the enemy was a common error amongst the military and civilian leaders of the great powers. In 1903 the Russian military attaché in Tokyo issued a glib assessment, when he claimed that the Japanese army was 'no longer the rabble of an Asiatic horde . . . it is nevertheless no modern European army. It will take them ten, perhaps a hundred years.'[8] John Hay, the Secretary of State, famously described the Spanish-American War in July 1898 as a 'splendid little war', though

---

[8] Cited in David Schimmelpenninck van der Oye, 'The Russo-Japanese War', in Frederick Kagan and Robin Higham, eds, *The Military History of Tsarist Russia* (Basingstoke, 2002), p. 185.

he was not blind to the difficulties the American forces faced.[9] The victories of General Baratieri over Ethiopian forces in early 1895 encouraged Francesco Crispi, the Italian prime minister, to view the war against Emperor Menelik in 1896 as a guaranteed success. In a clash between a civilised European state and a barbaric African state, Crispi assumed that the Italian forces would triumph easily. Neither Joseph Chamberlain, the Colonial Secretary, nor the War Office believed that the Boers had substantial military forces. The Boers were depicted as indisciplined, if tough. War seemed to offer the prospect of an easy settlement of political differences.

But others were less sanguine about embarking on wars against lesser powers. Officers studied each other's campaigns and were familiar with the challenges posed. General Kuropatkin, always aware of the frailties of Russian military power, noted: 'It is highly significant and ominous that recently, as Europeans fought in Asia and Africa, the foe has more and more proven to be their equals. British defeats in Afghanistan and the Sudan, and French setbacks in Tonkin, demonstrate that African and Asian peoples can battle Europeans with the hope of beating them.'[10] In South Africa, General Wolseley and Sir William Butler were well aware of the weaknesses of the British position and urged a build-up of forces before hostilities began. Sidney Sonnino, the Minister of Finance in Crispi's government, was so vehemently opposed to colonial adventures and wars in Africa on the grounds of their financial expense that Crispi and his generals had to pursue their aggressive strategy behind Sonnino's back. The wars of the late nineteenth century proved the pessimists, the Kuropatkins and the Sonninos of the world, correct.

Wars rarely went to plan. Costs escalated, the casualty figure rose, and popular opinion proved fickle, often turning against governments. The cost of the South African War rose from an expected £10 million at the outset to £217 million by the end of the conflict. It put severe pressure on the Victorian fiscal state, which had valued low taxes and low government expenditure. The Italian government spent 1.7 billion lire on the war against Turkey in 1911/12; in 1910/11, its total military expenditure had been 577 million lire. The war created a large budget deficit, undermining the fiscal and political underpinnings of liberal Italy. The USA spent $400 million on the Spanish-American War and the

---

[9] Joseph Smith, *The Spanish-American War: Conflict in the Caribbean and the Pacific, 1895– 1902* (London, 1994), p. 212.

[10] Cited in David Schimmelpenninck van der Oye, *Towards the Rising Sun: Russian Ideologies of Empire and the Path to War with Japan* (DeKalb, 2001), p. 90; Peter Holquist, 'Violent Russia, Deadly Marxism? Russia in the Epoch of Violence, 1905–1921', *Kritika: Explorations in Russian and Eurasian History*, 4, 3 (2003): 634–37.

subsequent campaigns against Cuban and Filipino insurgents. In 1897, the entire USA federal government expenditure had amounted to almost $366 million.

Pious notions of national identity were laid bare, as great powers found it difficult to bring wars to a successful conclusion. Of course, patriotism in wartime could bolster a government, as the Conservatives found to their advantage in the 1900 election. Campbell Bannerman, the leader of the Liberal party, then in opposition, criticised the 'barbarous methods', including the use of concentration camps, that Britain practised in the war against the Boers. The conduct of the war punctured the government's argument that the war was being fought to uphold the rights of Uitlanders, foreign residents in the Transvaal. Throughout the 1890s, the Spanish use of concentration camps against Cuban rebels had infuriated American public opinion. But the USA, having defeated Spain, came to copy some of their methods when fighting against insurgents in Cuba and the Philippines. In the latter, Emilio Aguinaldo's guerrilla war led General Arthur MacArthur to adopt 'reconcentration methods', while Brigadier-General Jacob Smith ordered his men to turn the land into a 'howling wilderness'.[11] American opinion turned against the war, whose conduct was so much at odds with the stated humanitarian aims.

On two occasions, Russia exemplified the potential domestic political risks of war. In 1877, Alexander II declared war against Turkey. The mix of geopolitical calculation and heady pan-Slavic populism accompanying the war distorted Russian strategy. Having made great gains in March 1878 at the treaty of San Stefano, including the creation of a united Bulgaria, a satellite state of the Tsarist empire, Russia was forced to row back at the Congress of Berlin. The strengthening of Austria-Hungary and Britain in the Balkans and the Near East, alongside the division of Bulgaria into two provinces, with one, Eastern Rumelia, remaining under Turkish sovereignty, led a leading Muscovite Slavophile, Ivan Aksakov, to tell the Moscow Slavic Society in July 1878 that the Congress of Berlin had been 'a funeral of whole countries'.[12] Russia had won the war, but lost the peace, due to the exhaustion of her army, which had been held up at the siege of Plevna in the second half of 1877. More men had died of typhus than had died in military combat – not an unusual statistic before the twentieth century. On the home front, the Finance Minister, Reutern, warned that the state could not sustain war expenditures, which increased to 1.075 billion rubles. Failure at the peace table, a demoralised

[11] Smith, *Spanish-American War*, pp. 221–25; Ben Wattenberg, ed., *Statistical History of the United States: From Colonial Times to the Present* (New York, 1976), p. 1104.
[12] Cited in David MacKenzie, 'Russia's Balkan Policies under Alexander II', in Hugh Ragsdale, ed., *Imperial Russian Foreign Policy* (Cambridge, 1993), p. 243.

army, and creaking finances added up to a revolutionary situation. A series of terrorist attacks began in January 1878 with the murder of General Trepov, the Chief of Police in St Petersburg, and ended with the assassination of Alexander II in March 1881.

Much worse was to befall the Tsarist regime during the revolution of 1905. Of course, the revolution was not simply the outcome of a disastrous war. Discontented workers, liberals, and others had long-standing grievances with the Tsarist regime. Nonetheless, the war provided the context for revolution. Defeats on the battlefield magnified the failings of the Tsarist regime. A left-liberal paper, *Russkoe bogatstvo*, claimed that Russian military 'impotence' was rooted 'in the unpreparedness and improvidence, as well as in other defects, characteristic of a bureaucratic system'. Calls for reform spread across society, while violence erupted. The Minister of the Interior, V. N. Plehve, was assassinated in the summer of 1904. Once revolution broke out in February 1905, political upheaval at home reinforced the weakness of the Tsarist regime abroad. Politically, financially, and militarily prostrate, there was hardly any room for manoeuvre in domestic and foreign politics throughout 1905 and early 1906. Instead of reinforcing great power prestige, war, along with the revolution, had brought Russian power to its lowest ebb since the Crimean War.

The scale of the Russo-Japanese War belied the short war myth, in which one decisive battle would deliver victory. Admiral Togo Heiachiro's attack on the Russian fleet in Port Arthur on 8–9 February 1904 gave Japan a commanding logistical advantage, but the war on land was one of attrition, rather than annihilation. The battle of Mukden was the final major land battle of the war and it lasted from January until March 1905, with 270 000 men on either side. Russian forces suffered ninety thousand casualties, Japanese forces seventy thousand. It was another naval battle, the sinking of Russia's fleet at Tsushima on 28 May 1905, which brought about an end to the war. Even then, peace owed more to the collapse of Russian credit and domestic stability.

Military observers paid close attention to the wars fought in East Asia and South Africa. To a certain extent, officers simply imbibed the lessons that they wanted to learn. This often meant that their analysis of the Russo-Japanese War and the South African War confirmed the emphasis on the offensive. Nor did their observations render war a less viable instrument of politics. As military observers mainly reported tactical and operational innovations, they tended to ignore the financial and social impact of wars. But their observations were more complex than this straightforward restatement of orthodox thinking. They noted the vast scale of the battlefields, the length of the battles, the ability of armies to send batch after batch of reinforcements, and the impact of new and improved technologies, particularly artillery. These observations did not necessarily feed through into a critical re-evaluation of tactical and operational doctrine. On the other hand, the experiences of war made clear their brutality. A French assessment of the South African War, published in January 1902, noted:

> The South African campaign has just reminded us, in an opportune fashion, of the inexorable characteristics of war and responds victoriously to those utopians, who harboured the hope of resolving all conflicts by arbitration and removing from the struggle between nations its character of brutality and savagery. We witnessed the destruction of an entire people, and even the women and children were not saved. It would be naïve beyond measure to be surprised by the nature of war, pushed to its extreme consequences by the obstinacy of two opponents.[13]

Wars had become contests between nations and societies, not just states and armies. The Balkan Wars confirmed the changing character of warfare, though many observers attributed the atrocities against civilians to the putative cultural backwardness of the region rather than as representing the essence of early twentieth century warfare.[14] Because the stakes were higher, the restraints on warfare would be cast aside, leading to extremely destructive conflicts. There was very little evidence, on the basis of the European experience of warfare between 1871 and 1914, to suggest that a general war between the great powers would be short, sharp, and decisive.

Indeed, the European military elites were well aware that the next general war would differ from the cabinet wars of the mid-nineteenth century. These wars, in 1859 and 1866, had ended after one or two battles, were characterised by restraint in terms of the conduct of war and the aims of the belligerents, and modified, rather than overturned, the international system. But this era was passing. For Moltke, the continued French resistance and irregular warfare following the apparently decisive victory over Napoleon III's forces at the battle of Sedan was the most striking feature of the Franco-Prussian War. In his final speech to the Reichstag, on 14 May 1890, he told his audience: 'The age of cabinet wars lies behind us. Now, we only have people's war [*Volkskrieg*]. Gentlemen, it could be the Seven Years' War, it could be the Thirty Years' War – woe

---

[13] Cited in Olivier Cosson, 'Expériences de guerre et anticipation à la veille de la Première Guerre mondiale: Les milieux militaires franco-britanniques et les conflits extérieurs', *Revue de l'Histoire Moderne et Contemporaine*, 50, 3 (2003): 144–45.

[14] See the contributions of Adrian Wettstein, Günther Kronenbitter, Markus Pöhlmann, and Florian Keisinger in Dominik Geppert, William Mulligam, Andreas Rose, eds, *The Wars before the Great War. Conflict and International Politics before the Outbreak of the First World War* (Cambridge, 2015), pp. 176–231, 343–58.

betide whoever plunges Europe into flames, whoever is the first to light the fuse to the powder keg.'[15] The people's war in 1870/1 was a challenge to the Prussian way of warfare. Defeating the enemy army and state was insufficient; it was necessary to defeat the enemy nation and society. The lessons of 1870/1 were ambiguous. German officers were certainly aware of the dangers of people's war. Colmar von der Goltz, who worked in the War History Department of the General Staff, examined the history of Léon Gambetta's army, which had been raised in the levée in 1870. Fritz Hoenig, a retired officer and well-known author, wrote a book in 1893 on the people's war in the Loire valley.

These may not have been the leading lights of the German General Staff, but even Schlieffen, writing in 1909, expressed doubts about the possibility of winning a decisive battle. He noted that battles lasted many days in the Franco-Prussian War and expected longer battles in the next European war. 'All the doubts about the horrible cost', he argued, 'the possible high casualties, as well as the phantom of danger threatening from anarchism have emerged from the background. Universal conscription, which uses high and low, rich and poor alike, as cannon fodder, has dampened the lust for battle.'[16] Yet he also doubted whether a war would last too long, owing to the collapse of business, trade, and credit upon which modern civilisation depended. This ambiguity about the next war was far removed from the clarity of his 1905 memorandum. Short wars escaped from the restraints of political and economic stability, but it does not follow logically that wars *had to be* short due to these constraints. The scenarios entertained by the German General Staff exposed the myth of the short war. They recognised that the French army might retreat behind the Loire, forcing Germany into a drawn-out campaign. In 1907, Alfred von Tirpitz warned the Secretary of the Interior, Arthur von Posadowsky-Wehner, of the need to build up food supplies in case a war lasted longer than expected. Moltke's decision not to invade the Netherlands, turning it into a 'windpipe' for Germany, confirms the view that German officers were not wedded to a short war myth.

Officers in the Austro-Hungarian army arrived at similar conclusions about the duration and nature of the next war. In an 1889 memorandum, entitled 'Future Wars', Beck pointed out that a general war involving between 7 and 8 million soldiers would be completely different to previous wars. This would render the conduct and consequences of a war uncertain. Otto Berndt, whose 1898 book, *Die Zahl im Krieg*, was used

[15] Cited in Stig Förster, 'Der deutsche Generalstab und die Illusion des kurzen Krieges, 1871–1914. Metakritik eines Mythos', *Militärgeschichtliche Mitteilungen*, 54 (1995): 66.
[16] 'War Today', originally published in *Deutsche Revue*, 1909 in Robert Foley, ed., *Alfred von Schlieffen's Military Writings* (London, 2003), p. 204.

widely in military schools, pointed to the French ability to continue their resistance after Sedan. He argued that there was no evidence to suggest that wars were getting shorter and predicted the next general war would last months, and probably years. In 1912, General Blasius Schemua, Conrad's successor as Chief of Staff, warned that the 'seriousness of a war is not sufficiently ingrained in the people. The next war will be a people's war, in the true sense of the word.' The war would continue until the destruction of the army and the occupation of the enemy's commercial heartlands. The state would have to mobilise all its resources and would fight until it was 'bled white'.[17] Conrad routinely referred to the next war as a struggle for existence. The apocalyptic language indicated that officers expected the next war to be fought on a gigantic scale.

The visions of future war in the officer corps of the French, British, and Russian armies are less clear. Doughty simply notes that the French army had not prepared for a long war before 1914. Future wars, Ferdinand Foch told cadet officers at the École supérieure de guerre, would be 'violent and short.' Like Schlieffen he reasoned that the cessation of social and commercial life following mobilisation could not long be endured by modern societies. Yet this reasoning was fallacious. Foch's recipe for decisive battle was as optimistic and far-fetched as Schlieffen's. If the decisive battle never transpired, then only catastrophic social and political upheaval could bring about an end to the war.[18] Peter Gattrell argues that the planners ignored Russia's narrow industrial base because officers expected a short war. Fuller agrees with Gattrell, arguing that Russian strategy was distorted by the fear that if they lost the first battle, they would lose the war. Much of this reasoning is deductive – because military planners did not prepare for a long war, they expected a short war. Yet, as the evidence from the Austro-Hungarian and German officer corps demonstrates, officers foresaw a long conflict, but they concentrated on mobilisation schedules and initial operations at the expense of planning for the economic, political, and social pressures of a general war. The narrow professional concerns of the officer corps, the unwillingness of civilian ministers to press for greater coordination of war planning, and the polycratic bureaucracies of many pre-war European states hindered planning for a long war. In Britain, Lord Kitchener, appointed Secretary of State for War on 6 August 1914, predicted that the war would last three years and that Britain would require an army of millions, rather than hundreds of thousands, of men. He could hardly have come to this conclusion in the days since Britain had declared war.

---

[17] Günther Kronenbitter, '*Krieg im Frieden*'. *Die Führung der k. u. k. Armee und die Groß-machtpolitik Österreich-Ungarns, 1906–1914* (Munich, 2003), p. 139.
[18] Ferdinand Foch, *Des principes de la guerre* (Paris, 1996), p. 130.

Yet even if soldiers believed that the next great power conflict might well bring catastrophe in its wake, they were not necessarily opposed to war. Some saw it as an inevitable occurrence in human history, while others saw it as a simultaneously creative and destructive conflict. These arguments undermined peace between the great powers. War became an end in itself, a phenomenon that could not be controlled or restrained by politics. Moltke the Elder, despite his prophecies of another Thirty Years War, argued that war remained a central and progressive driving force in human history. Erich von Falkenhayn, the architect of German strategy at Verdun, argued in the midst of the Russo-Japanese War that 'we must have a struggle for life with all its horrors, but also with all its glorious developments, if everything here is not to grow weary and be smothered in lies and sluggishness. If only it is not already too late.'[19] Moltke the Younger took a more resigned, fatalistic view of the likelihood and desirability of war. For him, it was a question of the existence of the German nation, a question that could not be evaded in the long term. Given that war was inevitable, Moltke persistently argued that the sooner, the better.

Within the Austro-Hungarian officer corps, similar claims about the inevitability and desirability of war were regularly advanced. According to Conrad, the maintenance of the status quo in the Balkans would only lead to internal decadence within the Habsburg empire. 'Only an aggressive policy with positive aims', he argued, 'can guard against catastrophe and achieve success. Whoever does not have the courage for such a policy, must be prepared for collapse.' General Potiorek, the commander in Bosnia-Herzegovina, called for an activist, aggressive foreign policy: 'If it happens without the use of arms, so much the better. But for God's sake, no lazy peace. A defeat on the field of battle against a great power would be preferable to that.'[20] In late 1912, Colonel Appel wished for a 'strengthening bath of steel', which would separate the chaff from the wheat. The prediction of collapse was accurate, but officers argued that it was preferable to a self-defeating peace, during which the internal bonds of the empire were shredded and foreign enemies grew more powerful. On this reading, values such as martial honour had primacy over material concerns, such as financial stability or the preservation of territory. In some ways, these positive visions of warfare, as the essential motor of history or a creative force, were a defence of the officer corps. While officers embraced modern technologies, they felt embattled by aspects of modern society. Consumerism, internationalism, and individualism were

---

[19] Cited in Holger Afflerbach, *Falkenhayn. Politisches Denken und Handeln in Kaiserreich* (Munich, 1996), p. 53.
[20] Jürgen Angelow, *Kalkül und Prestige. Der Zweibund am Vorabend des Ersten Weltkrieges* (Cologne, 2000), p. 414.

amongst the 'isms' charged with undermining traditional values, which would be essential in a future war – and to the status of the officer corps in society.

The experiences and visions of warfare generated between 1871 and 1914 pointed to a long and destructive conflict. But what did civilian political leaders think about the next war? Crispi had looked to war to create the Italian nation, since he had fought alongside Garibaldi, the great Italian soldier of the Risorgimento, in the 1860s. On becoming the first Italian prime minister from outside Piedmont in 1887, and deeply aware of the regional divisions in Italy, Crispi had pursued an aggressive foreign policy. He hoped that a military convention with Germany would be the precursor to a war against France. But he had to wait until 1896 to get his war, which turned into a disaster as Italy was defeated by Abyssinia. It was clear that most Italians did not share Crispi's positive view of war. Indeed, on 20 September 1895, on the twenty-fifth anniversary of the taking of Rome, while Crispi was out unveiling a statue to Garibaldi, a thief broke into Crispi's home and stole his military medals!

Few other politicians shared Crispi's views on warfare. Most were aware of the potentially catastrophic consequences of a major European war. Even if the military did not discuss the character of modern warfare in depth with their civilian masters, the latter were well aware of the consequences of the various wars fought in the forty-four years between Sedan and Sarajevo.

Nonetheless, there were so many war crises during this period that Wolfgang Mommsen has identified 'a topos of inevitable war'. The great power tensions, the scares in the press, and the partial mobilisations of the military and navy contributed to a sense that war was inevitable at some point, probably in the not too distant future. Arguably, this created a sense of fatalism, which reduced the psychological barrier to opting for war. If it were to be done, 'twas best done quickly. Yet, the fear of inevitable war had existed since the early 1870s – and for four decades, these fears proved unfounded. In February 1872, Austro-Hungarian military and political leaders believed that they had two years to prepare for war. During the multiple crises of 1885–7, the view was frequently expressed in European capitals that war was inevitable. Friedrich von Holstein, the leading figure in the Foreign Office after Bismarck's departure in 1890, warned his friend, Ida von Stülpnagel: 'Peace, like a person with a heart condition, can hold out for many years, but it can also come to a sudden end as a result of some small complication.'[21]

---

[21] Cited in Rainer Lahme, *Deutsche Außenpolitik 1890–1894. Von der Gleichgewichtspolitik Bismarcks zur Allianzstrategie Caprivis* (Göttingen, 1990), p. 24.

These crises had passed without resulting in a general war, but the 'topos of inevitable war' re-emerged during the Moroccan crisis of 1905/6 and the Bosnian crisis of 1908/9. It emerged even more strongly after the Second Moroccan crisis of 1911. Historians have tended to agree with the contemporary view that war became increasingly likely after 1911. The threat of war, which had loomed in the summer of 1911, faded in the latter part of the year, but its legacy included an intensified arms race, the outbreak of a series of wars in North Africa and the Balkans, and heightened nationalist sensitivities. In Russia, Austria-Hungary, France, and Germany, numerous examples could be found of the topos of inevitable war. The German ambassador to Paris, Wilhelm von Schoen, noted that the Second Moroccan crisis had shaken the French from their 'dreams of peace between nations'. He acknowledged that the French were not governed by 'a lust for aggressive war', but that they believed that 'sooner or later a war will become inevitable'.[22] William II told King Albert of Belgium on 6 November 1913 that war was inevitable within the next year, while Moltke, twice on the same evening, told King Albert that the sooner war came, the better.

Yet the significance of the topos of inevitable war is open to question. First, simply because political leaders predicted war does not mean that it was inevitable. After all, cries about the inevitability of war had dogged great power politics since the early 1870s, yet wars had been repeatedly avoided. Certainly, after 1911, there were signs – army bills, press wars, and the consolidation of alliances – that governments were preparing for the worst-case scenario of a general war, without necessarily wishing it to come about. But there were also plenty of voices who doubted whether war was inevitable. These voices, until recently, have been lost, as historians paid more attention to the perceived inevitability of war, which fitted into a neat explanation of pre-war international politics as riven by crises and belligerence and doomed to end in catastrophe. Nicolson was confident 'that the present equilibrium is the best chance of maintaining the peace'. He predicted that 'most countries will also be greatly preoccupied with their internal affairs. I myself really have no fears that there will be any serious friction between European powers, divergent as their views may be on many questions.'[23] The British ambassador to Berlin, Edward Goschen, told a colleague from the French embassy at the height of the Moroccan crisis: 'I told him I regarded the present situation like I regarded ghosts. I don't believe in them, but I am frightened of them. So I don't believe there will be war, but I am deadly anxious about

---

[22] Schoen to Bethmann Hollweg, 22 March 1912, *Grosse Politik*, vol. 31, pp. 397–401.
[23] Nicolson to Bunsen, 19 January 1914, TNA, FO 800/372, fol. 83.

it.'[24] In November 1912, just before the Russian mobilisation crisis, the German military attaché in Russia doubted whether the Tsar would risk a war, given the internal political difficulties that the regime continued to face.

Second, even apparently clear evidence, such as William II's conversation with King Albert, can be interpreted in different ways. King Albert, deeply concerned, relayed the information to the French government, and it soon found its way around the European diplomatic circuit. At the time, it was widely dismissed as an outburst by an emperor who was actually restraining the war party in Berlin. It was written off as one of William II's impetuous episodes. Only in the light of events in 1914 was it taken more seriously, as evidence of a planned war of aggression. But even then, this conclusion is open to dispute, given that William II had tried at the last moment to pull back from war against France in July 1914. In spring 1912, Falkenhayn lamented: 'I no longer share the view about the inevitability of war. His Majesty is completely decided to keep the peace under all circumstances and there is nobody in his circle to dissuade him from this dangerous decision.'[25] It is possible that William II either disguised his aggressive aims or else shifted to a more belligerent policy in the second half of 1913, when he also assured Archduke Franz Ferdinand of German support in a war against Serbia.

Nonetheless, it is striking that so many well-informed diplomats, politicians, and soldiers did not subscribe to the 'inevitable war' thesis before 1914. This undermines the argument that the prospect of inevitable war was a self-fulfilling prophecy. Instead, Friedrich Kießling has identified a very different topos – the 'topos of the avoided war'. The successful resolution of a series of crises between 1911 and 1913 had promoted confidence amongst European diplomats and politicians that war could be avoided. Combined with the experience of over forty years of general peace, politicians accepted the possibility of war, but did not really expect it.

In fact, many civilian politicians stressed the dire consequences of a general war and therefore had every incentive to avoid one. British Liberals were well known for their aversion to war, even Liberal imperialists, such as Grey. In June 1911, in the midst of the Second Moroccan crisis and bedevilled by a constitutional crisis and labour unrest, Grey predicted that the social revolution would occur in any state that went to war. Even the victor in a general war would emerge crippled from the

---

[24] Friedrich Kießling, *Gegen den großen Krieg? Entspannung in den internationalen Beziehungen, 1911–1914* (Munich, 2002), p. 38.
[25] Afflerbach, *Falkenhayn*, p. 99.

conflict. Fear of revolution in the wake of war had been an important strand of conservative thinking throughout the nineteenth century. Not surprisingly, given the consequences of the Crimean, Russo-Turkish, and Russo-Japanese Wars, this argument was articulated clearly by Russian conservatives. In February 1914, P. N. Durnovo, a member of the State Council, submitted a memorandum to Nicholas II. Worried that increasing antagonism between Russia and Germany would lead to war, he warned of 'the enormous losses by which war will be attended under present conditions of military technique . . . The result of such a war will be an economic situation compared with which the yoke of German capital will seem easy.' War would ruin trade, financial stability, agriculture, and most importantly, the monarchy. Political and social revolution would almost certainly follow.[26] Grey and Durnovo were at the opposite poles of European political culture, but they shared a common assessment of the consequences of a general war.

On several occasions, Bethmann Hollweg made clear that he saw war as a catastrophe. In a much-quoted speech to the Reichstag in April 1913, Bethmann Hollweg warned of a possible 'life and death struggle' between Slavs and Germans in the near future, but he also noted that Germany had good relations with the Tsarist empire. Indeed, the terrible consequences of a general war were transformed into an early form of the concept of deterrence. Between 1912 and 1914, Kurt Riezler, an adviser to Bethmann Hollweg, wrote two books: *The Demands of the Impossible* and *The Essential Features of Contemporary World Politics*. In these works, he stressed 'the postponement of military conflict', which he attributed to the expansion of European powers in Africa and Asia and the growing economic interdependence of the modern world. Indeed, the potentially ruinous consequences of war were becoming more evident by the day. Yet, each state continued to arm. But this was not in preparation for war; rather it was a means of building a military superiority that would enable it to wrest concessions from other powers. A policy of calculated risk could allow a state to achieve its goals without drawing its sword – its rivals would back down, particularly if the issue was not a priority. 'The more we all arm, the more the relationship between the advantages and disadvantages of war shifts to the latter and therefore in favour of peace.'[27] Riezler's arguments shifted between a policy of deterrence and one of calculated risk.

---

[26] Frank A. Golder, *Documents of Russian History, 1914–1917* (London, 1927), pp. 3–23.
[27] Andreas Hillgruber, *Deutsche Großmacht und Weltpolitik im 19. und 20. Jahrhundert* (Düsseldorf, 1979), pp. 91–96.

Some politicians even dared to hope that war belonged to the past and was banished, at least as far as great power conflict was concerned, from the modern era. When Conrad argued in favour of a preventive war against Italy in April 1907, Francis Joseph responded that a preventive war was unacceptable according to contemporary norms. Italy's war against Turkey in 1911 was widely condemned as a violation of the European sense of law and justice. It was seen as a blatant war of conquest, which could not be justified with any of the usual excuses about the threat to European life and property or the collapse of government structures in a failing state. At a Guildhall banquet in 1905, Arthur Balfour predicted: 'So far as human foresight can go, in future we shall not see wars, unless indeed we can conceive that either a nation or a ruler should arise, who feel that they must carry out their schemes of national aggrandisement, except by trampling on the rights of their neighbours. I can see no prospect of any such calamity to Europe. It would indeed be a tragic reversion to ancient days if Europe had again to make a coalition against any too ambitious Power.'[28] André Tardieu, a French journalist who had close connections to the Quai d'Orsay, informed a German audience in February 1910 that France would not embark on a war of vengeance nor Germany on a war of hegemony. It would be a 'crime, if we cannot resolve the quarrels of a lesser nature, which constitute the small change of international life, in a friendly nature'.[29]

These statements about the unacceptability of war were hedged with reservations. Balfour, speaking in the immediate aftermath of the Russo-Japanese War, could only have been referring to warfare between the great powers in Europe. Wars in the colonies, in Africa, and in Asia were justifiable on certain grounds. Yet the norms that governed the use of force in international politics were changing. In the 1870s and 1880s, Bismarck had ruled out a preventive war on the grounds that it would cause long-term political damage to the Kaiserreich. His successors on the European stage, for the most part, considered an aggressive war as unacceptable *tout court*. How, why, and when this shift in norms occurred remains to be researched, but the change in attitude was an important restraint in European politics before the First World War. The most important reservation was that nobody ruled out a great power war in defence of a vital national interest. The definition of the national interest was ambiguous, varying across the different capitals, in the minds of different statesmen, and at different times. But generally, a great power

28 Cited in Jason Tomes, *Balfour and Foreign Policy: The International Thought of a Conservative Statesman* (Cambridge, 1997), p. 145.
29 André Tardieu, 'Vergangenheit und Zukunft der französisch-deutschen Beziehungen', *Deutsche Revue*, February 1910, p. 7, Archives nationales, 324 AP/20.

war would not be waged over colonial differences, public insults, or the acquisition of territory, including Alsace-Lorraine, from another great power. The second problem with this reservation was that the concept of a defensive war was also ambiguous. In July 1914, one of the most significant problems facing the international system was that all the great powers claimed they were waging a defensive war.

Before 1914, war was seen as a legitimate, but not a normal instrument of policy in great power politics. War was the option of last resort, an instrument that could only be used in defence of a vital national interest. The potential consequences of a great power war were well known amongst politicians and soldiers. A general war was unlikely to be short and would have ruinous consequences for social, political, and economic stability. For many soldiers, these negative consequences of war were balanced by its perceived creative qualities; but neither diplomats nor politicians shared this positive view of warfare. But could civilian political leaders exercise control over their generals?

Civil–Military Relations before 1914

It has been a long-standing axiom of liberal thought that the army must be subordinated to civilian political control. The sphere of the professional soldier is preparing for and fighting wars. In theory, there is a neat division of labour between the civilian politician and the professional soldier, but the boundaries can become blurred. Historians such as Mombauer and Kronenbitter have argued that before 1914 officers exercised too much influence over political decisions. Moltke and Conrad, they contend, bear a good deal of the responsibility for the outbreak of the First World War. Of course, officers had to play a role in political decisions. The question is whether they managed to overrule their civilian and political masters. For the most part, governments kept control of their generals before 1914.

In states where the military brought about changes in government or in the regime, they exercised considerable influence, pushing for a more aggressive foreign policy. In 1912, the Japanese army brought down the government of prime minister Saionji Kimmochi, after he had refused the army's demand for two extra divisions to be sent to Korea. The army did not take over the reins of government, but it accelerated the shift towards a more aggressive foreign policy. The Serbian military destabilised European politics in the decade before the First World War, pursuing increasingly radical goals. Army officers led the coup of 1903, shooting the king and queen and then throwing their mutilated bodies out of a window in the royal palace. They then voluntarily surrendered power to a government of national unity. The new government shifted away from the pro-Austrian policy of the Obrenovic dynasty to a pro-Russian policy. The structure of the Serb military, with links to guerrilla groups (Chetniks) in Ottoman territories, made civilian control more difficult. In addition, the military continued to pursue its own policies. It pressed the prime minister, Pasič, to declare war on Bulgaria in the summer of 1913, as Serbia and Bulgaria vied for control of Macedonia. Only the hasty declaration of war by Bulgaria saved Pasič from giving in to the demands of the military. Colonel Dragutin Dimitrijevic, nicknamed Apis (Bull), had led the coup in 1903. He ran the Black Hand group, which was initially used in the struggle between the Balkan states for control of Macedonia. The government failed to control the Black Hand, which organised the assassination of Franz Ferdinand. This marked the disastrous culmination of military influence in Serbian politics before the war.

In the Ottoman Empire, a group of officers based in Macedonia, popularly known as the Young Turks, revolted in July 1908. They aimed to restore the liberal constitution of 1876, developing the internal cohesion and strength to resist the constant encroachments by the great powers on Ottoman territory. The course of Ottoman politics between 1908 and 1914 was complex, including coups and counter-coups. In January 1913, the Young Turks seized power again and until the beginning of the war, Enver Pasa, an officer, dominated Ottoman high politics.

Amongst the great powers, it was the two liberal, constitutional states, France and Britain, where relations between the civilian government and the military were most fraught. However, civil–military tensions arose from the inability of the military in the two countries to exert influence on political affairs. In France, the relationship between the army and the republic was often difficult. The monarchical bent of the officer corps meant that republican politicians entertained suspicions of the army. There was also a tension between the republican vision of the citizen-soldier and the professional military preference for a highly disciplined, trained soldier. These tensions came to the fore during the Dreyfus affair, which divided French opinion between the nationalist and Catholic right and the republican left. Paul Déroulède, leader of the League of Patriots, decided to use the occasion of the state funeral of President Felix Faure, who had died in the arms of his mistress, to launch a coup. He expected the support of the army units based around Paris. But the attempted coup fizzled out, as military support for Déroulède never materialised. In Britain, the military challenge to civilian authority was similarly anaemic. It occurred during the Home Rule crisis of 1914, when the officers, based at the Curragh outside Dublin, made it clear that they would not take action against the Ulster Volunteer Force. However, the authority of the government was quickly restored.

Coups were a drastic measure and influence was normally exercised in more subtle ways. Constitutional structures and personal relationships between officers and political leaders shaped the ability of the military to influence political decisions. In Britain and France, the military were integrated into civilian constitutional structures. The cabinet posts at the War Office and the Admiralty in Britain were held by civilian politicians. The prime minister headed the CID, at which strategy was debated and decided upon. Officers had to make representations to their civilian ministers, the Secretary of State for War and the First Lord of the Admiralty, who would then table proposals at cabinet level. Ultimately, military and naval budgets had to pass through parliament. There was a thick network of civilian institutions, therefore, which meant that officers had to make their influence felt through powerful advocacy and political networking. A figure like Sir Jackie Fisher became powerful through the force of his personality and his political skills. He befriended leading politicians, such as Balfour, Grey, and Churchill. He leaked material to journalists in order to put pressure on the government. Fisher was also effective at framing his arguments in ways that would appeal to the prevailing political wind. Henry Wilson was another dynamic officer, who developed a close relationship with Arthur Nicolson, the permanent under-secretary at the Foreign Office. Nicolson brought Wilson's views to the attention of Haldane and Grey. In this round-about way, Wilson emerged as a key influence on British military planning before 1914.

Fisher and Wilson were able to exercise influence because civilian politicians were predisposed to their solutions, be it the development of the Dreadnought or the sending of the BEF to northern France. It is more difficult to identify instances when British military and naval figures determined policy. Talks between the British and French armies from 1906 were conducted without the knowledge of the cabinet, but with the approval of Grey. These talks never represented a political commitment by Britain to come to French aid in the case of a general war, but they did deepen the relationship between the two entente partners. The entente had originally been a colonial agreement, but these talks were at the centre of a new dynamic in Anglo-French relations.

The French army was also embedded into a liberal constitutional framework. Unlike Britain, the Minister of War was not always a civilian. But this was less significant than might be thought. In 1900, President Loubet appointed General Louis André, who was charged with making absolutely certain the army's loyalty to the Third Republic. It was the political inclination of the general, not his membership of the military caste, which mattered. In 1872, the Third Republic set up a Supreme Council of War, which included the president and the premier, as well as senior generals. It was supposed to discuss all facets of military policy, while the Supreme Council of National Defence, established in 1906, had a broader remit, as the ministers of finance, colonies, and foreign affairs were members of this body. Krumeich and Doughty suggest that officers had considerable influence because of the frequent change of ministers and the strengthening of the position of High Command by Alexandre Millerand, the Minister of War, in 1912. However, even on planning matters, as we have seen, political concerns trumped Joffre's desire for an invasion of Belgium. Officers played an important role in the alliance negotiations with Russia in the early 1890s. Between 1912 and 1914, talks between the French and Russian general staffs consolidated the alliance. On both occasions, military policy fitted with broader political interests. Officers gave advice on foreign policy issues, but never determined foreign policy. In his memoirs, Joffre recounts a conversation with Caillaux during the Second Moroccan crisis. Caillaux asked if France had a 70 per cent chance of victory in a war against Germany, to which Joffre replied that he did not think so. 'Well then', concluded Caillaux, 'we'll negotiate.'[30]

The position of the military in the other great powers was very different, offering more room for influencing foreign policy and decisions on war and peace. In Germany, the military and navy had direct access to the Kaiser. The General Staff was independent of the Prussian Ministry of War, who represented the army in the Reichstag. The Kaiser was supposed to give coherence to these structures, as decision-making powers ultimately rested with him. But the pressures of work and the personality of William II militated against coherence. The lack of a forum like the CID made it potentially difficult for civilian leaders to exercise restraint on their military counterparts. One of the most notorious episodes in the history of the Kaiserreich, the so-called War Council of 8 December 1912, was a meeting of William II and his closest military advisers, including Moltke and Tirpitz. According to Fritz Fischer and John Röhl, this meeting set Germany on a course for a general European war eighteen months later. New navy and army bills, a press policy to prepare the public for war, and the strengthening of Germany's alliances were the key points raised at the meeting. Röhl argued that real power had shifted away from the civilian leaders, the Chancellor, and the Foreign Office to the military entourage of William II. The civilian government merely implemented the decisions taken at this meeting. Several

---

[30] Jean Claude Allain, *Joseph Caillaux. Le défi victorieux* (Paris, 1978), pp. 380–81.

historians have disputed the significance of the meeting. Apart from speeding up the passage of the new army bill, which was already on the agenda, 'the immediate results of the gathering were fairly slight'.[31] Power, in Mommsen's view, rested with Bethmann Hollweg and the civilian leadership, not William II's military advisers.

The evidence suggests that the civilian leaders, from Bismarck to Bethmann Hollweg, were able to prevent the generals from taking crucial decisions on war and peace. Generals urged preventive wars on a number of occasions – notably, in 1887 and in 1905 – but Bismarck and Bülow were able to restrain them. William II and Bethmann Hollweg turned a deaf ear to Moltke's cry of 'the sooner, the better'. Kiderlen made it clear that his threats of war against France in 1911 were bluff. He warned against any form of mobilisation, which might escalate into war. Whenever there was a clear opportunity to provoke a war or launch a preventive war before 1914, German politicians invariably rejected the option and kept their more belligerent generals in check.

Although the ultimate decision of war and peace lay with the Kaiser and the civilian leadership, the military and naval elite could shape the context in which foreign policy was conducted. From 1897, Tirpitz's naval programme was the single most important factor in rising Anglo-German antagonism. The fleet invested colonial disputes and economic rivalries with a greater strategic significance than had previously been the case. While the fleet was directed against Britain, Tirpitz also feared that the Royal Navy might 'Copenhagen' the German fleet before it was fully ready. He feared that Bülow's project for a Russo-German alliance, bringing together Britain's two greatest and most dangerous rivals, would lead to a pre-emptive strike against the German fleet by the Royal Navy. Tirpitz's programme and the consequent antagonism between the two countries restricted the foreign policy options for the Kaiserreich. When Bülow and Bethmann Hollweg tried to repair relations with Britain after 1906 and 1911, it was made more difficult by the legacy of the naval race. On the other hand, Bülow shared many of Tirpitz's goals and agreed on the need for a navy to promote German power around the globe. Politicians were aware of the implications of the Tirpitz programme. Generals demanded increases in the size of the army, but as we will see, arms races were the product of political factors, rather than generals working outside constitutional checks and balances.

In Austria-Hungary, the constitutional position of the army was somewhat similar to that in Germany. The Chief of the General Staff had direct

[31] Wolfgang Mommsen, *Imperial Germany, 1867–1918: Politics, Culture, and Society in an Authoritarian State* (London, 1995), p. 170.

access to the Kaiser. But the structures were more complex because there were two ministers of war, one in Austria and one in Hungary. As Franz Joseph entered the seventh decade of his reign, the heir to the throne, Franz Ferdinand, became an increasingly important centre of power in Habsburg politics and he had his own military circle. However, it is the impotence of the military that is striking. Conrad was one of the most aggressive proponents of preventive war in Europe before 1914. On numerous occasions, following his appointment as Chief of the General Staff in 1906, he urged war against Italy or Serbia, depending on circumstances. On each occasion, the foreign minister, Aehrenthal and Berchtold after February 1912, opposed his calls successfully. In 1911, as Italy fought in North Africa, Conrad insisted that Italian armament plans were designed for war against Austria. He called for a preventive war and he tried to conduct his own military diplomacy with Moltke, with a view towards preparing a convention for war against Italy. Aehrenthal became increasingly frustrated with Conrad's political machinations, which damaged Austro-Italian relations. In mid-November, Conrad made his final bid for a preventive war. Franz Joseph responded: 'My policy is a policy of peace. All must adapt to this policy of mine.' On 1 December, Conrad resigned. This was widely perceived as a victory for the peace party in Vienna.[32]

But Conrad was not finished. A year later, he was reappointed and was soon up to his old tricks. Franz Joseph and Franz Ferdinand, as well as the new foreign minister, Berchtold, continued to restrain him. In February 1913, during a crisis over the Serbian demands for a port on the Adriatic, Conrad reiterated his calls for a preventive war. Instead, Franz Joseph sent a peace mission to St Petersburg. Conrad was defeated time and time again. The attitude of Franz Joseph was vital, as he gave his support to the foreign minister, instead of Conrad. This enabled Aehrenthal and later Berchtold to prevent Conrad from translating his desire for preventive war into a reality.

Russian generals could hardly be blamed for causing the war against Japan. Some of them had warned of the fundamental weakness of Russia's military position in East Asia. One of the consequences of the war was a restructuring of Russian government. Ministers wanted to ensure that Nicholas II ruled through the bureaucracy, preventing the chaos that had afflicted autocratic court politics before the Russo-Japanese War. While Nicholas II would remain the fulcrum of power, political decisions were to be implemented by the bureaucracy. One of the centre-pieces of this

[32] Kronenbitter, 'Krieg im Frieden', pp. 360–67.

reform was the creation of the Council of Ministers in October 1905. The Council of Ministers was the forum for major policy decisions. This had significant implications for the influence of the military. Although generals retained a direct link to the Tsar, the real battles were fought amongst the ministers. Only in 1913 and 1914 did Nicholas II revert to his autocratic instincts. Until then, civilian ministers were successful in restraining the military. The Finance Minister, Kokovtsov, reined in military expenditure until 1913. In 1908, he offered the War Minister 7 million rubles, instead of the 207 million rubles requested, for the replenishment of war matériel. In October 1912, he refused a request for 63 million rubles to strengthen defences on the border with Austria.

It was possible for generals to act outside the framework of the Council of Ministers. In November 1912, Nicholas II, Sukhomlinov, and the commanders of Odessa and Kiev military districts ordered partial mobilisation. However, before sending the orders out, Nicholas II decided to consult with Kokovtsov and his foreign minister, Sazonov. Both were enraged, fearing that the partial mobilisation order might precipitate a general war. Sazonov criticised Sukhomlinov for even considering war as a policy option. 'We shall have a war anyway', the latter replied, 'we cannot avoid it and it would be more profitable for us to begin it as soon as possible.'[33] On the other hand, Stevenson has suggested that Sukhomlinov, conscious of the frailty of the Russian forces, wanted to use the crisis to get concessions from the civilian leadership.

Italian generals had minimal influence on foreign policy. The Chief of Staff was subordinate to Minister of War, who was often an officer, but the Foreign Ministry controlled the development of policy. The gap between war planning and foreign policy was well illustrated by the fact that Pollio was unaware of the neutrality agreements that Italy and France had reached in the early years of the century. His war planning was almost wholly predicated on the assumption that Italy would fight alongside Germany and Austria-Hungary. Decisions to undertake colonial campaigns were made in Rome by civilian politicians, though the details were plotted by generals. When campaigns escalated, as happened during the war in 1911, this was due to the war aims that the government sanctioned. This gap between the civilian and military created problems in Italian foreign policy, because the relationship between military means and political objectives was not always well understood by the generals' civilian masters.

---

[33] L. C. F. Turner, 'The Russian Mobilisation in 1914', in Paul Kennedy, ed., *The War Plans of the Great Powers, 1880–1914* (London, 1979), p. 255.

For the most part, the European military elites did not make the key decisions on war and peace, alliance policy, and crisis management. Civilian politicians managed to restrain their military counterparts, even when the constitutional structures made it difficult, as was the case in Germany, Austria-Hungary, and Russia. The prospect of a general war worried political leaders of all hues, and therefore, it is little wonder that they made strenuous efforts to restrain their generals. Military influence on foreign policy was generally restricted to issues on which soldier and civilian agreed. In other words, the military were not a significant determinant of policy. The military gave some colour and added tones to particular trends in foreign policy, be it the consolidation of an alliance or imperial expansion, but the lines on the canvas had already been sketched in by the civilian officials in the foreign ministries and chancellories. Despite the overwhelming evidence of the belligerence of European military elites and their readiness to fight a general war they knew could be catastrophic, they lacked the influence at the very highest level of politics to push Europe into war.

Arms Races and International Politics

When the French Three Year Military Service Bill was proposed in spring 1913, Tardieu wrote: 'We hope that Germany will greet with *sang froid* the armaments, which France judges necessary.' He argued that neither France nor Germany harboured any intention of attacking the other, but that the arms bills, passed on both sides of the Rhine in 1912 and 1913, were justified as acts of self-defence and measures that would maintain the balance between the two alliance blocs in Europe.[34] Poincaré and Bethmann Hollweg both justified armaments increases by pointing to their deterrent effect. The former, at a speech in Nantes, claimed that 'the peoples most faithful to the ideal of peace are obliged to remain prepared for any eventuality'.[35] Others were more sceptical that the Roman adage *vis pacem, para bellum* (if you want peace, prepare for war) had any merit. The British pacifist MP Wilfrid Lawson ridiculed the idea, likening it to telling a drunk 'if you want sobriety, live in a public house'.[36] The Russian foreign minister, Muraviev, setting out his stall for an international agreement limiting armaments, argued that 'in proportion as

---

[34] André Tardieu, 'Le devoir militaire de la France en face des armaments allemands', *La Revue de Foyer*, 1 April 1913, Archives Nationales, 324 AP/20.

[35] Klaus Wilsberg, *Terrible ami – aimable ennemi. Kooperation und Konflikt in den deutsch-französischen Beziehungen 1911–1914* (Bonn, 1998), pp. 88–90.

[36] Paul Laity, *The British Peace Movement, 1870–1914* (Oxford, 2001), p. 2.

the armaments of each power increase, so do they less and less fulfil the object which the Government has set before themselves'.[37]

Historians have been inclined to follow the arguments of Muraviev and Lawson, without discounting the defensive intentions that often informed increases in armaments. The arms race before the First World War was a fundamental structural problem in the international system, which undermined peace between the great powers. The arms race arose from geopolitical factors, the alliance system, and the heightening of suspicions between the great powers in the wake of a succession of crises. The arms race was not engineered by unscrupulous arms manufacturers nor by generals. The cumulative effect of the various army and navy bills before 1914 was to create a security deficit, in which political calculations were increasingly framed by an assessment of relative military strength. This militarisation of the international system influenced diplomacy, especially in 1912 and 1913. Although political leaders sought to prevent the arms race from escalating into a general war, it contributed to the erosion of the bonds of peace before 1914. Of all the military-related factors that contributed to the outbreak of the First World War, the arms race was by far the most significant.

The Second Moroccan crisis was a vital turning point in the character of the arms races between the European powers. Before 1911, there had been multiple arms races, but they were largely bilateral, affecting relations between two states, but not spilling over into a single, general, systemic arms race. The naval race between Britain and Germany or the armaments competition between Italy and Austria-Hungary between 1904 and 1907 are cases in point. By 1912, Britain had won the naval race against Germany. As Germany became more concerned with military defence against France and Russia, resources were diverted away from the navy. Naval construction had little place in the political strategy of Bethmann Hollweg, who wanted to repair relations with Britain. In 1912 and 1913, Anglo-German relations improved, due in part to the end of the naval race. The Austro-Italian race came to an end in 1908, as relations between the Habsburg and Russian empires deteriorated in the aftermath of the Bosnian crisis, so that Conrad turned his attention from the south to the east. In neither state was there sufficient finance to fund a lengthy arms race.

A second feature of the arms races before 1912 was that they were rarely simply about numbers. The quality of the weapons was also important.

---

[37] Cited in Jost Dülffer, 'Chances and Limits of Armaments Control, 1898–1914', in Holger Afflerbach and David Stevenson, eds, *An Improbable War? The Outbreak of World War I and European Political Culture before 1914* (Oxford, 2007), p. 95.

6. A Zeppelin and an airship fly over the manoeuvres of 1905 (IWM HU 68469A). Military leaders sought to exploit the nascent technologies of flight. The German army developed Zeppelin airships, but it was the French military that had a major advantage in this area before the First World War.

This was obvious in the case of the naval race, in which Britain's Dreadnought, with its new technology, guns, and speed, forced all other naval powers to follow suit. Naval parades during the First World War were partly designed to demonstrate national technological accomplishments to foreign audiences. There were also examples in the land arms races. In 1897, the French army developed its quick-firing 75 mm artillery piece. The improvement in accuracy and the ability to fire from a hidden position was a significant advantage over other armies. Developments in airpower became important before 1914. Once again, France enjoyed a head start over its rivals. Louis Blériot's flight across the Channel in 1909 was a technological triumph, which impressed German military observers. Paris hosted the 'Great Week of Aviation' in July of the same year. Other armies were compelled to follow France's lead. Although it was concerning to see a rival develop new weapons, the contest for technological supremacy never achieved the same intensity – apart from in the naval sphere – that characterised the quantitative race after 1911.

The First Moroccan crisis and the Bosnian crisis both sparked minor tit-for-tat arms races. In early 1905, French leaders were aware of their military weakness. In June, Rouvier told his Minister of War to 'get our frontier, our armaments, and our troops in a fit state as soon as possible, assuring him that no credit necessary would be refused'.[38] While French military training improved, Rouvier's most important step was to look to Britain and Russia for military assistance in the case of war. Russian support was out of the question, and it took several months before British and French officers began to discuss plans. Following the Bosnian crisis, the Minister of War, Schönaich, was able to get 164 million crowns to improve the state of the army. Austro-Hungarian military measures created fear amongst her neighbours, with Italy, Serbia, and Montenegro taking measures to improve their armed forces. In Serbia's case, this took the form of securing military matériel from France, while Italy spent 186.8 million lire on fortifications and 145.8 million lire on field artillery between 1908 and 1911. But it never escalated into a Europe-wide arms race.

The spiralling dynamic of army bills was what made the renewed arms race after 1911 so serious. In short, various arms races became interconnected and part of a larger whole. For instance, German army bills could be partly justified by the deterioration of Austria's position in the Balkans, which in turn sparked increases in the size of the Russian and French armies. The intentions of statesmen became less important than the cumulative effect of their decisions on the international system. Military capability of potential rivals became the determinant of fresh armaments increases. This undermined the political and diplomatic restraints on war. Fear of falling permanently behind in the arms race created a space for the concept of the window of opportunity – or as various generals put it 'the sooner, the better'. In these circumstances, none of the political leaders wanted a general war, but they were prepared to consider it. If the consequence of falling behind in the arms race was to become the object of great power politics, rather than an actor in great power politics, it meant that states had to make continually greater efforts to keep pace with their rivals – or if they feared running out of puff, then it created an incentive to risk war.

Two factors precipitated the arms race from late 1911. First, the Moroccan crisis, during which Germany was isolated amongst the great powers, led civilian and military leaders in Berlin to reconsider their security policy. Tirpitz wanted to pass another large naval bill, but Bethmann Hollweg and Moltke were able to outflank him by proposing an increase in the size of the army. The impetus for the 1912 bill came as much from the civilian leadership as it did from the military. Bethmann Hollweg and

---

[38] Cited in David Stevenson, *Armaments and the Coming of War: Europe, 1904–1914* (Oxford, 1996), p. 71.

Moltke had different long-term aims. The Chancellor sought to improve Germany's international position by building an effective military deterrent and forging a détente with Britain. Moltke identified France as Germany's 'most dangerous enemy', which could only be contained by military force. But for the moment, they were able to cooperate and the resulting 1912 Army Bill allowed for an increase of 38 890 soldiers.

Second, in February 1910, Russia decided on a comprehensive rearmament plan. A ten-year budget of 715 million rubles would be used to develop the strategic railway network, bring the field artillery up to date, and improve fortifications. The army itself was reorganised, as Sukhomlinov established a territorial mobilisation system. The rearmament plans of 1910 were tied in with the mobilisation plan, Schedule 18. There was also a naval construction programme, which involved almost 700 million rubles. Some historians have criticised the misallocation of resources – to the navy and the construction of railroads in Asia. Russia was always likely to rearm as time passed since the defeat in East Asia. Military weakness had made Russian diplomacy impotent during the Bosnian crisis. Restoring its great power prestige necessarily involved rearmament. A flourishing economy and the backing of the parties within the Duma removed two restraints on Russian rearmament.

The shifts in Russian and German armaments policy were followed by the Balkan Wars, which began in October 1912. These wars set the scene for the most intense year of the arms race, 1913. The wars were fought between Turkey and the Balkan League – Serbia, Bulgaria, Montenegro, and Greece. In the summer of 1913, the Balkan League collapsed and Bulgaria was defeated by the other three powers. No great powers were involved in the wars, but Austria-Hungary, in particular, suffered seriously from the shift in the regional balance of power. Serbia emerged from the wars with a battle-hardened army and its territory and population almost doubled in size. Austro-Hungarian officials believed that Serbia could put up to four hundred thousand men in the field. To Vienna, it represented a significant threat, which had to be confronted from a position of military strength. On 3 October 1913, the Austro-Hungarian Ministerial Council approved an army bill that saw the peacetime strength of the Habsburg army increase to six hundred thousand and its wartime strength to 2 million men. While the army remained weaker than its likely opponent, Russia, the crises of 1912 and 1913 had eased the constitutional, political, and financial restraints on Austro-Hungarian military power.

The weakening of Austria-Hungary's position also had an impact on German armaments policy. On 17 November 1912, the General Staff officer Colmar von der Goltz penned a memorandum, arguing that

Germany would fight alone against the Triple Entente. Military analysts had become increasingly pessimistic about Austrian military support. As Austrian strategy concentrated increasingly on Serbia, it would
leave Germany to fight the great powers. Only by maximising its military strength could Germany defend itself. Moltke wanted an increase
in the annual conscription rate of 150 000 men, but Bethmann Hollweg
managed to reduce it to 63 000, still almost double the increase in the
1912 Army Bill. Bethmann Hollweg was convinced that Germany needed
to rearm. He pointed to the French threat, in particular the increasing
speed of French mobilisation, while in a notorious Reichstag speech he
spoke of the great struggle to come between Slav and Teuton. The German Army Bill of 1913 was certainly shaped by the General Staff, but it
reflected Bethmann Hollweg's concerns about the geopolitical changes,
which had been unfavourable to Germany and Austria-Hungary. Historians have seen the 1913 bill as Germany's last gamble in the arms race,
a desperate attempt to stay ahead of the combined power of Russia and
France. Financially and demographically, Germany was stretched. In the
immediate term, German leaders deemed France to be their most dangerous opponent, but they also feared that Russia was merely warming
up. By 1917, Russian rearmament would be complete and the Tsarist
empire would be vastly superior to Germany. The next few years, after
the implementation of the 1913 Army Bill increases, became the military
window of opportunity.

   In the spring of 1913, the outlines of the Russian 'Big Programme'
emerged. The financial restraints on armaments, which Kokovtsov had
imposed with considerable success, were less effective as Russian economic growth accelerated. The programme included an increase of more
than two hundred thousand men in the size of the Russian army, three
times the increase in the German Army Bill of the same year, as well
as the deployment of a new army corps in Warsaw, more field artillery,
and the construction of more railway lines to Russia's western front.
Yet Nicholas II delayed approval of the programme until November
1913, and the Duma only voted the budget for the programme on 22
June 1914. Russia's rearmament programme did not have any time to
take shape before the war broke out. It was the potential of Russian
power that frightened German leaders. The gap between the reality and
future potential of the Russian army created a window of opportunity for
Germany.

   Germany's 1913 Army Bill forced France to join the race. In 1913, the
Three Year Service Law was passed. This increased the length of service
for each conscript from two to three years, increasing the size of the army
at the point of mobilisation by 50 per cent. France, with a population

only two-thirds the size of Germany's, had already conscripted over 80 per cent of males of military age, effectively the whole of the militarily fit male population. The only way to increase the size of the army was to increase the length of service. Krumeich has argued that the Three Year Law was also inspired by France's need to show Russia that it was committed to an early offensive against Germany. However, it was first and foremost a reaction to Germany's 1913 Army Bill. 'Bethmann Hollweg has been the best architect of the Three Year Law', wrote Poincaré in his diary on 7 April 1913.[39] The increase in the size of the German army forced the French government to react. Politicians dominated the formulation of the Three Year Law, which had to be steered through the Chamber of Deputies and became one of the most contentious issues in the May 1914 general election. On 31 January 1913, the French military attaché in Berlin, Serret, reported on the planned increases in the German army. In the first half of February, there was a series of conferences, chaired by Premier Aristide Briand. The Minister of War, Eugène Etienne, advocated a three-year service bill, and he was supported by Joffre and Jules Cambon, the ambassador to Berlin. While the supporters of the Three Year Law won a slight majority in the 1914 elections, contemporary commentators thought it possible that the law would be revised if international tensions continued to ease as they had done since late 1913.

The arms race after 1911 destabilised the international system. The balance between the two power blocs was undermined as Russian military power increased greatly and was expected to continue to grow until 1917. At the same time, Austria-Hungary's position had deteriorated. The arms race also militarised international relations. The use of concepts such as the armed peace, armed diplomacy, and deterrence became more widespread than had been the case before 1911. High-risk diplomacy, backed by military force, became more acceptable. Throughout the multiple crises between 1911 and 1913, statesmen had successfully controlled the use, or prospective use, of military power. However, it only needed to go wrong once. One caveat should be added. By the first half of 1914, the arms race had receded. Armies looked to bed down the increases of the previous years. Finance ministries reasserted the importance of balanced budgets. It was possible, therefore, that the arms race would have faded and statesmen would have agreed an acceptable balance between the different powers. The chance of this was scuppered by the July crisis. Of course, there was one power, Russia, which had not decelerated its pace of rearmament, but there were no signs of

[39] Cited in François Roth, *Raymond Poincaré* (Paris, 2000), p. 262.

discussions for further increases in the size of the Russian army after Nicholas II had approved the 'Big Programme'. The distinctions made by contemporaries between current and potential power gave rise to the idea of a window of opportunity, in which the declining powers, Germany and Austria-Hungary, had an incentive to attack the rising powers, Russia and France. Whether this opportunity would be seized, however, remained a decision that politicians, not soldiers, would take.

4   Public Opinion and International Relations

In 1881, a rising star in the British diplomatic establishment, Francis Ottiwell Adams, wrote from Paris to the foreign secretary, Lord Granville: 'Up to that time [the political crisis of 1877] it may be said that there was no public opinion at all throughout the country... From that time forward, a public opinion has been gradually growing. Journalism has become comparatively free, & the Government could no longer fetter that freedom nor control the whole press as of yore... The very idea of a war with a neighbour raises a scare, & if I may say so, they are like boys at school, who having been severely chastised by their master, are still smarting from the pain, & will do almost anything to avoid the chance of another such punishment.'[1]

Adams was entirely wrong that there had been no public opinion in France before the 1877 crisis, but his letter contained four astute insights. First, it identified the importance of the changing structures of the public sphere, in which public opinion could be expressed. Second, he examined the range of popular attitudes, which in this case wanted to preserve peace. Third, it was significant that he was only interested in public opinion in terms of its impact on government policy. For him, public opinion only existed if the governing elites were influenced by it. Finally, it was also significant that he felt it necessary to write a lengthy analysis for the British Foreign Secretary. Public opinion could influence the government of the state in which it was expressed – for example, French public opinion influenced the French government – but it could also influence the perceptions and attitudes of other governments; for example, French public opinion could influence the formulation of German foreign policy. National public opinions could also interact with each other across borders, either escalating tensions in press wars or cooperating with each other to improve relations.

Historians have differed widely about the significance and role of public opinion in international politics before the First World War. For some,

---

[1] Adams to Granville, 5 August 1881, British Library, Add MS 64796, fols. 168–71.

public opinion was largely irrelevant to foreign policy, which was formu-
lated by a small number of politicians and officials. These elites may have
been aware of public attitudes about international affairs, but they never
took them into account when developing policy. Others, such as E. D.
Morel, argued that the war was the result of secret diplomacy. Had public
opinion been more influential, they argued, war would have been avoided.
Another strand argues that belligerent public opinion created an atmosphere of chronic tension between the great powers, which transformed
minor issues into fateful questions of national prestige. Criticisms have
been levelled at governments' inability to control public opinion. The
modernisation of politics, with the emergence of populist movements,
the growth of the press, and the increased size of the electorates throughout Europe, undermined the stability of the international system, where
politics had traditionally been conducted by an elite who generally acted
with restraint.

The public sphere became an increasingly important site for politics, including international politics, in the late nineteenth century. It
expanded rapidly between the 1870s and the First World War, due to
technological, commercial, and political developments. Popular attitudes
to international affairs obviously varied from country to country and
from decade to decade. Noisy minorities called for armaments, imperial expansion, and war. At the risk of generalising, public opinion was
largely inclined towards the peaceful conduct of relations between the
great powers, though people were also prepared to support a defensive
war. The relationship between the state and public opinion also varied.
For the most part, governments exercised some influence over public
opinion, but they were unable to manipulate it effectively and consistently. On the other hand, governments were often able to resist the
clamour of public opinion, especially when it veered towards the most
extreme solutions. Governments were also influenced by foreign public
opinion, when nationalist and militarist popular movements and press in
one country directed their furies at the government of a different state.
Press wars between different societies could escalate very quickly, confusing and poisoning the atmosphere in which diplomacy was conducted. Of
course, there were internationalist networks – pacifists, religious groups,
and socialists, for instance – that worked together to improve relations
between states, but their influence on the international system tended to
be slight.

The Changing Structures of the Public Sphere

Public opinion was communicated through the press, books, parliaments, various associations, and other public fora, such as universities

and churches. Throughout the late nineteenth century, the public sphere expanded. There were more newspapers, more interest groups, and more voters. Literacy increased. Technology transformed public awareness of international politics. The transmission of news became more rapid. In 1865, it took twelve days for the news of Lincoln's assassination to reach London. In 1881, London papers knew of President Garfield's assassination within twenty-four hours. In 1900, it took a telegraph message sixty minutes to reach Bombay from London. Two news agencies dominated the international distribution of news: Reuters, based in London, and Havas, based in Paris. Time and space shrank. Jules Verne's novel *Around the World in Eighty Days* was published in 1873. In 1889, the American journalist Nellie Bly, sponsored by Joseph Pulitzer, took up the challenge. He completed the voyage in seventy-two days, meeting Verne en route. One of the consequences of this transformation was that it made foreign affairs more important to the general public. Small regional papers often carried several columns with foreign news items. In 1893, the number of foreign correspondents in London was sufficient to establish the Foreign Press Association.

The space within which public opinion could be articulated varied from state to state – and even within states, depending on regional variations in literacy patterns and civil society. Representative assemblies, the media, associations, and interest groups were the main channels for the expression of public opinion.

In Britain, the House of Commons played an important role in mediating public opinion. Parliament was the source of political power in Britain as governments required a majority in the House of Commons to pass the annual budget. Members of Parliament did not consider themselves as simple organs of their constituents' opinion. They believed that they had a role in shaping public opinion. MPs were also bound by party ties and discipline, which were increasingly important from the 1870s onwards. The franchise was extended in 1867 and 1884, giving more than 5.5 million men the vote. The relationship between the government, the House of Commons, and public opinion also changed in the 1860s and 1870s. A change in government was now normally preceded by an election, whereas previously governments had changed without the popular drama of an election. This made public opinion a more important force in high politics than had been the case after the first Reform Act of 1832. Shifts in public opinion became a more important preoccupation in political life.

In Britain, the press was free of any formal censorship, though politicians and diplomats leant on editors to modify their views on certain occasions. The most respected newspaper was *The Times*, whose editorials were read with as much interest by diplomats in foreign capitals as by those in London. Other papers, such as the *Manchester Guardian*, the *Westminster Gazette*, and the *Daily Telegraph* were closely associated with a political party. But the landscape of the British newspaper business was changing in the late nineteenth century, as the first mass dailies made their appearance. The liberal proprietor of the *Daily News*, Samuel Morley, declared that 'I went into the *Daily News* not to make money, but to advocate principles.'[2] But newspaper owners were increasingly preoccupied by profit. The *Daily Mail* sold around 1 million copies a day during the Boer War. In 1907, it sold between 850 000 and 900 000 copies each day. Kennedy Jones, the managing editor, warned his journalists: 'Don't forget, you are writing for the meanest intelligence.'[3] There was a tendency to sensationalism in the journalism of papers aimed at a mass audience. As far as international affairs were concerned, sensationalism was fed by wars, imperial expansion, war scares, outbursts of xenophobia, and more wars. The underpinning of journalism changed from the political, which aimed to convince readers of the merits of a particular policy, party, or idea, to the commercial, which aimed to sell as many papers as possible by entertaining readers. The spread of cinema in the early twentieth century also transformed the transmission of news. In 1914, there were 568 cinemas in London and 1 million people went to the cinema each day in Britain. These new technologies, argues Rüger, created 'a dynamic public market, in which politics and culture were increasingly inseparable'.[4]

The strength of civil society in Britain provided the basis for the establishment of societies, which contributed to public debate on international politics. For some associations, such as Protestant missionary organisations, foreign policy was tangential to their central concerns. By 1914, there was a wide range of associations, from the Peace Society to the National Service League, which had a primary interest in international affairs.

The Chamber of Deputies did not have the same importance in French politics, as parliament did in Britain. However, the Chamber was elected by male suffrage, which made it more representative of public opinion than the House of Commons. Changes of government were far more frequent, but they were not necessarily accompanied by an election. The

---

[2] Cited in Stephen Koss, *The Rise and Fall of the Political Press in Britain*, vol. I, *The Nineteenth Century* (London, 1981), p. 307.

[3] Cited in Dominik Geppert, *Pressekriege. Öffentlichkeit und Diplomatie in den deutsch-britischen Beziehungen, 1896–1912* (Munich, 2007), pp. 39–41.

[4] Jan Rüger, *The Great Naval Game: Britain and Germany in the Age of Empire* (Cambridge, 2007), pp. 51–56.

formation of a new government involved bringing in a new premier and some new faces to the cabinet, but several members of the previous cabinet were often retained. Party discipline was much more lax than in Britain. Deputies were often seen as representatives of interest groups, not voters. In any case, deputies generally ignored foreign policy until the debate on the Three Year Service Law in 1913 and 1914. In 1907, two questions related to foreign policy were asked in the Chamber, and the following year, when the Bosnian crisis erupted, four questions were asked.

This did not mean that the French public was uninterested in foreign affairs. In the second half of the 1880s, the Boulangist movement, which had a strong revanchist bent, marked a significant shift towards mass politics. An 1881 law enshrined the freedom of the press. French journalists wrote extensively on foreign policy issues. In fact, there were very close links between the world of politics and journalism. Gabriel Hanotaux, foreign minister between 1894 and 1898, and his successor, Théophile Delcassé, had been journalists. The most respected French paper was *Le Temps*. André Tardieu, close to diplomatic circles in France and abroad, wrote for *Le Temps* from 1903 until the First World War. Other important newspapers were *Le Matin, Progrès de Lyons*, and *Depêche de Toulouse*, which was on the centre-left of French politics. Four major papers – *Le Matin, Le Petit Journal, Le Petit Parisien*, and *Le Journal* – attracted a daily readership of 4.5 million and accounted for 40 per cent of papers sold in France. Provincial newspapers were dependent on the Parisian ones for much of their content about foreign affairs. In provincial towns and cities, the 'petite presse', costing five centimes, flourished, with 4 million copies sold daily in 1914. France was the birthplace of the cinema industry and in rural areas travelling cinemas enabled much of the population to have access to the new medium and newsreels about foreign, imperial, and military affairs. In France, there was also a wide range of popular associations and movements. In 1901, the Law of Associations removed all restrictions on the right of association – with the important exception of religious orders. Even before this legal guarantee, associative life had flourished in France. The associations interested in foreign policy issues, such as pacifist groups and Déroulède's League of Patriots, were centred on Paris and to a lesser extent on the other major urban areas, such as Lyon and Marseille.

In Germany, the Reichstag, the German parliament, was also elected by male suffrage. Yet it was weaker than its counterparts in France and Britain. Power centred on the person of the Emperor, who had the right to appoint and dismiss ministers. Courting favour with the Emperor was more important than winning plaudits in the Reichstag. The Reichstag had one important role, which offered it some leverage over policy – it had to pass the annual budget. Again, this right was diluted by the fact that military budgets were set for a seven- or a five-year period after 1871. But from the late 1890s, as expenditure on first the navy and then the army increased, the Reichstag became a more important forum for national political debate. Ministers had to cobble together majorities to pass the huge naval and military budgets. The Budget Commission of the Reichstag questioned ministers on foreign policy issues. Power also shifted away from the Kaiser following certain episodes, such as the *Daily Telegraph* interview in 1908. William II was deemed incompetent and the criticism of his personal rule undermined his credibility. By the eve of the First World War, the Reichstag had assumed a central position in German political life.

The German press, reflecting the federal structure of the Kaiserreich, was more regionalised than in France and Britain. Newspapers, such as the *Rheinland Merkur*, the *Frankfurter Zeitung*, and the *Kölnische Zeitung*, were of national importance, as was the *Berliner Tageblatt*, based in the capital. Others papers were associated with particular political parties, such as *Vorwärts*, the organ of the SPD, and the *Kreuzzeitung*, close to the Conservatives. Censorship in most German states had been eased since 1848. Passed in 1874, the Press Law guaranteed freedom of expression. By 1914, there were more than forty-two hundred papers in Germany. The mass press was less developed in Germany than in Britain, though publishers such as Ullstein saw newspapers as a commercial enterprise, not a statement of political ideology. Cinemas were also spreading throughout Germany, with 1.5 million people visiting them each day. As politics modernised in Germany, popular associations emerged. Foreign policy concerns played an important role in stimulating the establishment of these associations, such as the Colonial Society and German Navy League.

In the other European great powers, public opinion was more restricted, due to legal restrictions and the weakness of civil society. The most notable change came in Russia, where politics was transformed by the 1905 revolution. Nicholas II established the Duma, or parliament, in the constitution of 1905. However, its composition and role were quickly circumscribed. The first two Dumas were dissolved. It was only after Stolypin had gerrymandered the constituencies before the elections of 1907 that the Duma became an important political institution. Restricted voting rights and the rigging of constituencies meant that the Duma represented only a small section of Russian society. Moreover, the Tsar still retained complete control over military and foreign policy. But ministers were forced to take the Duma into account, particularly as it passed some of the annual budget. Political realities led ministers to acknowledge the importance of the Duma. As Rediger said of his own position, 'the Minister of War has to answer not only to the Emperor but also to the legislature'.[5] Mass-circulation newspapers emerged in Russia in the 1870s. The founder of *Moskovskii Listok*, N. Z. Pastukhov, told his reporters to write for 'my janitors and shopkeepers', but after the 1905 revolution the 'kopek' dailies flourished.[6] Censorship remained in place after 1905, but the press was relatively free to articulate its own position on foreign policy. Major papers employed former diplomats to write on foreign policy. There were 125 papers in 1900 and 856 by 1913. The largest selling daily paper in Moscow, *Russkoe Slovo*, sold between seven hundred thousand and eight hundred thousand copies per day. Though pan-Slavic associations had been a feature of Russian politics since the 1860s – a Slavic Congress met in Moscow in 1867 – interest in foreign affairs appears to have been limited to urban areas. The public sphere was much more restricted in Russia, but public opinion had come to play a more important role in political life.

Within the Habsburg empire, there were multiple publics. Ethnic groups created their own public sphere, while there were separate parliaments in the Austrian and Hungarian halves of the empire. The scope for parliamentary influence on foreign policy was extremely limited. Passing the budget required several levels of approval, from the Austrian House of Deputies and the Hungarian parliament, before delegates from both sides of the empire agreed on the budget. Although the House of Deputies was elected by universal male suffrage after 1907, in 1910 Karl Stürgkh was appointed Austrian prime minister and he ruled by emergency decree. But in other ways, the public sphere was highly developed within the Habsburg empire, although it was largely divided along ethnic lines. For example, every fifteenth Slovene belonged to the Hermagara Fraternity. The Polish Club was influential in Austrian politics. The pan-Germans organised in Austria as well as in the Kaiserreich. The flourishing public sphere seemed to threaten the existence of the empire. 'A foreign war against the Slavs', Leon Trotksy observed, 'also means an internal war for Austria-Hungary.'[7] Ethnic groups sought autonomy within the

---

[5] Cited in David Schimmelpenninck van der Oye, 'To Build a Greater Russia: Civil–Military Relations in the Third Duma, 1907–1912', in Eric Lohr and Marshall Poe, eds, *The Military and Society in Russia, 1450–1917* (Leiden, 2002).

[6] Louise McReynolds, *The News under Russia's Old Regime: The Development of a Mass-Circulation Press* (Princeton, 1991), pp. 105, 225–43.

[7] Cited in Tamara Scheer, 'The Habsburg Empire's German-Speaking Public Sphere and the First Balkan War', in Geppert, Mulligan, Rose, eds, *Wars*, p. 303.

framework of the empire; others forged close links with allies in different states.

The major restrictions on the public sphere in Italy were the highly restrictive franchise, the weakness of civil society, and widespread illiteracy. The latter two factors were particularly important in the south. The public sphere did expand before the First World War. The franchise was extended to all adult males in 1912. Parliament was central to Italian politics, as cabinets required a majority and budgets had to be passed. The system of *trasformismo* meant, however, that much of parliamentary politics was conducted by backroom deals. Party allegiances were weak, which allowed Prime Ministers to use a range of tactics to build a majority. The emergence of modern political parties began in the twentieth century. In the years before the First World War, an increasing number of associations with an interest in foreign policy were established. The Italian Nationalist Association was founded in December 1910. Italian imperialists could join the Italian Geographical Society (1867), the Dante Alighieri Society (1884), and the Italian Colonial Institute (1905), which was the smallest of these groups. There was also an Italian Navy League, set up in 1897.

The expansion of the public sphere, evident amongst the great powers, was part of a global phenomenon. In the USA, the public sphere was underpinned by a combination of highly representative institutions, the mass press, and a thick network of associations and groups. In Japan, the 1889 constitution had an extremely restricted franchise. But public opinion found other outlets. Sixty-six Japanese newspapers sent 114 journalists to cover the war against China in 1894/5. In the Ottoman Empire and the Balkans, the public sphere was also expanding before 1914. In the wake of the Young Turk revolt of 1908, the constitution of 1876 was restored, establishing a parliament. Press censorship continued, but writers managed to publish books and pamphlets in significant quantities. In states such as Bulgaria and Serbia, press and parliament played an increasingly prominent role in politics before the First World War. In Bulgaria, a reported fifty thousand people gathered in front of the 'Sveti Kral' Church in Sofia to demonstrate support for the declaration of war in 1912.[8]

Between the wars of national unification and the First World War, the public sphere had expanded rapidly, creating new contexts for the conduct of international relations. The pace of change quickened around

---

[8] Nikolai Vukov, 'The Great Expectations: Political Visions, Military Preparations, and National Upsurge in Bulgaria at the Onset of the Balkan Wars', in Geppert, Mulligan, Rose, eds, *The Wars*, p. 134.

the turn of the century, as technological and commercial innovations established new spaces within the public sphere, such as the cinema and the mass daily paper. Constitutional change, including the widening of the franchise and the easing of censorship, also expanded the public sphere, as did the formation of popular organisations and the increasingly formal organisation of political parties, reliant on mass membership. This expanded public sphere could not be ignored in international politics.

Popular Attitudes towards Foreign Policy

Politicians regularly condemned the press for poisoning relations between the great powers. However, the argument that the public mood throughout Europe on the eve of the First World War was belligerent has been undermined by research on popular attitudes at the outbreak of war. The resignation, despair, and fear that characterised the mood of large swathes of the public in 1914 is hard to reconcile with the image of Europe as an armed camp, bristling with martial fervour. There was a broad spectrum of attitudes, ranging from those who were committed pacifists to those who saw war as an end in itself. Most people clustered somewhere between these two extremes around a vaguely defined notion of defensive patriotism.

Amongst the great powers, the strongest pacifist movement flourished in Britain. In 1816, the Peace Society was founded, rooted in Britain's Nonconformist religious milieu. The Quakers were at the forefront of the pacifist movement. By the 1840s, radicals and free traders, such as Richard Cobden, added their numerical weight and intellectual prestige to the movement. By the end of the nineteenth century, there were a variety of pacifist associations in Britain, drawing on networks of humanitarians, the churches, and working-class groups. The Peace Society, the Workman's Peace Association, and the International Arbitration and Peace Association all vied with one another. The numerical strength of pacifism in Britain meant that there was greater scope for the formation of splinter groups and in-fighting. Although it boasted the strongest pacifist movement in Europe, pacifism never represented British mainstream opinion about international politics. Henry Cremer, a working-class pacifist leader, was disappointed by the change in London working-class politics, which had marginalised its 'internationalist, republican' elements.[9]

Pacifist influence was limited by more widely held understandings of the national interest. British public opinion was generally willing to wage

[9] Paul Laity, *The British Peace Movement, 1870–1914* (Oxford, 2001), pp. 155–62.

war and adopt a tough stance in defence of its perceived imperial interests. Disraeli's aggressive policy towards Russia in 1878 won popular support, as did Gladstone's government's decision to invade Egypt in 1882. However, as these two great rivals discovered, popular opinion turned quickly when campaigns went badly and government policy lacked coherence. Setbacks in Afghanistan, South Africa, and the Sudan contributed to Disraeli's defeat in the 1880 election and Gladstone's electoral demise in 1885/6. In the so-called khaki election of 1900, fought largely on the South African War, the Conservatives trounced the Liberals. Liberal candidates who supported the war tended to fare better than those who opposed it.

Fighting an imperial war was one thing, but fighting a general European war elicited very different responses from the British public. Popular navalist and militarist associations attracted reasonable support. A large proportion of the British population was exposed to naval and military organisations, exhibitions, and literature. The Navy League, established in 1895, claimed eighteen thousand members by 1900, but by 1907, only twenty-seven hundred members had voting rights. In 1908, 112 MPs were members. By way of comparison, in the same year, thirty-two MPs were involved in the London Universal Peace Congress. Following the South African War, the National Service League was founded to promote universal conscription. Headed by Lord Roberts, a popular general, the League claimed two hundred thousand members in 1912, of whom one hundred thousand were active. Around one hundred MPs were associated with the National Service League. The Territorial Army, which had been set up by Richard Haldane, the Secretary of State for War in the Liberal government, attracted 270 000 volunteers, many from a working-class background. During the visit of the Royal Navy to London in July 1909, around 4 million people visited the vessels. The invasion scare stories of William le Queux, Erskine Childers, and others were popular with Edwardian readers and regularly serialised in the popular press.

Yet the significance of these numbers is open to dispute. They did not represent a bellicose strand in British public opinion, which would have supported a war of aggression. For many, reading le Queux's novels or attending a naval display was a form of leisure activity, not an affirmation of militarism or navalism. There was an element of irreverent comedy in the music hall songs about soldiers, with General Redvers Buller, who presided over the fiasco of 'Black Week' in South Africa in December 1899, earning the nickname 'Reverse Buller'. Thomas Cook, the tourist company, organised luxury cruises so that people could see the full majesty of the Royal Navy. The emotions of the audiences at the launch of ships were complex. Workers could admire the triumphs of modern science, show pride in their contribution, disdain elites, and ignore the foreign policy context. There was also a certain amount of social etiquette and political pragmatism involved in supporting the various military and naval associations. Conservative MPs were prominent in the National Service League, while Liberals predominated at pacifist meetings. Only a few from either party saw these issues as their primary concern. To the extent that the public were interested in military and naval affairs, their attitudes were defensive – service in the Territorial Army to defend Britain against a possible invasion or cries for extra dreadnoughts during the naval crisis of 1908/9 to prevent Germany from gaining a decisive lead reflected the defensive orientation of popular attitudes. Popular novels were invariably about the invasion of Britain, not Britain's conquest of the territory, even the colonial territory, of another great power. Of course, the martial deeds and heroism of soldiers around the globe were celebrated in the press and books, but there was little interest in war as an end in itself amongst the British public.

For much of the second half of the nineteenth century, the British public expected a general great power war would pit it against Russia, and possibly France. Public hostility to Russia reached its height in the Crimean War and again during the Eastern crisis of the 1870s. Even after the 1907 entente, popular opinion never warmed to Russia in the same way as it had to France after the 1904 entente. There were widespread criticisms of Russian domestic and foreign policies. Liberals were disappointed that the 1905 revolution had not produced a genuinely parliamentary regime. MPs went out of their way to support the Duma, while others, such as the radical Liberal, Robert Spence Watson, supported Russian revolutionary papers and groups based in Britain. Russian attempts to stifle constitutional reform in Persia by supporting the authoritarian Shah also angered Liberals. On the other hand, Russia's defeat against Japan and the Anglo-Russian entente of 1907 meant that Russia was no longer regarded as a military threat. The prospect of war against Russia faded from public debate in the decade before the First World War.

Le Queux's *The Great War in England in 1897*, published in 1894, depicted a Franco-Russian invasion of Britain. By the early twentieth century, popular attitudes towards Germany led to a spate of novels in which the Kaiserreich was the primary enemy. Commercial rivalry, the legacy of the Franco-Prussian War, and a brief outbreak of colonial rivalry in 1884/5 caused some change in popular attitudes. However, it was during the South African War that attitudes altered radically. Influential British journalists, such as Valentine Chirol, the foreign editor of *The*

Times, George Saunders, the German correspondent of *The Times*, Leo Maxse, editor of *The National Review*, and James Garvin, editor of the *Observer*, wrote articles warning about the German threat to the British empire, the growth of the German fleet, and the Anglophobia of German public opinion. Many of these men admired German military and economic achievements, but it was Germany's apparent success that made it appear such a formidable threat. 'They have every qualification for taking our place', Garvin wrote to Northcliffe in 1909, 'and are bound to aspire to it more ardently as time goes on.'[10] Germany was blamed for a host of problems, from trying to stifle fair competition with British manufacturers to attempting to overthrow Britain's global position. While it was admired for its economic success and social welfare provision, it was also regarded as illiberal, militaristic, and technocratic. Anglo-German antagonism was about the clash of two political cultures, as well as more traditional geopolitical and military concerns.

As usual, popular attitudes came in many different shades. Conservatives were more likely than Liberals to regard Germany with scepticism. The development of British antagonism towards Germany was not linear. The press campaigns of 1902 and 1903 were followed by a lull. Indeed, the victory of the free trade Liberals in the 1905 general election signalled that Joseph Chamberlain's Tariff Reform League and its message of commercial rivalry with Germany had limited appeal. The naval crisis of 1908/9 and the Moroccan crisis of 1911 exacerbated popular antagonism towards Germany. But even then, there was a wide range of opinion in the British press. Despite the infamous *Daily Telegraph* interview of 1908, in which William II had suggested that the German people wanted a war against Britain, the Kaiser came to be regarded as a guardian of peace. After the Moroccan crisis, Anglo-German press wars, an important feature of international politics in the first decade of the twentieth century, virtually ceased. 'Public opinion in both countries', Herbert Asquith, the prime minister, noted in early 1913, 'seems to point to an intimate and friendly understanding.'[11] The ending of the naval race, the cooling of colonial rivalries, and diplomatic cooperation in the Balkans led to an improvement in Germany's image in Britain on the eve of the First World War. In other words, the realities of international politics were the main determinant of public attitudes in Anglo-German relations. In 1914, few expected and even fewer wanted a general European war. But if it came, there was a reservoir of ideas,

---

[10] Cited in Andreas Rose, *Zwischen Empire und Kontinent. Britische Außenpolitik vor dem Ersten Weltkrieg* (Munich, 2011), p. 69.

[11] Cited in Geppert, *Pressekriege*, p. 414.

memories, and identities upon which the population would draw in a defensive war.

In France, the spirit of revanche, of revenge against Germany and the reconquest of the lost provinces of Alsace and Lorraine, was weak. Even General Boulanger, who rose to prominence as an allegedly revanchist politician in the late 1880s, denied that he wanted war. The Boulanger movement dissipated quickly after he was sacked from his post as Minister of War by a government fearful of his revanchist reputation. Paul Déroulède had been active within the Boulangist movement, putting the League of Patriots at the general's disposal. Although the League claimed to have two hundred thousand members, police reports put the figure at fifty thousand, with membership concentrated in urban areas. Déroulède, who became the leading advocate of revanche, had fought in the Franco-Prussian War. After the war, he wrote *Les chants du soldat*, which sold 87 627 copies. Yet the vast weight of French opinion was opposed to a war of revanche. In February 1886, Jules Grévy, the premier, told Déroulède that 'a democracy does not make war'.[12] Thoughts of revenge became largely formulaic in French public opinion. Few would consent to giving up the lost provinces, but even fewer would agree to starting an aggressive war to regain them. As the socialist leader Jean Jaurès put it: 'Neither war, nor renunciation.'[13]

Indeed, French opinion became largely pacifistic after the 1870s. There was little support for war as an instrument of policy, perhaps not surprising when one considers the experiences of 1870/1. Boulanger, Déroulède, and their followers made considerable noise and attracted international attention, but they represented a small segment of French public opinion. Rémy de Gourment claimed in 1891 that he had outgrown the kind of hurrah patriotism that could lead to war: 'Personally I would not give in exchange for these forgotten territories either the little finger of my right hand – it helps me to support my hand when I write, or the little finger of my left hand – it helps me to flick ash from my cigarette.'[14] War between the great powers was seen as destructive and a barrier to the progress of civilisation. In 1884, the first pacifist society in France, the Puy du Dôme Group of the Friends of Peace, was set up. By 1913, there were twenty-eight different peace societies with around one hundred thousand members in France. French pacifists promoted international law

---

[12] Bertrand Joly, *Déroulède. L'inventeur du nationalisme français* (Paris, 1998), pp. 40, 110, 359.

[13] Bertrand Joly, 'La France et la revanche, 1871–1914', *Revue d'histoire moderne et contemporaine*, 46, 2 (1999): 325–47.

[14] Cited in H. L. Wesseling, *Soldier and Warrior: French Attitudes toward the Army and War on the Eve of the First World War* (Westport, CT, 2000), p. 19.

and arbitration as the most effective means of maintaining peace. There were a host of other associations committed to peace but not included in these figures. The French left produced the strongest anti-militarist movement in Europe, though they routinely differentiated themselves from bourgeois pacifists on the grounds of their different domestic and foreign policy programmes. The use of troops in policing operations led to fatal consequences. Events such as the shooting of protesting textile workers in Fournies in northern France contributed to the spread of anti-militarism amongst the working class.

The Third Republic began to stage elaborate military festivals from Bastille Day in 1880. These were attended by thousands – in fact, it was estimated that between 150 000 and 200 000 attended military parades at Longchamps, outside Paris. It is important not to over-interpret the public interest in these military displays. They were theatrical, an opportunity to show off new weaponry. For many in the audience, attending a military parade was a form of leisure activity, a day out, not a statement of militaristic fervour. To the extent that the military parades were politicised, they were a means of creating a republican military tradition. Revanchist nationalists stayed away from the official parade and held their own ceremony, which involved laying a wreath at the statue of Strasbourg, where the loss of the two provinces was commemorated.

France's most aggressive policies came in the imperial sphere with the establishment of colonies and protectorates in northern and western Africa. Yet a lack of interest marked popular attitudes to the empire. François Garnier, a French colonial explorer, remarked in 1873 on the 'profound indifference' towards colonies. There were groups that supported French imperial expansion. They ranged from religious leaders with humanitarian and anti-slavery motives, like Cardinal Lavigerie, to economists, like Paul Leroy-Beaulieu, who pointed to the commercial benefits of colonies, to political leaders like Jules Ferry, who saw colonial expansion as a means of restoring French great power prestige. Colonial supporters were few, but influential. The French Colonial Union, founded in 1893, had only 1219 members in 1900, but it counted amongst its members leading professional, commercial, and political figures. The Colonial Group, composed of members from the Chamber of Deputies, was organised by Eugène Etienne, a businessman and a gifted journalist, who wrote for *Le Figaro* and later became Minister of War.

Colonial expansion influenced popular attitudes to foreign policy by diverting attention from revanche to the historical rivalry between France and Britain. After the British occupation of Egypt in 1882, perfidious Albion, rather than Germany, ranked as France's primary rival.

Girardet has argued that one of the significant consequences of the First Moroccan crisis was that it conflated European and colonial issues. For the first time, Germany was the rival in both Europe and in North Africa. 'Yes, I rejoice about Morocco', wrote Maurice Barrès, anti-Semite, nationalist, and successor to Déroulède as leader of the League of Patriots, 'because it is a European affair, which can serve us on the Rhine.'[15] Wesseling has argued that colonial expansion led to the promotion of more aggressive values in public opinion. The cult of the warrior, the ideal of the regeneration of the nation through sacrifice, and the spirit of adventure were stimulated by exploits in the colonies. The French public may have been agnostic about colonial expansion but they embraced some of the values associated with it. In the wake of the First Moroccan crisis, these values were associated with the defence of France against German aggression. Historians have identified 1905 as a crucial moment of change in French attitudes towards foreign policy from being 'indifferent or pacifist' to being 'positive, self-assertive, and if not warlike, at least aware of the danger of war'.[16]

The Second Moroccan crisis had a longer-lasting impact on French public opinion than the first one. Foreign policy issues had faded from the political agenda after 1906, but the German decision to send a gunboat to Agadir in 1911 and the subsequent crisis marked the return of foreign affairs to the centre of French public opinion. Debates on war, peace, and military service, notably the Three Year Service Law of 1913, occupied politicians and public alike until the outbreak of war in 1914. Raymond Poincaré, premier and then president of the Third Republic, seemed to embody the new spirit of French public opinion. Poincaré had been ten years old when the Prussians occupied his home town in 1870. Because of his roots in Lorraine, contemporaries often associated him with revanche. In fact, he represented and articulated the defensive patriotism around which the majority of French public opinion gathered in the years before the war. In his first speech as premier, in January 1912, he called for the maintenance of cordial relations with Germany on the basis of 'mutual respect of interests and dignity'. He emphasised the need to bolster French military power and to consolidate relations with Russia and Britain.

A stoic acceptance, but not a desire, that war could occur characterised the new mood in France. Yet most hoped that war could be avoided. Paradoxically, the maintenance of peace required the preparation for war. It also required national unity, on the grounds that a fractured

[15] Raoul Girardet, *L'idée coloniale en France de 1871 à 1962* (Paris, 1972), p. 99.
[16] Eugen Weber, *The Nationalist Revival in France, 1905–1914* (Berkeley, 1968), p. 8.

nation would weaken national defence. J. Sansboeuf, the president of the Society of Veterans, argued that this mood of patriotism was not aggressive, but 'the concrete expression of the unity of the nation'.[17] But if most Frenchmen could still hope for peace, there was less agreement on the military preparations required to maintain it.

In 1913, the Three Year Service Law was passed, but it remained a central issue in the elections the following year, the most significant test of public opinion on the eve of the war in any of the great powers. It was clear that the majority in the Chamber of Deputies, voting on it in 1913, saw this as a defensive measure, a reaction to the army bills passed in Germany in 1912 and 1913. Etienne, now Minister of War, told the deputies that France 'wants peace and rejects any idea of aggression. But it wants peace with dignity and security.'[18] Yet support for the law was fragile. In spring 1913, Louis Barthou, the premier, ordered prefects to ban street demonstrations against the bill. In May 1913, conscript soldiers revolted against the prospect of an extra year's service. On the left, opponents decried the extension of military service as the act of a reactionary government and the negation of the French tradition of the nation in arms. Members of the Radical party, centrists in the Third Republic, had doubts, calling for an examination of alternatives, even as they supported the bill. The Radicals continued to duck and weave at their party congress in Pau in October 1913. The congress suggested a return to the two-year military service system, but it was not included in the ministerial programme of the party.

In the elections of May 1914, there was a slight swing to the left. The Three Year Law had been an important issue in the campaign. Those who supported it pointed to the rising international tensions, affirmed their desire to maintain peace, and generally played down any aggressive rhetoric. The Radicals remained divided after the election. After several attempts, René Viviani formed a government. The results of the election showed that the right was in retreat, but the left was not yet strong enough to force a revision of the Three Year Law. The slight swing to the left signalled a shift away from the nationalist reawakening that had swept Poincaré to the forefront of French politics after the Second Moroccan crisis. The expectation of a general war had eased in late 1913 and 1914. The underlying mood of defensive patriotism had endured since the First Moroccan crisis, providing a basis for mobilisation in 1914. Nonetheless, the First World War was neither wanted nor expected by a majority of

---

[17] Jakob Vogel, *Nationen im Gleichschritt. Der Kult der 'Nation im Waffen' in Deutschland und Frankreich 1871–1914* (Göttingen, 1997), p. 200.

[18] Wesseling, *Soldier and Warrior*, pp. 93–94.

Frenchmen in the early summer of 1914. After surveying the opinion of French youth in 1912, Agathon declared that war had 'recovered its prestige' and was embraced by a new generation. The more prosaic prediction of Jaurès, just before his assassination in July 1914, that the crisis 'will be like Agadir: there will be ups and downs, but things cannot *not* be settled', was a more accurate reflection of French opinion.[19] In short, the basis for mobilising the nation for a defensive war had been laid in the years before 1914, but it would require the declaration of war to trigger this defensive patriotic sentiment.

The wars of unification changed popular liberal, bourgeois attitudes towards the military in Germany. Conflict over the military budget had brought about a constitutional crisis in Prussia in the first half of the 1860s. By 1871, however, the National Liberals, the largest party in the new Reichstag, had come to regard the army as the embodiment of modern values – efficiency, discipline, and civilisation. The triumphs at Königgrätz in 1866 and Sedan in 1870 provided a different context for attitudes to war, peace, and international politics in the Kaiserreich than the other great powers, each of whom had suffered major defeats on the battlefield or, in the case of Britain, stood on the sidelines. It is too easy to assume that the creation of the Kaiserreich by war led the German public to venerate all things military. While certain strands of public opinion articulated an extremely aggressive view of international politics, the great majority of Germans were prepared to defend the Reich, but not to launch a war of aggression. Indeed, German National Liberals saw conscription as a guarantee against wanton wars of aggression, as the costs of war would be borne by all sections of society.

Radical nationalism emerged as a force in German politics in the 1880s and 1890s. Radical nationalists saw unification in 1871 as a prelude to further expansion, which was necessary to preserve the German people or *Volk*. They posited extreme all-or-nothing choices, which allegedly faced the German nation. 'The new century finds Germany faced with a momentous decision', declared *Alldeutsche Blätter* on 1 January 1900: 'do we wish to sink to, at best, the level of a second rate power or do we wish to become . . . a master race, the bearers of culture for the whole of humanity.'[20] This perception of international politics led to calls for an ultra-aggressive foreign policy that prioritised the interests of the German people over the constraints of the international system. Advocates of this position spotted vital interests around the globe, far removed from the

---

[19] Ibid., p. 67.
[20] Cited in Peter Walkenhorst, *Nation-Volk-Rasse. Radikaler Nationalismus im Deutschen Kaiserreich 1890–1914* (Göttingen, 2007), p. 168.

restrained geopolitical understanding of a Bismarck, which was rooted in central Europe. They considered war to be a regenerative force, indeed an end in itself. The task of the state was to transform Germany into a society prepared for war and to choose the most appropriate time to launch the inevitable great power war. Politics no longer served as a restraint on warfare, but as a means of preparing for war. In the view of radical nationalists such as Paul Samossa, losing a war would not be catastrophic, as it would sweep away the materialistic culture of the Wilhelmine Kaiserreich and spark a renewal of traditional German values.

The authors of these radical nationalist tracts were members of associations such as the Pan-German League (1891), the Colonial Society (1887), the Navy League (1898), and the Army League (1912). In 1912, the membership of the Pan-German League numbered around 17000, the Colonial Society more than 41000, the Navy League more than 320000, and the Army League 33000. The following year, the Army League counted ninety thousand members. These associations mobilised members of the professional and lower middle classes, many of whom were disenchanted with established political structures and the perceived feebleness of foreign policy. For example, Heinrich Claß, who became chair of the Pan-German League in 1908, came from a National Liberal background, but ended up writing a tract called *If I Were the Kaiser*. Criticism of the government from the right of the political spectrum was a novelty in the 1890s, but became a prevalent feature of political debate by the eve of the First World War.

The dissemination of military values was not limited to these groups. Over half of all German males were conscripted into the army for up to three years. The army considered itself the school of the nation, but it is not clear what impact military service had on the average conscript's view of international politics. Military and naval spectacles were a frequent part of German social life. There were plenty of commemorative dates and important occasions, which had to be marked with a military parade. Regular celebrations took place on the anniversary of the battle of Sedan, though it never achieved the status of a national day of celebration. Parades were held to mark the Kaiser's birthday and the autumn manoeuvres. In 1895, there was a series of celebrations to mark the twenty-fifth anniversary of the war, while in 1913, the centenary of the Battle of the Nations at Leipzig received top billing in the calendar of official celebrations. The construction of the German fleet was transformed into a public spectacle. Ship launches became increasingly complex, choreographed, and expensive. These celebrations became a stage for the creation and promotion of national identity, military preparedness, and local civic pride.

The audiences for these events were large. On occasion, they were carefully selected, either by invitation or by placing a high cost on a ticket for a seat in the main stand. These events, however, were not a straightforward transmission of militarist values to the masses. Those attending the events had their own motivations. For many, as in France and Britain, it was a day out, an opportunity to see famous soldiers, admire new technologies, and eat and drink. In 1908, pub owners in Berlin protested at the restrictions put in place by the police, which would prevent spectators from quenching their thirst in the local watering holes. Some suggested that the regularity of military parades dampened popular enthusiasm, while the French military attaché noted in 1913 that the crowd 'did not stir with excitement'. The celebrations for the opening of the Kiel Canal in 1895 were seen as an opportunity for locals to make money. Workers invited to the launch of ships had particularly ambivalent feelings. The launch of a ship was the moment when they lost their jobs and mourned colleagues who died during the building of the ship.

This range of reactions to military celebrations suggests that attitudes to war and the military were far more complex than the radical nationalists would have wished. In fact, radical nationalist groups were a small, if articulate and influential, minority. A survey of the German press in the decade before the First World War demonstrates that war was considered neither inevitable nor in positive terms. During the First Moroccan crisis, only 25 per cent of press articles on the crisis mentioned war as a possible solution. Nor did all of these articles regard war as a positive solution to the crisis. *Vorwärts*, which wrote most often about the possibility of war, was highly critical of German diplomacy. In the Second Moroccan crisis, a much higher percentage (60 per cent) of articles saw war as a possible outcome, but once again, many of these articles predicting war were found in left-wing papers. By the time of the July crisis, the proportion of articles predicting war had fallen to 33 per cent. Press reports were increasingly pessimistic about Germany's deteriorating international position, as it was seemingly encircled by the entente powers. Nonetheless, there was little support for a preventive war as a means of escape from this dilemma.

By 1912, the largest party in the Reichstag was the SPD. Traditionally an advocate of disarmament, arbitration, and international harmony, the evolution of the SPD's foreign policy towards an acceptance of war as an instrument of national defence illustrates the widespread appeal of defensive patriotism in Germany. In the Erfurt programme of 1891, the SPD called for the creation of a citizens' militia to replace the standing conscript army. The formation of a militia was a stock military policy in liberal and socialist circles in the nineteenth century, but it bore no relation to the security requirements of a great power. In the summer of 1911, the SPD organised a number of demonstrations against a general war, climaxing in Berlin in early September with a crowd of 250 000. The recovery of Russian power forced the SPD to reassess its attitude to foreign policy and war. In May 1914, Hugo Haase, a senior SPD figure, argued that the main weapon of the party against war – the general strike – might backfire by leaving one country open to an attack. A general strike could cripple the German war effort and enable the Russians to triumph. The prospect of Russian victory frightened SPD members, who regarded the Tsarist regime as barbaric and backwards. So while the SPD would not support a preventive war, it became clear that Russian aggression would induce the SPD to vote for war credits. Its attitude had evolved towards one of defensive patriotism.

The perceived Russian threat was important in forcing the SPD to modify its views on foreign and military policy. The German public's perception of potential enemies was coloured by international events and one's place on the political spectrum. Britain was the focus of German public anger at the turn of the century due to the South African War. Commercial, imperial, and colonial rivalry sustained widespread popular antagonism towards Britain in the early years of the century. A brief flaring of Anglophobia occurred during the Second Moroccan crisis, but thereafter popular German attitudes towards Britain became more positive. The spectre of a war of revanche meant that France remained a constant threat in the eyes of large sections of the German public. Yet advocates of a Franco-German reconciliation could be found at various times amongst the Catholic, socialist, and National Liberal parties. Further, while there was an assumption of French revanchism, many commentators pointed to French political and military decline, a result of its weak state and parliamentary institutions.

Fear of France and Britain was muted on the eve of the First World War – they were either incapable of attacking or did not intend to attack Germany. The most significant change in attitudes was towards Russia, admired by German (especially Prussian) conservatives in the 1860s and 1870s. Geopolitics, the presence of Polish minorities, and the autocratic bent of both governments facilitated this positive perception. By the 1880s, a variety of factors led much of German opinion to take a more critical, even fearful, view of their Tsarist neighbour. Amongst the radical nationalist milieu, the rise of a racist world-view meant that international politics was seen as a struggle between peoples and races, not states. The Russians were considered Slavs, and the Germans Teutons, who were destined to struggle for European and global dominance. Paul Lagarde was one of the earliest advocates of this idea, calling for a war against

Russia in 1884. The victory of the Balkan states in 1912 and 1913 spread fear of the 'Slav peril' beyond the radical right. Claß saw the Balkan Wars in terms of a defeat for the German race at the hands of the Slavic race, even though neither Germany nor Austria-Hungary actually fought. The more extreme demands of the pan-Germans for a preventive war were not widely shared, but many agreed that Russia presented a threat. Different groups defined the Russian threat in different ways – the SPD and liberals saw Russia as a threat to the rule of law, constitutional rights, and social welfare programmes, the pan-Germans saw Russia as a racial threat, and most Germans were concerned at the growth of Russian military power. Russia, therefore, provided a threat around which the different strands of German public opinion could rally in a show of defensive patriotism. By 1914, German public opinion in general accepted war as a possibility, if not a likelihood. While army bills of 1912 and 1913 had received considerable support, this support was predicated on the assumption that the army was preparing for a possible war of national defence.

The contours and trends of Russian public opinion are more difficult to assess. Within Russia's restricted public sphere, there was a wide range of attitudes to international politics, ranging from an aggressive pan-Slavism to the Christian pacifism of Leo Tolstoy, the most famous Russian novelist of the nineteenth century. Tolstoy had been critical of the pan-Slavist movement in the 1870s and the alliance with France in the 1890s, which he considered a ploy for the Third Republic to ensure Russian military support in the reconquest of Alsace and Lorraine. There was a small group of liberal pacifists, such as Pavel Miliukov, who worked on the Carnegie Commission on the Balkan Wars in order to inform Russians about the horrors of war. Despite the work of these very different pacifists, martial culture had an increased prominence in Russian culture after the Russo-Japanese War, according to Joshua Sanborn: 95 per cent of reservists signed up in 1914, a far higher figure than ten years previously.

What brought about this transformation and what did it signify? The humiliating defeat in the Far East and consequent blow to Russia's great power prestige, a succession of diplomatic setbacks in the Balkans, a more favourable view of France and Britain, and rising antagonism towards Austria-Hungary and especially Germany were the major influences and trends in Russian public opinion between 1904 and 1914. The Balkans were the most important foreign policy concern to the Russian public, whereas the Russian government conceived its policy in the Balkans in terms of the wider problem of the collapse of Ottoman power and the opening of the Straits.

The pan-Slavic movement's most notable success was to place the Balkans at the centre of Russian public debate on foreign policy. The movement had emerged in the 1860s, centred on intellectuals in Moscow, notably the journalist Mikhail Katkov. In numerical terms, it never achieved much strength. In 1874, there were 704 members of the Slavic Committee. It was more successful in promoting its ideas. Even before the Bosnian crisis of 1908, there was evidence of interest in the pan-Slavic idea, as St Petersburg hosted a Slavic week in May and Prague hosted a pan-Slavic congress in July. The association between Russian patriotism, pan-Slavism, and events in the Balkans sharpened with the Austro-Hungarian annexation of Bosnia in 1908. *Novoe Vremja* criticised Austria-Hungary in late September for its attack on Slavs, not its violation of the treaty of Berlin: 'Every attack against this idea [of pan-Slavism] . . . is considered as intolerable by Russian society. The Slavic idea is simply the completion of the Russian idea, the idea of Russian patriotism – and Russian patriotism expresses itself in the Slavic ideal.'[21] While there was no single party associated with or representing the pan-Slavic movement in the Duma, they were united in their condemnation of Austria-Hungary's annexation. The Balkans, therefore, became the touchstone of Russian public opinion on foreign policy issues after 1908.

One of the consequences of the Bosnian crisis was the increasingly widespread antipathy towards Germany, which lasted until the outbreak of the war. Although Austria-Hungary had annexed the province, Russian public opinion considered Vienna as a dependency of Berlin. There were several strands to anti-German opinion in Russia. Pan-Slavs depicted the struggle in a similar way to pan-Germans, as one between two races. Political allegiances were determined by race, not the territorial boundaries of the state. Since the 1870s, trade wars and commercial rivalry had soured relations. In late 1909, two Moscow businessmen, Rianbusinski and Konovalov, founded *Utro Rossii*, which took a strong stance against German interests. The Octobrists, Progressives, and Cadets regularly warned Nicholas II of the dangers of a dalliance with Germany. They argued that Germany simply wanted to split Russia's entente with Britain and alliance with France, as a means of making the Tsarist empire dependent on Germany. It was also a happy coincidence that their domestic political goals would be strengthened by an alliance with the two liberal powers in the west. The Liman von Sanders crisis in 1913/14, the first direct confrontation between Russia and Germany in the Ottoman

---

[21] Caspar Ferenczi, *Außenpolitik und Öffentlichkeit in Rußland, 1906–1912* (Husum, 1982), pp. 170–72, 188.

Empire, was followed by a press war between the two countries in the spring of 1914.

Russian conservatives had a more favourable view of Germany. These included former ministers, such as Peter Durnovo and Sergei Witte, as well as the right-wing newspaper editor Prince V. P. Meshchersky. They argued that Russia and Germany shared common ideological and foreign policy interests, which the western powers, France and Britain, were trying to upset. Durnovo, in particular, feared that Russia would get dragged into what he saw as an inevitable war against Britain. The result would be a catastrophe for Russia, which would bear the burden of fighting – and Britain would be the sole beneficiary. But these views were limited to a small section of public opinion. For the most part, educated professionals, businessmen, and the military considered Germany as Russia's principal enemy in a future war.

Conservatives feared the consequences of a general war. The attitude of Russian public opinion towards war had been shaped by a sense of powerlessness after 1905. War was simply not an option for the best part of a decade. The press shifted awkwardly between a recognition of Russian weakness and an unwillingness to accept peace at any price. *Novoe Vremja* called Russia's capitulation to German and Austro-Hungarian pressure in the spring of 1909 a 'diplomatic Tsushima', recalling the disastrous defeat of the Russian navy at the hands of the Japanese just four years earlier. The same paper warned that while 'Russia is powerless . . . Russian anaemia will disappear more rapidly than they [Germany and Austria] believe.'[22] The consequence of military weakness was a greater public readiness to support a more assertive policy. Defensive patriotism in the Russian case included the assertion of great power prestige. Russian public opinion conceived of the Balkans as a testing ground for great power status. The vision of the Russian national interest in the Balkans was constructed in terms of prestige, racial and religious affinity, and a national historical mission. Arguments couched in the language of territorial interests or national security were less important. The broader definition of what constituted defence of the national interest in Russian public opinion was a destabilising element in the international system before 1914.

Public opinion in the Austro-Hungarian empire was more disparate than in the other great powers. In the Habsburg empire, popular attitudes to foreign policy were largely determined by nationality. Hungarian public opinion was opposed to the incorporation of more Slavs into the empire and supported, for the most part, the alliance with Germany as a

[22] Ibid., pp. 205–18.

bulwark against Russia. Yet the Hungarian parliament proved reluctant to fund increases in military expenditure until 1912. Hungarians were often uninterested in foreign policy issues. As Miklos Bartha, the Hungarian opposition leader, put it: 'Foreign policy – for us that is Franz Joseph's territory.'[23] German Austrians were also natural supporters of the Dual Alliance with the Kaiserreich. Support for the Dual Alliance owed much to the growing concerns about the rise of Slavic nationalisms. The alliance with Germany provided both military security against Russia and a defence against domestic challenges from Slavic minorities. Polish deputies in the Reichsrat, who accounted for around 80 of the 516 deputies, also supported the Dual Alliance as a bulwark against Russian aggression, despite Germany's harsh treatment of its Polish minority. Other groups, such as the Czechs, were critical of the Dual Alliance, which was a hindrance to the achievement of their national goals within the framework of the Habsburg empire.

Attitudes towards war also varied depending on whether a general war was deemed an opportunity or a danger. At the beginning of the First Balkan War, there was a series of mass meetings in Budapest and other Hungarian cities to protest against any possible intervention in the war. At around the same time, Josef Redlich, an Austrian liberal, noted that 'the great public does not believe in the possibility of a war between the great powers. Such is the way that liberalism, socialism, and pacifism has deadened the opinion of the educated. However, in Russia, in fact, the primitive lust of man for war has spread through all sections of society.'[24] Redlich was critical of the desire for peace, which he noted in Austrian society, because he thought it would weaken the Habsburg empire's foreign policy. On several occasions, he urged a preventive war against Serbia. According to his own testimony, he was in a minority. Others looked forward to war as a means of achieving national independence. At a meeting of Polish nationalists in August 1912, Pilsudski saw the forthcoming Balkan War and possible Austro-Russian conflict as an opportunity to win independence. The local governor, Bobrzynski, was so concerned that he tried to clamp down on public discussion of international politics in late 1912. Taking the lowest common denominator of public opinion in the Habsburg empire, there was general support

[23] István Diószegi, 'Das politische und wirtschaftliche Interesse Ungarns an der gemeinsamen Aussenpolitik', Habsburgermonarchie, pp. 382–86; Lothar Höbelt, 'Die deutsche Parteien, das Reich und der Zweibund', in Helmut Rumpler and Jan Paul Niederkorn, eds, Der Zweibund 1879. Das deutsch-österreichisch-ungarischen Bündnis und die europäische Diplomatie (Vienna, 1996), p. 395.

[24] Diary entry, 17 October 1912, Fritz Fellner, ed., Schicksaljahren Österreichs, 1908–1919. Das politische Tagebuch Josef Redlichs (Böhlau, 1953), vol. I, p. 162.

for the alliance with Germany and a concern about the deterioration of Austria-Hungary's position, but little desire for a general war. Indeed, even a victorious local war against Serbia promised only an escalation of tensions between the various nationalities.

Public opinion in Italy developed a more aggressive bent in the years before the First World War. Admittedly, this aggressive attitude towards foreign policy was developing from a low base. The Italian futurist, Filippo Marinetti, criticised 'a tenderness of heart and an almost feminine sensitivity which are absolutely Italian'.[25] But there were more concrete reasons for the suspicions and doubts that many Italians held about the army. First, the army had been an instrument of suppression in the years after unification, conducting bloody campaigns in southern Italy. Second, the army was also used to quash strikes. In 1898, the army shot eighty civilian protesters in Milan. The decoration of the commanding officer led to public outcry and the collapse of the Rudini government. Finally, not only was the army an instrument of internal suppression; it was also inept on foreign fields, as the humiliating defeat at Adowa testified. The army lacked prestige and ordinary Italians, to the dismay of their political leaders, showed little enthusiasm for wars of imperial expansion.

In the years before the First World War, nationalist associations became a more prominent feature of Italian political life. Their emergence and resonance owed much to the failings of Italian foreign policy since 1870. In 1906, the Italian Geographical Society, dominated by aristocrats, elected the future foreign minister San Giuliano as its president. He wanted the Society to promote public interest in imperial expansion. The Italian Navy League, set up in 1897, had fifteen thousand members by the time it was granted a Royal Charter in 1907. The Dante Alighieri Society, which supported irredentist aims in the Tyrol and imperial expansion in Africa, had fifty thousand members by 1911. In December 1910, the Italian National Association was founded in Florence amidst calls for more active foreign policy. Intellectuals, such as Luigi Federzoni and Gabriele D'Annunzio, were at the forefront of the nationalist movement, but it also attracted support from businessmen and property owners, who were concerned at the rise of socialism. They had little direct political success – in the 1913 elections the Italian Nationalist Association only put forward five candidates. But this in no way represents the impact of their ideas, which they disseminated successfully through pamphlets and the press.

[25] Cited in John Whittam, *The Politics of the Italian Army, 1861–1918* (London, 1977), p. 172.

Italian foreign policy had traditionally faced a choice between expansion in Africa, where France was its major rival, or irredentist claims, in which the Habsburg empire was the potential enemy. While governments had to make choices, nationalist public opinion did not. The Italian Navy League depicted France and Austria-Hungary as rivals for naval supremacy in *mare nostrum*, the Mediterranean. The Dante Alighieri Society complained about the Habsburg 'slavicisation' of Trieste, which was dominated by ethnic Italians, but also supported the war against Turkey in North Africa. Yet in reality, the nationalist public recognised that irredentist claims could only be made good during a general war, whereas imperial expansion was a more feasible option. Antagonism towards France dated back to the wars of unification and the French occupation of Rome. It continued after 1870, due to clashes in North Africa, the unequal contest for supremacy in the Mediterranean, and trade wars. Even after diplomatic relations improved at the turn of the century, vehement criticisms continued, including a campaign in the leading Italian papers in 1906 and 1907. The press depicted France as a decadent, revolutionary, unstable state. Feelings flared up again in 1912 after the Italian navy seized two French vessels suspected of transporting war matériel to the Turkish forces. Despite the rise of nationalist opinion in the years preceding the First World War, there was little popular impulse towards participating in a general European war in 1914. Indeed, nationalist opinion in Italy had turned away from foreign policy towards domestic concerns – in June 1914 socialist protests about the military had sparked a week of rioting, demonstrations, and counter-demonstrations.

In the Balkans and Ottoman Empire, popular opinion on the eve of the First World War was shaped by the experiences of the wars of 1912 and 1913. Intellectuals were the most prominent supporters of war and nationalism in the Balkan states, but the contours of popular opinion are not clear. It is telling that while opposition leaders and university students in Serbia and Bulgaria pressed for an aggressive foreign policy between 1911 and 1913, desertions in the Bulgarian army rose rapidly in the spring of 1913 – therefore between the victory in the First Balkan War and the outbreak of the second, in which Bulgaria was defeated. This suggests a gulf in attitudes between a small elite urging an aggressive foreign policy and the mass of those doing the fighting. Intellectuals did not shy away from fighting, as the example of Ljuka Jovanovic, a Serbian proponent of a Yugoslav state, who died in the Second Balkan War, suggests. In Turkey, intellectuals had lost faith in the international system and looked to war as a means of avenging their defeat at the hands of the Balkan League in 1912 and promoting a national awakening. School textbooks carried stories about atrocities perpetrated against Muslims in Rumelia, which was now under Bulgarian control. Popular authors argued that the task of the state was to prepare for war. By 1914, many leading intellectuals in the Balkan states and Turkey advocated war. When they wrote of war, however, they meant a renewal of hostilities from the Balkan Wars, not a general European war. The First World War was unexpected, but also welcomed as an opportunity in many circles.

On the eve of war, therefore, public opinion in Europe did not demonstrate a widespread desire to go to war. Around Europe, war was accepted as a possibility, though certainly not an inevitability. Indeed, the probability of a general war seemed to fade from European minds in the first six months of 1914. Public opinion in most states was prepared to fight a defensive war, but not a war of aggression and not even a preventive war. Defensive patriotism characterised large swathes of European opinion, though pacifists and radical nationalists were an important presence in public debate. Defensive patriotism could mean different things to different groups – the preservation of territorial integrity, support for an ally, the maintenance of national security by means of armaments and naval bills, or the upholding of national dignity and prestige. If two or more different interpretations of defensive patriotism came into conflict, then the preservation of peace became more difficult. That said, the defensive orientation of European public opinion and the fears about the consequences of a general war were important bonds of peace in the early twentieth century. Any shift towards a more belligerent attitude in public opinion before 1914 was muted.

Governments and Public Opinion

In January 1904, Izvolski, then the Russian minister at Copenhagen, met his British counterpart, Edward Goschen. 'He said that a Free Press was a clumsy weapon', recalled the British diplomat, 'but a controlled Press a clumsier weapon still.'[26] The expansion of the public sphere and the increasing importance of public opinion in international politics posed challenges and presented opportunities to political leaders. Many statesmen and diplomats would have preferred to ignore public opinion. As Otto Hammann, head of the German Foreign Office press bureau said of Kiderlen, 'Popular psychology [*Volkspsychologie*] was not his strong suit.'[27] Governments variously tried to manipulate, ignore, and keep

---

[26] Diary entry, 25 January 1904, in Christopher Howard, ed., *The Diary of Sir Edward Goschen, 1900–1914* (London, 1980), p. 83.

[27] Cited in Thomas Meyer, *Endlich eine Tat, eine befreiende Tat. Alfred von Kiderlen-Wächters Panthersprung nach Agadir unter dem Druck der öffentlichen Meinung* (Husum, 1996), p. 140.

pace with public opinion. While governments could be swayed in certain directions by public opinion, they generally resisted more extreme demands. Public opinion created parameters beyond which statesmen could not venture, but these parameters were normally set quite generously and the statesmen often shared the assumptions of their public.

The British Foreign Office was the only one amongst the great powers not to establish a press bureau before the First World War. This did not indicate a failure to appreciate the importance of public opinion in international politics nor an absence of attempts to influence the press and public opinion. Ministers kept in regular contact with journalists, normally having a few journalists with whom they were in regular contact. Friedrich Tretz of the *Münchner Neueste Nachrichten* told Lord Acton in 1912 'that although England possesses no Press Bureau yet, owing to different social conditions, the editors of the leading London dailies keep in more constant touch with the governing classes than is the case in Germany'.[28] Diplomats also corresponded regularly with journalists. Chirol exchanged views regularly with ministers, as well as diplomats such as Charles Hardinge and Arthur Nicolson. Grey was in regular contact with J. A. Spender of the *Westminster Gazette*. Politicians and diplomats regularly asked journalists to pursue a certain line of argument. In June 1904, Hardinge warned Chirol that a future Anglo-Russian agreement was being put in jeopardy by the tone of 'mocking contempt' in *The Times*.

British governments had an ad hoc approach to the press. Ministers and officials leaked stories, cajoled editors, and dined journalists on a case-by-case basis in order to serve their wider political aims – after 1904, the maintenance of the ententes with France and later Russia and the securing of naval supremacy against Germany. In autumn 1908, Fisher leaked figures about the rate of German naval construction to the press in order to stoke support for an increased rate of construction in Britain. In 1911, during the Second Moroccan crisis, the British press supported Lloyd George's Mansion House speech, in which he clearly warned Germany that Britain would intervene to support France. Securing public support was a useful tactic to serve a wider political strategy. In this respect, public opinion was an instrument, not a determinant, of policy. Generally successful, British press policy – to the extent that a policy can be said to have existed – depended on good relations between politicians and journalists and a degree of patriotic self-censorship on the part of the latter.

---

[28] Geppert, *Pressekriege*, p. 63.

Neither journalists nor public opinion were always pliant. Public antipathy to Germany swelled in the early twentieth century, although Lansdowne, the foreign secretary, tried to maintain good relations with Germany. Journalists such as Maxse and Garvin, concerned about the growing threat from Germany, wanted Britain to forge much closer relations with France and Russia. Regular attacks in the press culminated in their campaign against the proposed Berlin–Baghdad railway, a project that was supported by the German government. Lansdowne had intended to support the railway, on the grounds that it would probably be built and that it was better for Britain to have some influence on the project, rather than stand aside. His intentions were overwhelmed by the press campaign and the opposition from within the cabinet by Joseph Chamberlain. In the spring of 1903, Lansdowne refused to guarantee loans by British bankers for the building of the railway. This effectively stalled the project, blocked what the German government considered an important imperial interest, and accelerated the growing Anglo-German antagonism. Lansdowne lamented the 'anti-German fever', while Nicholas O'Connor, the attaché at Constantinople, regretted that 'too much influence is exercised by movements of opinion due to causes, which are probably less permanent in their character'.[29] The growing Anglo-German antagonism had its roots in geopolitical and naval threats, but the hostility of popular attitudes on both sides of the North Sea contributed to worsening relations.

The victory of the Liberal party in the 1905 election led to the appointment of Grey as foreign secretary. While he was a firm supporter of the ententes with France and Russia and suspicious of German intentions, many of the backbench MPs in his party sought better relations with Germany, which, in turn, were a prelude to reducing naval expenditure. In the years before the First World War, public pressure on foreign policy was directed towards détente with Germany. After the Second Moroccan crisis, pressure from backbench MPs on Grey increased. In 1911, John Brunner, a highly respected Liberal MP, was elected chair of the National Liberal Federation. He made détente with Germany a major issue, arguing that peace in Europe was vital to the future of the Liberal party and could only be secured by improved relations with Berlin. This pressure led Grey to send Haldane to Berlin to discuss the naval race. While the Haldane mission failed to achieve concrete results, Grey was prepared to improve relations with Germany in order to prevent a

---

[29] Memorandum by Lansdowne, 14 April 1903; O'Connor to Lansdowne, 28 April 1903, in G. P. Gooch and Harold Temperley, eds, *British Documents on the Origins of the War* (London, 1927), vol. II, pp. 187–88, 191–93.

European war. His main concern was that public pressure to improve relations with Germany should not disrupt Britain's existing friendships with France and Russia, where suspicions might arise that détente with Germany meant Britain was less committed to the Triple Entente.

The structures of British government ensured politicians and the public generally shared the same set of assumptions and perceptions of international politics. Politicians were rarely bounced into major shifts in policy by public sentiment. During the naval scare of 1908/9, neither Grey nor Reginald McKenna needed the public to let them know that the German navy was a potential menace to British security. Nonetheless, public opinion did set some bounds on foreign policy. Foreign secretaries regularly invoked public opinion as a reason for not entering into a full alliance with another state. Only parliament could decide on whether Britain would go to war and that decision would always depend on circumstances, they said. Although some officials, such as Nicolson, wanted a full alliance with France and Russia, this was impossible, given the role of parliament and public attitudes to Russia. One of the tensions in Grey's foreign policy, which was exposed in the July crisis, were the different understandings he, his officials, the cabinet, and the public at large had of the entente with France and the commitments it implied or did not imply.

Despite its constitutional structures, the influence of French public opinion on the foreign policy of the Third Republic was limited. The Chamber of Deputies showed little inclination to press foreign ministers on their diplomacy. Deputies were more interested in domestic political issues, such as church–state relations. The Quai d'Orsay and French ambassadors also exerted a strong influence on the formulation of policy, far away from the prying eyes of the press. In fact, the strength of French diplomats weakened ministerial control over foreign policy, with the exception of strong figures, such as Delcassé and Poincaré.

Indeed, foreign ministers seemed to have paid more attention to the press than to the Chamber of Deputies. Each evening Delcassé dictated statements to Robert de Billy, head of the Press Office, which were to appear in the papers the following day. He used some papers to float ideas about the direction of foreign policy, without implicating himself. Others, notably Le Temps, Journal des Débats, and, until Delcassé's quarrel with the editor in 1903, Le Figaro, supported French policy and acted as the quasi-official press. The French Foreign Office secretly employed journalists, such as Henry des Houx and André Tardieu. The latter fell out with Stephen Pichon, yet another journalist who became foreign minister, in 1909, but Poincaré brought him back into favour in 1912. Poincaré set up a magazine called La politique étrangère in December 1912 to promote his views on foreign policy. It carried warnings about Germany's hegemonic ambitions in Europe, the necessity of building up French military power, and the importance of the entente with Britain and the alliance with Russia. These publications were aimed at a small, elite section of public opinion. Nonetheless, this amounted to a significant effort to influence public opinion as to the merits of a particular foreign policy. They would hardly have made this effort if they considered public opinion to be of little importance.

As in Britain, public opinion set certain limits on the options available to French foreign ministers, but rarely determined policy. A war of revenge was out of the question, but so too was a full reconciliation with Germany. Jules Ferry's brief cooperation in the colonial sphere with Bismarck during 1884 and 1885 was dogged by criticism and ultimately he found it impossible to steer a course between meaningful cooperation with Germany and the maintenance of popular support at home. Ferry's fall from grace was quickly followed by the rise of General Boulanger. His short-lived popularity demonstrated that noisy revanchism could not push the government into a war that neither it nor the country wanted. Poincaré's foreign policy outlook may have embodied the ethos of the national reawakening, but it was hardly forged by the heightened sense of defensive patriotism after 1911. He had already set his foreign policy course, before public opinion was able to influence it. On the major questions of colonial and foreign policy in North Africa, pressure groups were only partly able to shape policy. After the confrontation with Britain at Fashoda in 1898, the Groupe Coloniale favoured a barter with Britain, involving acknowledgement of British supremacy in Egypt for a similar French position in Morocco. It was not until 1903 that Delcassé came to share their view, and, even then, other factors had influenced his change of mind.

For much of Bismarck's Chancellorship, German public opinion seemed pliant, supportive of the government's foreign policy. Bismarck sought to preserve foreign policy from the vagaries of public sentiment. His successors were equally keen to maintain control over decision-making in foreign policy. Facing criticism over relations with Britain from members of the Pan-German League, Bülow declared that he could not make policy 'from the perspective of the beer-stand'.[30] Yet the German government had called into existence the radical nationalist groups, which would criticise Bülow's and Bethmann Hollweg's foreign policy

---

[30] Martin Mayer, *Geheime Diplomatie und öffentliche Meinung. Die Parlamente in Frankreich, Deutschland und Großbritannien und die erste Marokkokrise, 1904–1906* (Düsseldorf, 2002), p. 102.

from the turn of the century until the outbreak of war. Since Bismarck's day, the government sought to manipulate the press. The Foreign Office had a Press bureau, which became increasingly important in the late 1890s, when Bülow became foreign secretary and then Chancellor. Its powerful head, Otto Hammann, later claimed that Bülow was so obsessed with the press that he dictated press releases before his breakfast. Other ministries followed – the Reich Navy Office in 1897, the Colonial Office in 1907, and the Prussian Ministry of War in 1912. Hammann built up the press office, kept in regular contact with favoured journalists, and ignored more critical ones. These ministries also established, supported, and sought to instrumentalise popular pressure groups, such as the Navy League and the Pan-German League.

By the turn of the century, the government had lost control over public opinion. For a start, the different press offices often worked at cross purposes. More importantly, it was impossible to manipulate the radical nationalist associations. Stig Förster has identified a tension in German politics between the radical militarism of the nationalist associations and the conservative militarism of the government. Radical nationalists consistently attacked the government over its weakness in the foreign policy arena. At the Pan-German Conference in 1902, Claß delivered a stinging criticism of *Weltpolitik*, mocking the gap between rhetoric and achievement and condemning the government for selling out the Boers. At around the same time, the Navy League also stepped up its criticism of naval policy. By the eve of the war, these organisations were the most vehement critics of what they considered to be Germany's weak foreign and military policies.

The most disastrous mismanagement of public opinion occurred in 1911, when Kiderlen sought to manipulate radical nationalist opinion to achieve his goals in Morocco. Kiderlen had little interest in the role of public opinion in foreign policy and disliked Hammann intensely. While he maintained close links with some journalists, he saw the press and public opinion as instruments of foreign policy, not as actors. In the spring of 1911, as the situation in Morocco deteriorated, Kiderlen stepped up his contacts with members of the Pan-German League, giving Ernst von Reventlow a donation of 2500 marks and meeting with Claß on 19 April. While the press got hold of the idea that Kiderlen was seeking compensation in Morocco, he wanted compensation in central Africa. Although the Pan-German League saw the sending of a gunboat to Agadir as a defence of German prestige and honour and a liberation from the pusillanimous policy of recent years, it had no interest in acquiring compensation in central Africa. By August, Kiderlen's tactics had begun to unravel. Resignation and anger, particularly in the radical nationalist press, spread. At a meeting of the Pan-German League in December, there were demands for Kiderlen's resignation. A combination of raised expectations and secret diplomacy led to a severe setback for German foreign policy. Public opinion, fostered by the German government, had transformed the Moroccan question into one of prestige in 1905 and 1911 – and on both occasions, German prestige suffered a setback.

During the Second Moroccan crisis, as public opinion became increasingly charged within Germany, Hammann feared that it could precipitate a war. On 5 September 1911, the *Kölner Zeitung* entitled its leading article 'War or Peace'. While it argued that neither the French nor German public wanted war, it contributed to a febrile atmosphere. Kiderlen never intended to go to war over Morocco, and one of the restraints on war was, in fact, the public mood. Despite the influence of the radical nationalists on public opinion, it remained clear that the German public would support a war neither over Morocco, nor over other peripheral interests, such as the Balkans. German leaders recognised that war would require the consensual mobilisation of the population. While naval, imperial, and military policy were the subject of persistent attacks by the radical nationalists – attacks that occasionally swayed policy or determined the outcome of disputes amongst the elites – the defensive patriotism of the majority of Germans acted as a restraint on war. Moreover, after the Second Moroccan crisis, when Bethmann Hollweg took more control of foreign policy, radical nationalist influence declined. Bethmann Hollweg was less susceptible to the pressures and attractions of public opinion than Bülow.

After the 1905 revolution, the Russian Foreign Ministry developed a more active approach to influencing public opinion. They tried to build public support for their policies by influencing the press and meeting with the leaders of the parties in the Duma on a regular basis. All the major papers had former diplomats in their employment, the Foreign Ministry gave regular subsidies and bribes to papers, such as *Golos Moskvy* and *Novoe Vremja*, and articles were regularly placed in the press. In November 1905, the government set up a new official paper, *Rossija*. Senior ministers and generals used public opinion as an instrument to advance their own agendas at the highest levels of government, in the Council of Ministers, or in military reforms. During the negotiations of the Anglo-Russian entente, Izvolski placed articles in the press in order to strengthen his hand against those in high places who were critical of the accommodation with Britain. He was also adept at orchestrating debates when he wanted the Duma to show the rest of the world the unity of Russian opinion. The army also developed links with Duma leaders, notably the Octobrist leader, A. I. Guchkov, as a means of building support for the military budget and by-passing obstacles to reform.

Yet public opinion began to exert its own pressures on Russian policy. After the Austro-Hungarian annexation of Bosnia, public opinion expressed outrage. Izvolski had tried to garner support amongst the Duma leaders for his ill-fated deal with Aehrenthal. After the débâcle, he then held a secret meeting with the Duma leaders, in which he prepared them for Russia's capitulation. Between 1909 and April 1912, no foreign minister appeared in front of the Duma. There was widespread criticism in the following years of military weakness, the attempts of the government to develop friendlier relations with Germany, and Russia's often ineffective diplomacy during the Balkan Wars. Within the lower ranks of the officer corps, the influence of pan-Slavism mushroomed. In 1913, the War Minister, Danilov, criticised Guchkov for demoralising soldiers with pan-Slavist propaganda. The rising popularity of pan-Slavism and antagonism towards Germany limited the government's room for manoeuvre, though it did not force the government into a decision it did not want to make. The 1910 Potsdam agreement between Russia and Germany received a cool reception in the Russian press. In 1912, Sazonov adopted a tough stance at the outset of the Balkan Wars, in an effort to appease domestic public opinion.

Russian leaders had become more susceptible to the pressures of public opinion because they recognised the importance of national cohesion during wartime. The introduction of universal conscription in 1874 made the moral qualities of the rank and file more important. The nation, an alternative source of political legitimacy, increasingly challenged the autocratic Tsarist regime. The war against Japan accentuated fears that the masses were not sufficiently nationalised to sustain a war effort. The military resumed their efforts to propagate military values throughout the population. But this attention to public opinion could serve as a restraint on war. Just weeks before his assassination, Stolypin wrote to Izvolski, arguing that Russia needed a period of peace. War without public support would destroy the Tsarist regime: 'Russia cannot sustain and cannot emerge victorious from a war unless it is a popular war.'[31] As pan-Slavist ideas became more popular and the possibility of a war against Germany was increasingly accepted, one of the restraints on a general war was eroded. Arguably, it was the weakness of the Tsarist regime, reflected in its concern for popular legitimacy, that made Russian ministers more susceptible to the pressures of public opinion in 1914.

---

[31] Abraham Ascher, *P. A. Stolypin: The Search for Stability in Late Imperial Russia* (Stanford, 2001), pp. 259–60.

In the Habsburg empire, diplomacy remained largely immune from the pressures of public opinion. Nonetheless, the Foreign Ministry set up a press bureau during the 1860s, as the imperial government shifted away from a negative policy of press censorship towards a more positive engagement with public opinion. Aehrenthal, using his wide range of contacts, devoted considerable attention to portraying the annexation of Bosnia as a success. At the same time, he tried to control press attacks against Italy, fearing an escalation of tensions with Austria-Hungary's southern neighbour. By 1912, public concern at Austria-Hungary's deteriorating international position and the costs of maintaining security were more evident. The nationality issue, military conscription, and the burden of financing armaments ensured that the makers of foreign policy could never disregard public opinion. The relationship between national minorities and foreign states exacerbated Austria-Hungary's sense of insecurity. The military were prone to overestimate the destabilising effect of nationalist agitations. To that extent, public opinion within the empire shaped the context, but did not determine the direction of policy.

Until 1911, Italian foreign policy was largely shielded from popular politics. Crispi's foreign policies, aimed at strengthening the Italian national identity, backfired. Mass protests followed the defeat at Adowa. A restrained foreign policy after 1896 neither required nor invited public support. Only after the Bosnian crisis did popular concern about Italian foreign policy emerge, reaching a highpoint during the Moroccan crisis. The recognition of France's dominance in Morocco led to calls for the assertion of Italian influence on the North African coast, in Libya. The government, backed by the public, declared war on Turkey in September. San Giuliano's original war aim was to set up a protectorate in Tripoli, but the pressures of public opinion contributed to the radicalisation of Italian war aims. The establishment of a protectorate had been the cover for imperial expansion in Egypt, Morocco, and Bosnia (until 1908), and it was a solution that the Ottomans were willing to accept in 1911. In a major speech on 7 October, Giolitti rejected chauvinist demands for annexation. Yet, one month later, on 5 November, the Italian government declared it was establishing full sovereignty in Libya. Giolitti considered that only annexation was compatible with Italian dignity's and would satisfy nationalist associations. The war would drag on until spring 1912, weakening both Italy and the Ottoman Empire. Giolitti and liberal Italy in general had come under increasing pressure, both in terms of domestic political reform and foreign policy achievements. While the war delivered a short-term boost to Giolitti's popularity, its longer-term consequences opened wide fractures in the Italian body politic. Nonetheless, in 1914 there was no public pressure on the government to join the European war.

During the Balkan Wars, public opinion in both Serbia and Bulgaria played an important role in forcing governments to adopt a more belligerent stance. Geshov's government in Bulgaria came under pressure in late 1911, as Radoslavov, the leader of the opposition National Liberals mocked: 'We have not spent 950 million leva on the army just to look at it in the parade.' Geshov ended his attempts to cooperate with Turkey and instead formed an alliance with Serbia in early 1912, the core of the Balkan League. In the aftermath of the First Balkan War, the Serbian government came under popular and military pressure to attack Bulgaria. The Serbian premier, Pasič, was losing control over his foreign policy by the time Bulgaria launched a pre-emptive strike.

The efforts of government to control public opinion in the late nineteenth and early twentieth centuries were often futile. On the other hand, public opinion rarely forced governments to change their foreign policy. Public opinion set bounds on the policies governments conducted, but statesmen often shared the assumptions of their publics, or the bounds were so widely set that it is difficult to say that the foreign policy of a particular state was largely determined by its public opinion. Public opinion could also act as a restraint, as statesmen recognised the desire for peace amongst broad sections of the population. Russian and German statesmen came under increasing pressure, but they had managed to resist popular demands for a more active foreign policy in 1912 and 1913.

The Transnational Impact of Public Opinion

The impact of public opinion was not restricted within national borders. Foreign ministries paid close attention to public opinion in other countries and even tried to influence foreign opinion. According to Hammann, the era in which Germans 'did not need to care about the opinions of the Brazilians and Chinese' was over. 'Public opinion has achieved an influence on political decisions, which was previously unheard of.'[32] This was an exaggerated acknowledgement of the increasingly complex ways in which public opinion could influence international politics. It was also a factor that was often beyond the control of governments, as the impact of transnational networks, international organisations, and press wars on the international system before 1914 testify. From students taking

---

[32] Meyer, *Endlich eine Tat*, p. 62.

courses abroad, to anarchists smuggling pamphlets from one country to another, to religious networks, contacts between different societies transcended borders and defied state control.

Governments were concerned not only with their own domestic public, but also with the currents of public opinion elsewhere. Manipulating public opinion abroad was an important policy instrument before 1914, as governments assumed that a favourable public perception would redound to their credit. The Habsburg Foreign Ministry mobilised its contacts in the European press during the Bosnian crisis, with some beneficial results. But the attempts of governments to influence foreign public opinion failed more often than they succeeded. Raffalovich, a Russian agent in Paris, distributed around £8000 per month to the French press in early 1905 in an attempt to convince the French public that lending money to the Russian state was a sound piece of business. The French bankers thought otherwise and abandoned the loan negotiations in March. German diplomats blamed Russian and French press agents for turning British public opinion against the Reich in the early twentieth century. They approached British journalists, such as Moberley Bell, the editor of *The Times*. They subsidised the new *Empire Review*, after its editor agreed to attack Maxse's *National Review*. Bernstorff, who joined the London embassy in 1903, believed that winning over public opinion was the key to improving Anglo-German relations. But by 1905, the embassy had given up, as British journalists proved less amenable than the German diplomats had hoped.

The Turkish government kept cuttings from more than one hundred foreign newspapers, so concerned was it about its image abroad. It intervened with foreign governments and the press to try to hinder the publication of damaging articles. It also sought to promote a more positive image at international events, such as world fairs. At the World Archaeology Congresses, it presented a modern, secular image. But western visitors to the Turkish pavilions at world fairs were often more interested in the exotic, such as Arabian horses, while in Budapest in 1896, visitors were admitted to see Muslims praying in the mosque. Worst of all, neighbours used the fairs to promote a negative image of Turkey. The Bulgarian pavilion at the St Louis World Fair in 1904 staged an exhibition of burnt-out villages in eastern Rumelia. If Turkish efforts to improve their image abroad faced a mix of prejudice and the difficulty of explaining away massacres in the Balkans and Armenia, the contest in cultural diplomacy between Germany and France was more equal. Both great powers used cultural contacts to promote their influence in Belgium. Cavallier, vice-president of the Chamber of Commerce in Nancy, argued that participation in the Brussels exhibition of 1910 was important as a demonstration of France's continued economic and cultural vitality. The German display of sympathy on the seventy-fifth anniversary of Belgian independence, in 1905, was much appreciated, but the publication of a pan-German atlas showing Flanders as part of the Reich caused consternation.

Cultural and public diplomacy had more of an impact when it aimed to strengthen existing relationships. During a visit of British parliamentarians to their counterparts in the Duma in 1912, Sazonov claimed 'that the mutual trust and sympathies of the two countries are not limited to the highest circles, but are founded on a broad basis'.[33] Parliamentary visits between France, Britain, and Russia took place in 1909, 1910, and 1912. Although the visits were designed to promote the Duma within Russia, they contributed to a strengthening of ties between the entente partners. Improving mutual perceptions on either side of the Channel was part of the prelude to the Anglo-French entente. In Germany and Austria, associations such as the Pan-German League, the German School League, and the Central European Economic Association straddled the border, each promoting the common interests of Austria and Germany in foreign, cultural, and economic affairs. On the other hand, the interference of an ally's public opinion in their partner's domestic affairs could grate. During the Badeni crisis in 1897, over the requirements for officials in Austria to master languages other than German, the criticisms of Vienna's policy by prominent German intellectuals angered the foreign minister, Goluchowski. Russian foreign policy faced major challenges in 1905 and 1906, when, while attempting to raise a loan in France and Britain, it found large sections of public opinion in these countries had a positive view of the revolution. These transnational currents of public opinion complicated relations between governments.

Press wars between newspapers in two or more countries undermined the stability of the international system. Admiral Yamamoto, during a visit to the USA in 1907, noticed that anti-American articles from the Japanese press were reprinted in American papers, fuelling antagonism between the two societies. Similarly, Roosevelt confided to the Secretary of War, Elihu Root: 'Our people wantonly and foolishly insult the Japanese in San Francisco... Undoubtedly these irritating articles in the newspapers and irritating actions may arouse a bitter feeling in Japan, which will make the Japanese people feel hostile to us and predispose them to war should the occasion arise.'[34] Press wars increased the

---

[33] Ferenczi, *Außenpolitik und Öffentlichkeit*, p. 283.
[34] Masuda Hajimu, 'Rumors of War: Immigration Disputes and the Social Construction of American–Japanese Relations, 1905–1913', *Diplomatic History*, 33, 1 (2009): 17–19.

influence of extremist opinion, complicated diplomatic negotiations, and created concerns about another government's intentions. 'There are certain English writers who are worth a battleship a year to Germany', wrote Spender, 'and certain pan-German professors who are the equivalent of the whole Navy League in this country . . . These campaigns tend to produce the very dangers which they allege.'[35] Geppert's study of press wars between Britain and Germany before the First World War charts a series of press campaigns on both sides of the North Sea, which contributed to the rising antagonism between the two countries. Articles printed and speeches made in one country were rapidly disseminated in the other, sparking a hostile response, which then led to a flurry of highly charged articles, while diplomats on either side accused the others of failing to restrain their press.

Anglo-German press wars reached a highpoint during the South African War. Criticism in the German press far outstripped the attitude of the German government towards Britain, but so widespread was the assumption that the press was in the hands of the German Foreign Office that British officials often mistook press criticism for the attitude of the German government. At the end of the war, there was an acrimonious exchange between Bülow and Chamberlain. Defending the British army against charges of barbaric conduct, Chamberlain noted the poor treatment and murder of civilians at the hands of other armies, including a reference to the German army's shooting of French civilians in 1870/1. Public opinion mobilised in Germany, turning on Chamberlain as the embodiment of British imperialism, an imperialism motivated by profit and greed. Bülow responded to Chamberlain's speech with an attack on the British Colonial Secretary in the Reichstag in January 1902. By doing so, Bülow became caught in a press war, which bolstered his domestic position but damaged relations with Britain. Likewise, Chamberlain's popularity in Britain received a boost.

Rhetoric and articles employed in one country, often with a domestic political goal in mind, flew across borders with sometimes unforeseen repercussions. The Anglo-German press wars contributed to the deterioration of relations between the two countries in the early twentieth century. As governments sought to justify to domestic audiences their increased naval expenditure by pointing to the size of the German or British fleets, their propaganda was twisted in the other country into a display of aggression. Indeed, naval and military displays were aimed at foreign as well as domestic audiences. Increasing numbers of foreign

[35] Geppert, *Pressekriege*, p. 233.

correspondents covered fleet reviews, so that the public staging of naval power not only served to reassure the domestic audience about national security, but also served as a highly visible deterrent to other societies. However, the impact was to stoke anxieties in other countries, which, in turn, fuelled popular support for increased military expenditure.

During the First Moroccan crisis, articles heightened tensions in both Germany and France. In *Die Kreuzzeitung* in June 1905, Theodor Schiemann, who had links with the German Foreign Office, claimed that British naval support would be of no use to France in a continental war. This caused uproar in France and even Bülow was angry with Schiemann. In October, *Le Matin* published a piece claiming that Britain had agreed to attack Schleswig in northern Germany if war broke out on the continent. Thomas Sanderson, the permanent under-secretary in the Foreign Office, called this article a 'whopping falsehood', but it created concern in Berlin.[36] These articles hardened public opinion on both sides, making the resolution of the crisis more difficult.

The most portentous press war before the war broke out in early March 1914, when the *Kölnische Zeitung* argued there was a danger of war in three to four years, as Russian military power increased. This was an implicit argument for a preventive war, which was taken up by other German papers. The Russian press responded, claiming that Russia could take the offensive in a war against Germany. Officials on both sides denied inspiring the articles, but neither diplomats at the time nor historians since believed the denials. The fact that it took two weeks for the German government to reject the implications of the *Kölnische Zeitung*'s statement was considered proof of their tacit, if not actual, support of the press campaign. The articles whipped up public sentiment and were also taken as an indication of government policy. The deterioration in relations between the German and Russian governments since the Liman von Sanders crisis was replicated at the level of public opinion.

Although governments could foment press wars, they also recognised the dangers of these bouts. In a telling, but exaggerated, speech, Bülow claimed that 'most of the conflicts, which the world has seen in the last ten years, have not been called forth by princely ambition or ministerial conspiracy, but through the passionate excitement of public opinion, which, through the press and parliament, has swept along the executive'.[37] Governments tried to put a stop to press wars by asking journalists to desist

[36] Mayer, *Geheime Diplomatie und öffentliche Meinung*, pp. 208–13, 238–39.
[37] Cited in Bernhard Rosenberger, *Zeitungen als Kriegstreiber? Die Rolle der Presse im Vorfeld des Ersten Weltkrieges* (Cologne, 1998), p. 33.

from attacks or placing an authoritative denial in the official press. Journalists also made efforts to improve relations. In 1906 and 1907, British and German journalists went on tours of the other country. Ludwig Stein, editor of *Nord und Süd*, organised special issues on Austro-Italian and Anglo-German relations in 1912. There were also some sporadic efforts in the French and German press to improve relations after the Moroccan crisis.

The press wars and outbreaks of public antagonism had long-term effects on the stability of the international system. Governments rarely adopted a more aggressive foreign policy to assuage domestic public opinion, but diplomats often thought that the foreign policy of a country reflected its public opinion. Bülow complained that other states' perception of German foreign policy was shaped by what their diplomats read in the German press, particularly the radical nationalist press. Press campaigns were read in two ways. Either diplomats suspected that press campaigns had been officially orchestrated and therefore the belligerent tone of the articles reflected the real intentions of a particular government or else they feared that the government was too weak to resist extremist opinion. In either case, this meant that diplomats and officials placed a high value on press articles and public opinion when they assessed the direction of another state's policy.

Between the Moroccan crisis and the outbreak of the First World War, German policy makers were concerned by the potential consequences of the nationalist awakening in France and the rise of pan-Slavist opinion in Russia. As tensions between Austria-Hungary and Russia increased in late 1912, Kiderlen feared that while the Russian government wanted peace, 'it is very weak against pan-Slavist agitators'.[38] Bethmann Hollweg expressed similar concerns in February 1914, hoping, but doubting, that more responsible elements would control the pan-Slavist influence on foreign policy. Pan-Slavic opinion, therefore, not only influenced Russian policy, but also German policy. Diplomats, soldiers, and ministers in Berlin based their assessments of Russian policy on the aggressive pan-Slavist rhetoric as well as on the more pacific reassurances of Russian diplomats. Similar concerns shaped German policy towards France in 1912 and 1913. The German ambassador to Paris, Wilhelm von Schoen, sent regular reports on French public opinion to Bethmann Hollweg. These usually distinguished between what he considered an excitable revanchism and a more sober-minded desire to avoid war. Schoen concluded that the majority of French people did not want war, but he

---

[38] Ralf Forsbach, *Alfred von Kiderlen-Wächter (1852–1912)* (Göttingen, 1997), vol. II, p. 723.

feared that a single incident could be used to whip popular opinion into a fury, which no government could resist. Yet Schoen also noted that pan-German leaflets, 'which few people [in Germany] take seriously', were used by French papers to portray Germany as a threat. So while he considered French revanchism to constitute a threat to peace, he dismissed pan-German propaganda as a minor irritant.

Diplomats elsewhere were unwilling to discount German radical nationalist opinion. Copies of pan-German tracts and newspaper articles were regularly sent back to the Foreign Office, while French and Russian diplomats also took these publications seriously. Eyre Crowe, an increasingly important figure in the Foreign Office before 1914, argued that British policy had to take German opinion into account, precisely because it reflected government policy. During the Russo-German press war, he commented that 'No German government, not the Emperor, will be driven into war by popular clamour. On the contrary, the necessary popular clamour, will be engineered by the German government if it wishes to go to war. Public opinion alone is of no account whatever.'[39] Assessments of public opinion revealed the degree to which diplomats stereotyped states. In the case of Russia and France, the state was considered weak and therefore susceptible to following the whimsies of popular opinion. In Britain, the government was considered beholden to public opinion, due to its parliamentary structures. In Germany, the state had a reputation for being strong and therefore was supposed to be able to control what the press printed. These stereotypes did not reflect the complex links between governments and the press, but they demonstrate the difficulty (faced by diplomats as well as historians) of interpreting the relationship between public opinion and international relations before the First World War.

The efforts of international pacifist, socialist, and religious organisations to strengthen peace and to prevent war faced enormous challenges. Pacifists and socialists developed strong transnational links in the decades before the First World War. The Second International was formed in 1889 to bring together the various European socialist parties under one umbrella. From 1904, the prevention of war became a major theme at meetings of the International. Differences between national groups and their lack of influence over government policy undermined the attempts of European socialists to coordinate their anti-war strategies. In 1910, the Bureau of the International, its permanent secretariat, was given the task of coordinating responses in the case of war, but the Bureau was

---

[39] Crowe minutes on 'The Feeling in Germany towards War', 16 March 1914, FO 371/2092, fol. 27.

far too weak to undertake this task. European pacifists also held regular meetings, but like the socialist movement, their aspirations were scuppered by internal divisions and governmental indifference. French and German pacifists found it difficult to resolve their differences over Alsace and Lorraine. When Benjamin Constant d'Estournelles, the French pacifist, spoke before the Prussian Upper House in 1909, it made little impact on Franco-German relations. The Scottish-American steel magnate turned philanthropist, Andrew Carnegie, was an energetic sponsor of the peace movement in Europe. He supported a meeting of Christian pacifists that was scheduled to take place in the southern German town of Constance on 1 August 1914. The realities of international politics overtook the event. While pacifistic and socialist attitudes towards war placed boundaries on individual government policy, their ambitions to reshape the international system were never matched by their achievements.

In the late nineteenth and early twentieth centuries, the rapid expansion of the public sphere meant public opinion was increasingly important in international, as well as domestic, politics. For the most part, public opinion was inclined towards defensive patriotism. Most Europeans wanted to preserve peace, but were prepared to fight a war in defence of certain, limited national interests. Moreover, governments rarely followed the more extreme sections of public opinion. In fact, the formulation of foreign policy was largely shielded from the pressures of public opinion. Statesmen often shared the same assumptions and understandings of the national interest as the public, but this does not mean that popular pressures shaped their policies. For the most part, public opinion acted as a force for peace in Europe before 1914. Statesmen recognised that a general war would also have to be a popular war, presented as one of national defence. While this constituted an important restraint on war, it was also possible that two sides could claim they were waging a defensive war and that these claims would be accepted by their publics.

Examining the relationship between public opinion and the formulation of foreign policy in terms of cause and effect – either that the public pushed the government towards war or that the government manipulated the public into supporting a war – is only part of the story. A full analysis must take into account the interaction of different national publics, the role of transnational organisations, the efforts of governments to shape foreign public opinion, and the ways in which governments made sense not only of their own public opinion, but also that in foreign states. Public opinion provided a context in which international politics was conducted.

Diplomats analysed the press as well as their colleagues' statements, as they sought to understand the foreign policies of their allies and rivals. Public gestures and opinions were scrutinised for deeper meanings, where none might exist. It made international politics more uncertain and more complicated, eventually contributing to the erosion of peace in 1914.

5   The World Economy and International Politics before 1914

'In recent times,' Otto Neurath, one of Austria's leading economists, wrote in 1910, 'great wars are not as damaging as might have been expected either to the defeated or to the victorious side and, that on the contrary, something like an economic boom can be observed during or shortly after the war . . . the economic risk of war is relatively small under the present humane system of waging wars.'[1] The financier-turned-politician, Paul Rouvier, offered a very different view at the height of the Moroccan crisis in August 1905: 'As long as there was money, one fought, when the coffers had been emptied, one made peace. Now, everything revolves around credit. Nations are closely bound to each other by the links of credit. A war in Europe would bring about a general disaster.'[2] Where Neurath claimed that economic factors were not a restraint on war, Rouvier saw the complex web of relations in the world economy as a bond of peace. In general, the Frenchman's assessment was more accurate. Merchants, bankers, and industrialists saw the maintenance of peace as an important foundation for business. Profit, not peace, motivated them, but profit required a stable international system. They were willing to cooperate, regardless of nationality, and chafed at the restrictions imposed by governments on commercial transactions. However, the growing interdependence of the world economy brought in its wake frictions, tensions, and rivalries. Trade wars were a regular feature of international politics. Governments used finance as an instrument to advance their interests. Clashes over economic spheres of influence provided the grit of many diplomatic crises. Global interdependence created new vulnerabilities for states and societies, which naval and military planners targeted.

The term 'globalisation' has been used to describe the emergence of an interconnected world economy in the late nineteenth century. While

---

[1] Otto Neurath, 'War Economy', in Thomas Uebel and Robert Cohen, eds, *Otto Neurath. Economic Writings: Selections, 1904–1945* (Vienna, 2004), pp. 160–61.

[2] Cited in René Girault, *Emprunts russes et investissments français en Russie, 1887–1914* (Paris, 1973), p. 425.

the term itself was not used before the First World War, contemporaries were acutely conscious of the ways in which societies and economies were connected. Statistics also support the claim that national economies were integrating into regional, imperial, and global economies. In 1913 prices, global trade had increased from $1.7 billion in 1850 to $18.7 billion in 1913. This growth occurred in three unequal phases. In the heyday of free trade, between 1850 and 1872, world trade increased at an average of 4.8 per cent per annum. During a period of weaker economic growth and the raising of tariffs, between 1872 and 1894, world trade grew by an average of 2.6 per cent per annum. In the twenty years before the First World War, from 1894 to 1913, annual average growth rates rose to 4 per cent per annum. Significantly, world trade grew more quickly than the global economy between 1870 and 1913, an annual average of 3.4 per cent and 2.1 per cent, respectively. This meant that trade had become an increasingly important part of many national economies. A further sign of increasing global market integration was the convergence of prices, so that by 1910 a bushel of wheat in Liverpool was only 16 per cent more expensive than in Chicago, the heart of the American wheat market. Lower transport costs and more information about prices, transmitted by telegraph and radio, made for a more competitive, integrated market.

Capital flows were an equally important indication of globalisation before 1914. The City of London was the centre of global financial integration, with $18.3 billion lent overseas in 1914. France was the next largest creditor, with $8.6 billion in foreign loans, while Germany, a recent exporter of capital, had $5.6 billion in foreign loans. The USA, Russia, Turkey, and China ranked amongst the largest debtor nations. The spread of the Gold Standard, adopted by Britain in 1821, enabled the transfer of vast sums of money by minimising the risk of currency fluctuations. After unification, Germany joined the Gold Standard, giving it a decisive advantage as a system for organising global currency relations. Russia's decision to join the Gold Standard in 1897 was a triumph for its modernising Minister of Finance, Sergei Witte. By the eve of the war, all the major world economies were on the Gold Standard.

The concerns of European workers about competition from cheaper Asian labour at the turn of the century illustrated the increasing integration of the world labour market. Debates about tariff barriers often emphasised the benefits for workers as well as for entrepreneurs. Patterns of mass migration reflected the development of regional and global economies: 19 million Chinese emigrated to South-East Asia in the nineteenth century, while tens of millions of Europeans made the voyage to North America. Half of the (comparatively meagre) population increase in France between 1895 and 1911 came from immigrants, mainly from eastern Europe.

The increasing flow of capital, labour, and goods across borders suggested that the world economy was developing its own dynamic, independent of the constraints of the nation state. On the other hand, there was a strain of thought that argued for the subordination of economic interests to the national interest. Max Weber mocked political economists for 'devising recipes for universal happiness'. According to the German sociologist, 'if our work is to have any meaning, it lies, and can only lie, in providing for the future, for our descendants'. The interest of the nation would determine economic policy, no matter the consequences for the international system. 'As far as the dream of peace and universal happiness is concerned', he concluded, 'the words written over the portal into the unknown future of human history are: "lasciate ogni speranza" ['abandon all hope'].'[3] The pursuit of the national interest at the expense of the wider international economic system was justified, even though it would stimulate economic rivalries to compound the political tensions between the great powers. The economy was subsumed into a framework of power politics. Weber's view was widely shared. Figures as diverse as Sergei Witte, William McKinley, and Joseph Chamberlain conceived of economic policy in terms of national power.

The politics of the international economy steered an awkward course between cooperation and rivalry in trade and finance. Some historians have identified economic issues as a contributory factor to great power tensions and war. Andreas Etges argues that conjuring up the existence of economic threats added to war readiness in Germany, while Jacques Thobie claims that economic rivalries became bound up with imperial rivalries to explosive effect. Paul Kennedy's study of Anglo-German antagonism makes a powerful case that the roots of the conflict lie in the shifting economic weight of the two countries from the late nineteenth century. The naval race and colonial rivalry were products of these economic circumstances. The relationship between military and economic power exercised contemporaries, becoming part of the calculus of the balance of power. However, economic rivalries never translated into war – indeed some contemporaries believed that they had replaced war between the great powers. Crises did occur, but were resolved by a combination of patience and restraint. Short of strangling another great power's economy, statesmen considered economic issues as important, but not vital, interests.

---

[3] Max Weber, 'Der Nationalstaat und die Volkswirtschaft', May 1895, Inaugural Lecture in Peter Lassman and Ronald Speirs, eds, *Weber: Political Writings* (Cambridge, 1994), pp. 13–16.

Economic Power and Military Power

The relationship between military power and economic resources has long been recognised, though the precise contours of this relationship remain a matter of debate. The military strength of any power reflected the size of its population, its industrial base, its level of technological development, its agricultural sector, and its financial power. Contemporaries played close attention to the shifts in the world economy. In 1900, Gustav Schmoller, one of the foremost German professors of national economy, warned that 'the three enormous empires of conquest [Britain, the USA, and Russia] threaten to subjugate all smaller states, even to destroy them, to choke them economically, extinguish the light of life, with their craving for territory, their maritime and land power, their trade, their exports, and their expansive power'.[4] A few years later, speaking at Glasgow, the flourishing second city of the empire, Chamberlain warned his audience: 'I have been in Venice . . . which had at one time a commercial supremacy quite as great in proportion as anything we have enjoyed. Its glories have departed. When I was last there I saw the great tower of the Campanile . . . The other day, in a few minutes, the whole structure fell to the ground. Nothing was left of it but a huge mess of ruin and rubbish.'[5] Schmoller and Chamberlain were well aware of the economic statistics, which became an essential part of political debate, but these statistics could be read in different ways, according to the particular category the analyst privileged. The importance of financial reserves, manufacturing capacity, agricultural supplies, and population size to national power varied. Different states were more effective at mobilising certain sources of power, be they conscripts for their armies or tax to pay for armaments. Assessing national power was not a scientific calculation; it was a matter of judgement, in which raw statistics merged with perceptions. Contemporaries often misjudged the power of their rivals, but these misjudgements affected policy decisions.

Chamberlain was one of many at the turn of the century who was concerned about the relative decline in British manufacturing. Table 5.1 suggests there was reason to be concerned. Germany and the USA had outstripped Britain and their lead in industrial potential was accelerating, while other countries had closed the gap. Industrial power – the construction of railroads, the production of artillery, the building of naval vessels – was an essential foundation of military power. States had their own arsenals, which produced a large amount of their military hardware.

---

[4] Sonke Neitzel, *Weltmacht oder Untergang. Die Weltreichslehre im Zeitalter des Imperialismus* (Paderborn, 2000), pp. 88–90.

[5] Cited in Aaron Friedberg, *The Weary Titan: Britain and the Experience of Relative Decline, 1895–1905* (Princeton, 1988), p. 23.

Table 5.1 *Total industrial potential, Britain = 100 in 1900*

Country/Year	1880	1900	1913
Austria-Hungary	14	25.6	40.7
Britain	73.3	100	127.2
France	25.1	36.8	57.3
Germany	27.4	71.2	137.7
Italy	8.1	13.6	22.5
Russia	24.5	47.5	76.6
Japan	7.6	13	25.1
USA	46.9	127.8	298.1

Source: Paul Bairoch, 'International Industrialization Levels from 1780 to 1980', *Journal of European Economic History*, 11, 2 (1982), 292.

There were also some large private firms that concentrated on military production, such as Krupp in Germany, Vickers in Britain, Schneider-Creusot in France, and Steyr in Austria-Hungary. In terms of capacity to manufacture supplies for their own war effort, Germany, France, and Britain were the only self-sufficient European powers on the eve of the war. Firms in these countries exported arms around the world, often to potential enemies of their respective great power governments.

Industrial potential did not automatically translate into military power. The Russian case illustrates this well. In 1904, Russia enjoyed a vast superiority in industrial development over Japan, but it was badly defeated in the subsequent war in East Asia. During the war Russia had to import 175 million rubles' worth of matériel, principally from France and Germany. Despite an economic boom in the years before the First World War, Russia still did not have a sufficiently well-developed industrial base and its economic backwardness proved a significant weakness in the war against Germany. Its relative technological backwardness and its low productivity meant although it had the largest GNP of the initial belligerents, it was unable to translate this into a decisive military advantage (see Tables 5.2 and 5.3).

Yet before dismissing Russia's industrial power as of little account in comparison to that of the German empire, it is worth noting that contemporaries paid attention to the trend of Russian economic growth. In his speech to the Reichstag in April 1913, Bethmann Hollweg warned that 'the astonishing development of economic relations of this enormous empire, blessed with inexhaustible natural treasures, goes hand in hand with the reorganisation of the army'.[6] Russian economic growth

---

[6] Cited in Günter Wollstein, *Theobald von Bethmann Hollweg. Letzte Erbe Bismarcks, erste Opfer der Dolchstosslegende* (Göttingen, 1995), p. 76.

Table 5.2 *Volume of GNP, in 1960 US dollar prices, in millions, 3 year annual average, except for 1913*

Country/Year	1880	1890	1900	1910	1913
Austria-Hungary	12 297	15 380	19 400	23 970	26 050
Britain	23 551	29 441	36 273	40 623	44 074
France	17 381	19 758	23 500	26 869	27 401
Germany	19 993	26 454	35 800	45 523	49 760
Italy	8 745	9 435	10 820	12 598	15 624
Russia	23 250	21 180	32 000	48 830	52 420
Serbia	382	432	560	700	725

Source: Paul Bairoch, 'Europe's Gross National Product, 1800–1975', *Journal of European Economic History*, 5, 2 (1976), 281.

Table 5.3 *Volume of GNP per capita, in 1960 US dollars, in millions, 3 year annual average, except for 1913*

Country/Year	1880	1890	1900	1910	1913
Austria-Hungary	315	361	414	469	498
Britain	680	785	881	904	965
France	464	515	604	680	689
Germany	443	537	639	705	743
Italy	311	311	335	366	441
Russia	224	182	248	287	326
Serbia	240	250	260	282	284

Source: Paul Bairoch, 'Europe's Gross National Product, 1800–1975', *Journal of European Economic History*, 5, 2 (1976), 286.

alarmed German leaders, even if they recognised the continued weaknesses that afflicted the Russian economy. The window of opportunity was an economic phenomenon as well as a military one.

Russia's greatest weakness was financial, and here lay Britain's greatest strength. Arms races were not just about the size of population or industrial capacity, they were also based on the financial condition of the great powers. The financial sinews of war were as relevant to the twentieth century as they had been in the early modern world, when soldiers and monarchs recognised the truism that 'victory will go to whoever possesses the last escudo'. Raising money had been central to Britain's rise as a great power in the eighteenth century, and her banking system, credit-worthiness, and ability to extract tax from the national wealth underpinned her great power status after 1871. Martin Daunton has shown how the British tax system was underpinned by a high degree of consent, which encouraged payment, rather than evasion. This remained the case after the bitterly contested budget of 1909, in which Lloyd George imposed his so-called super-tax on high earners. With this new source of revenue, British government expenditure doubled in a twenty-year period to £305 million in 1913. Moreover, Britain's greater wealth per capita meant that its tax levels remained relatively low compared to those of its European rivals.

At the same time as Lloyd George was pushing his budget past the opposition of the Conservatives and the House of Lords, the German government was trying to ease its fiscal crisis. The Reich's debts had reached 4.1 billion marks by 1908. Bülow's attempts to raise old taxes and introduce new ones were repelled by stiff Conservative opposition. The central government in Germany never had the same tax-raising instruments as Britain, relying largely on excise and duties. This hampered Germany's ability to compete in the naval race with Britain. Bethmann Hollweg also struggled to find the money to pay for the army bills of 1912 and 1913. His attempts to persuade Conservatives that a one-off levy to pay for the 1913 Army Bill was a patriotic duty fell on deaf ears. Instead, he had to rely on a coalition, including the SPD, that had voted against the army bills. Whether the Reich could have continued to raise money for further armaments increases remains a moot question, entwined with constitutional concerns. During the Second Moroccan crisis, the withdrawal of French capital from Germany caused a panic on the Berlin stock market. It also illustrated the importance of what Karl Helfferich, the Deutsche Bank official, called 'financial war readiness'. In France, which had stronger financial institutions than Germany, but faced similar difficulties in extracting tax, there was a recognition amongst some financial and military officials that the 'opening of hostilities must find France as ready financially as militarily, as the best way to have peace is to be ready to wage war'. Despite this, neither country devoted sufficient resources, financially, politically, and intellectually, to their economic preparations for war.[7]

The constitutional arrangements of the Habsburg empire also stifled attempts to increase levels of taxation, so that Austro-Hungarian military expenditure remained the lowest of the great powers. Extracting tax from national income was as much about the strength of the state as it was about financial power. Tables 5.4 and 5.5 offer a useful statistical overview, showing that of the European great powers Russia was the

[7] Boris Barth, *Die deutsche Hochfinanz und die Imperialismen. Banken und Außenpolitik vor 1914* (Stuttgart, 1995), pp. 437–45; Martin Horn and Talbot Imlay, 'Money in Wartime: France's Financial Preparations for the Two World Wars', *International History Review*, 27, 4 (2005): 712–27.

Table 5.4 *Military expenditure of the great powers, in £ million*

Year	Britain	Italy	Germany	Russia	US	Japan	France	Austria
1900	69.6	14.1	43.2	44.5	39.3	13.7	41.5	11.4
1906	62.2	14.8	57.1	109.3	50.9	40.9	46.2	13.7
1911	67.8	22.9	68.1	71	65.2	23.2	60.8	17
1912	70.5	29.9	72	86.2	65.7	22.8	62.8	20.6
1913	72.5	39.6	93.4	101.7	68.9	22	72	25

Source: J. M. Hobson, 'The Military-Extraction Gap and the Wary Titan: The Fiscal Sociology of British Defence Policy, 1870–1913', *Journal of European Economic History*, 22, 3 (1993), 464–65.

Table 5.5 *Comparative real military burdens of the great powers*

Year	Britain	Italy	Germany	Russia	US	Japan	France	Austria
1911	100	100	96	132	35	190	138	73
1912	100	125	96	138	29	170	130	81
1913	100	158	122	160	30	160	149	100

Source: J. M. Hobson, 'The Military-Extraction Gap and the Wary Titan: The Fiscal Sociology of British Defence Policy, 1870–1913', *Journal of European Economic History*, 22, 3 (1993), 479.

most stretched in financial terms on the eve of the war. However, these tables disguise the politics of financing military expenditure. The Duma approved the budget for the 'Big Programme' in June 1914 without any of the intense political battles that had dogged the budget plans of the other great powers, suggesting a greater political readiness to shoulder a high defence burden in Russia.

For the most part, contemporaries regarded empire as a boost to a great power's economic resources and military power, not as a drain on it. A number of historians have questioned this, arguing that the empire was a drain on British economic performance before the war. High expenditure to defend the empire diverted resources away from more productive sectors of the economy. As threats to British security in Europe mounted, the empire became an important source of military power in the years before the First World War. As the naval race escalated, Britain placed pressure on colonies to contribute more to imperial defence. Australia and New Zealand paid for two dreadnoughts, which were stationed in European waters. During the South African War and First World War, volunteers from the colonies fought in the British army. Likewise, the French were able to recruit soldiers from Morocco and their African colonies, a fact which German military officials noted. British strategists also looked to colonies, notably Canada, to provide food supplies during a future European conflict. So in terms of demographic, financial, and agricultural resources, the colonies added to British military potential. The contribution of the German and Italian colonial empires to their military power was negligible and represented a diversion of scarce resources from more vital security interests in Europe. German colonial possessions were a hostage to some likely enemies, virtually impossible to defend once the Royal Navy seized control of the seas in wartime.

Russia and Germany had the largest populations of the European great powers, though this discounts the ability of the British and French governments to tap into their empires for recruits. After 1871, the German population rose from just under 41 million to 67 million on the eve of the war. Russia's population, however, was about two and a half times the size of Germany's, with 175 million in 1913. While French policy makers feared Germany's demographic advantage, German leaders worried about the 'Slavic hordes' that constituted the Russian army. France and Britain had populations of 40 and 45.6 million, respectively, while Austria-Hungary with a population of 52 million and Italy with 35 million made up the rest of the great powers. But as ever, these raw statistics covered a multitude of different interpretations. The establishment of the French protectorate in Morocco in 1911 alarmed some German observers. Yet German military analysts argued that the French army would be tied down in Morocco, maintaining the colonial order and would not be in a position to recruit large numbers of Moroccans into a French force to fight in a European war. Contemporaries also paid attention to levels of education and social and national cohesion, which affected the value of sheer numbers in any military conflict. In these areas, Britain, France, and Germany appeared to be more cohesive societies on the eve of war than Italy, Austria-Hungary, and Russia.

The economic bases of military power had shifted between 1871 and 1914, but the nature of this shift remained a matter of contention amongst contemporaries. Economic interdependence and the importance of economic strength for military power created new vulnerabilities. British naval planners, in particular, sought to target German food supplies and its credit system. The pattern of German economic growth enabled it to surge ahead of France, but it also rendered it more vulnerable in war. If Britain's industrial and demographic power had been eroded in the late nineteenth century, it still remained the foremost financial power in the world, while its empire had grown and contributed to its prestige and military muscle. Russia remained an enigma. Its potential power was obvious to all, but chronic weaknesses remained in terms of poor infrastructure, a low level of education, and relative technological backwardness. These problems were quickly exposed in the First World War, but on the eve of the conflict, many contemporaries were fixated by Russia's growing economic and military power. The USA, already the largest economy in the world, had a strong navy, but it never threatened nor needed to translate its economic power into military power on the same scale as European states. While contemporaries watched American economic growth with great interest and some anxiety, it remained an economic, rather than a military, rival. And it is to these economic rivalries, particularly in trade and finance, that we now turn.

Free Trade, Protectionism, and International Politics

The abolition of the protectionist Corn Laws in 1846 by Robert Peel's Conservative government marked the transition of the world's most powerful economy to a free trade system. There were many reasons for repealing the Corn Laws, but one of the arguments, which Richard Cobden, a leading proponent of free trade, put forward, was that free trade would consolidate international peace. In domestic terms, the repeal of the Corn Laws was associated with the decline of the landed aristocracy, which had thrived on war; in terms of foreign policy, Cobden argued that commercial rivalry would replace military conflict and that the mutual benefits of free trade and the deepening bonds of commerce between nations would promote peace. Cobden's hopes were soon dashed by the Crimean War, when he found himself a marginal figure in British politics. In the 1860s, the free trade system spread throughout much of Europe. The starting point was the Cobden–Chevalier treaty of 1860 between Britain and France, which eased tensions between the two countries that had arisen in the war.

Once Europe's two leading economies had signed up to a free trade system, others followed suit. The basis of the trade treaties was access to national markets on the principles of 'most-favoured-nation status', according to which countries got access to another market on the same terms as other rivals. It did not mean the abolition of tariffs. In 1862, the German Customs Union and France concluded a trade agreement. By the mid-1860s, a further ten countries had concluded trade treaties with France, containing the most-favoured-nation clause.

'Free trade is God's diplomacy', Cobden told the French Emperor, Napoleon III, 'and there is no other certain way of uniting people in the bonds of peace.'[8] Throughout the 1860s, British diplomacy sought to create an international order based on commercial exchange, not military power. Cobden died in 1865, but his followers were to be sorely disappointed with the results of British commercial diplomacy. Wars between Austria and Prussia in 1866 and between France and Prussia in 1870 demonstrated the continued primacy of power politics in international affairs. Trade did not act as a restraint on the policies of the great powers. Napoleon III and Bismarck were both supporters of free trade, but they were also the leading exponents of power politics on the continent. The same argument might be made about Lord Palmerston, the British prime minister during the Crimean War. Bismarck was prepared to instrumentalise trade policy for his political ends, as he excluded Austria from the German Customs Union in 1865. Concerns about international trade rarely interrupted the geopolitical calculations of these statesmen. Moreover, other powers suspected that free trade served British interests more than their own national interests. Access to markets gave British industry an advantage, while industries in late-developing economies found it difficult to meet the British challenge.

From the 1870s, the free trade system came under sustained attack. Tariffs were raised throughout Europe and the USA, with the exception of Britain, where the requirement for cheap imported food and raw materials made free trade as much a material interest as a political principle. The nation was elevated to the guiding principle of trade policy. The language of protectionist arguments was couched in terms of a foreign threat to the national interest. Jules Méline, the French Commerce Minister, made clear in his 1891 report on customs duties that the objective of commercial policy was to defend French jobs 'by thwarting the excessive inroads of foreign competition'.[9] Gustav Schmoller set up the Association for Social Policy (*Verein für Sozialpolitik*) in 1873, which aimed at the 'development of national ideals in economic policy'. He and his supporters condemned free trade as a disguise for the promotion of the British national interest, favoured protectionist tariffs for nascent industries in the newly unified Reich, and viewed the international economy as being shaped by ruthless commercial competition between nations. In the USA, following the end of the Civil War, proponents of tariffs argued that closing the American market to foreign goods would enable the USA to achieve economic independence from Britain. A new school of American political economists included figures such as Henry Carey

---

[8] Cited in Cornelius Torp, *Die Herausforderung der Globalisierung. Wirtschaft und Politik in Deutschland 1860–1914* (Göttingen, 2005), p. 121.
[9] Cited in Herman Lebovics, *The Alliance of Iron and Wheat in the Third French Republic, 1860–1914* (Baton Rouge, 1988), p. 5.

Baird, who claimed that 'protection was a policy, which not merely rested on foundations of justice, but it was vindicated by all history'.[10]

The victory of the Union in the American Civil War ensured that tariffs remained high after 1865. In Europe, the shift towards raising tariffs began in the early 1870s, but without causing any significant trade wars. Russia raised its tariffs during the Russo-Turkish War of 1877/8 in order to fund its military campaign. In 1879, the Reichstag introduced agricultural and industrial tariffs. Raising revenue, the slowdown in the economy following the crash of 1873, and protecting German agriculture were important motivations for Bismarck. Other countries, including France, Italy, and Austria-Hungary, were slowly disentangling themselves from the network of commercial treaties in the 1870s. The Austro-Hungarian tariff bill of 1878 was supported by industrialists, but opposed by Hungarian agrarians. However, by the early 1880s, Hungarian farmers had joined the ranks of protectionist supporters. Also, 1878 was the year in which Italy introduced tariffs to protect industry against foreign competition, though a treaty with France in 1881 allowed French products to compete effectively on the Italian market. In France, the transition to protectionism took longer. An 1875 inquiry showed that the majority of French chambers of commerce supported the system of commercial treaties. In the 1880s, opinion amongst businessmen and farmers began to shift. In January 1892, the Chamber of Deputies passed the Méline tariff bill, which protected French agriculture.

Although the rise of protectionism in the 1870s and early 1880s had not caused any significant trade wars, the increased role of the state in trade policy and the justification of tariffs as a necessary protection for the nation laid the basis for trade wars in the late 1880s and early 1890s. The most notable were between France and Italy and between Germany and Russia. It should be noted that these trade wars were framed by larger political differences – Franco-Italian tensions in the Mediterranean and the worsening relations between Russia and Germany in the wake of the Balkan crisis of 1885/7 and the failure to renew the Reinsurance Treaty in 1890. Governments used trade issues as an instrument of great power politics. In short, economic questions did not determine, but were subordinate to, political concerns.

For Italy, the trade war with France in the late 1880s was a costly, but necessary, means of establishing its economic and political independence from its wealthier, more powerful neighbour. In 1886, 44 per cent of Italian exports went to France, while 22.9 per cent of imports came from France. This dependence on the French market was compounded

---

[10] 'An Advocate of Protection', *New York Times*, 1 March 1883.

by Italian reliance on French banks for capital. The trade war started with tit-for-tat measures: the French rejection of a navigation treaty in January 1886 was followed by the Italian repudiation of the 1881 trade treaty between the two countries. French tariffs on Italian agricultural produce had a devastating effect on the agrarian economy in the south. But the freedom from French industrial competition allowed industries in the north to develop. The trade war, therefore, divided the country, but in the long term it forced Italy to diversify its economic relations. While German banks and companies assumed a prominent role in the Italian economy, it did not become a dependent relationship. Italy's alignment within the Triple Alliance was reinforced by its economic relations.

Months after concluding the Reinsurance Treaty, Bismarck blocked Russian attempts to raise a state loan on the Berlin money market. This financial measure was followed by a trade war that lasted from 1887 until the conclusion of a trade treaty in 1894. It is still not clear whether Bismarck made the connection between his economic and foreign policy, but it is likely that he saw political benefits. The measures would remind Russia of the necessity of good relations with Germany, shore up the position of agriculture, and pay domestic political dividends at home. Russia used the economic confrontation to develop relations with French banks and to provide breathing space for the development of its industry. Between 1888 and 1890, Russia increased its tariffs on industrial products by 28 per cent. Two factors influenced the ending of the trade war. In 1891/2, Russia suffered from a brief famine. The decision of the Finance Minister, Ivan Vishnegradski, to continue exporting agricultural produce worsened the scale of the disaster. Second, the new German Chancellor, Leo von Caprivi, had set about negotiating a series of trade treaties with other continental European states. This meant that Russia was commercially isolated. In early 1894, the two governments agreed on a commercial treaty. This treaty granted most-favoured-nation status to Germany, so that while Russian tariffs remained high, German exporters were not at a disadvantage compared to other European rivals. Russian agricultural exports also benefited.

The trade war between Russia and Germany emphasised the subordination of economic interests to foreign and security policy. Caprivi's use of militarised language to describe the trade war with Russia was particularly revealing. In his speech to the Reichstag on 12 December 1891, he warned of 'a war of all against all' over trade. He warned that European states would have to stop 'draining the blood from each other, because in the economic struggle they will need to exert all their energy'.[11] After

[11] Torp, *Herausforderung der Globalisierung*, pp. 181, 186–87.

the treaty had been signed, the Chief of the General Staff, Alfred von Waldersee, commented bitterly that 'out of fear we have capitulated in front of Russia and we now help to improve the economic position of the enemy, which is armed to the teeth against us – at the expense of the interests of our agriculture'.[12] Considerations of national security shaped Caprivi's trade policy. He carved out an area of German economic dominance in central Europe as he concluded treaties with the Balkan states, Austria-Hungary, and Italy. Control of or access to a large market and primary material was important in case of war. Witte, who had become Finance Minister by the time the treaty was signed, entertained a similar view of the need to develop an economic basis for national security and independence. 'There is a radical difference', he told Nicholas II on 22 March 1899, 'between Russia and a colony: Russia is an independent and strong power. She is proud of her great power, by which she guards jealously not only the political, but also the economic, independence of her empire; she too wants to become a metropole.'[13] Political considerations played a role in ending the trade war, as German leaders reflected on their growing isolation in Europe, while neither side wanted the trade war to escalate into a military conflict.

The rhetoric surrounding economic relations between Germany and Britain became more aggressive from the late 1880s onwards. German merchants accused their British counterparts of envy, while British companies complained that German rivals took advantage of a protected domestic market to sell at a high price at home and a lower price abroad. The 'Made in Germany' Act of 1887, in which markings on merchandise were introduced in Britain, symbolised tensions in the economic sphere. Jackie Fisher identified 'German commercial hostility' as the most important factor in deteriorating relations between the two countries. In the early 1900s, Joseph Chamberlain called for an imperial preference, in which the governments in the empire would set higher tariffs on imports from outside the empire. Britain would export its industrial goods to the colonies, and the colonies would export food and raw materials back to the home country, a happy symbiosis in Chamberlain's view. His main aim was to strengthen the empire by tightening economic bonds. In Germany, his growing popularity was viewed with alarm. However, Chamberlain's programme was decisively rejected by voters in the general election of 1906. The incoming Liberal government was associated with the doctrine of free trade. The foreign secretary, Sir Edward Grey,

[12] Cited in Barbara Vogel, *Deutsche Rußlandpolitik. Das Scheitern der deutschen Weltpolitik unter Bülow 1900–1906* (Düsseldorf, 1973), p. 19.
[13] Cited in Girault, *Emprunts russes*, p. 247.

reassured the German government on several occasions that commercial rivalries between the two countries were not a cause of 'political estrangement'. Tirpitz justified the construction of the fleet on the grounds that Germany needed to defend its growing overseas commerce. But this was largely rhetoric, as Tirpitz's construction programme focused on battleships to win command of the sea, not cruisers to defend trade routes. Prophets of Anglo-German commercial rivalry were often intellectuals, politicians, or sailors, who had a strategic, rather than a commercial, axe to grind. Granted, economic issues did contribute to the rivalry, but these economic issues were framed by wider geopolitical and military considerations.

Rounding off the survey of Germany's various trade rivalries, it was significant that concerns in France about the commercial strength of their neighbour increased sharply after the First Moroccan crisis – in other words, political differences prompted people to see economic relations in a new light. German companies were integrated into the French economy, either through deals with local companies, the establishment of subsidiary firms, or the acquisition of mining rights. French companies, such as Renault, set up branches in Germany. From early 1907, articles in the press, business interest groups, and even officials at the Quai d'Orsay called for limits to German commercial penetration of France. *Echo de Paris* asked whether German business influence in France constituted a 'national danger'. Various schemes, such as the requirement of state approval for certain business ventures (mining rights, for example) or heavy taxes on the repatriation of capital to Germany, were floated, but the government took no action.

If the growth of German industry in the late nineteenth century was impressive, it was overshadowed by the expansion of the American economy. Foreign trade was less important to the American economy than it was to the smaller European economies, but American exports accounted for 11 per cent of world trade. By the eve of the First World War, American industry accounted for 32 per cent of global industrial production, more than the combined total of Germany and Britain. American protectionism – the McKinley tariff of 1890 imposed an average duty of 49 per cent on goods liable to custom duties – and its huge trade surplus with European states produced a mix of frustration and fear amongst businessmen. American economic competition stimulated debates about economic union of some form within Europe. In 1904, Julius Wolf, a German national economist, founded the Central European Economic Association, which called for a system of economic preference on the continent. His plans, however, were unrealistic, as states within Europe were unlikely to join an economic union in which Germany would be the dominant force. Walther Rathenau, the director of the German corporate giant, AEG, warned that the USA would be the only beneficiary from a European war: 'the American economy would develop on such a different level that all other economies would be subordinate to it'.[14] In the early twentieth century, French observers worried about American economic dominance. 'If one spent six months watching with one's own eyes', wrote a French observer at the St Louis World Trade Fair in 1904, 'as they march by, a population of solid, tall, active, intelligent, and well-fed people, who do in eight hours, what we do in twelve with the help of the most advanced machinery, one wonders what the near future has in store for Europe.'[15] European concerns about American economic dominance were bound up with other factors, notably fear of Americanisation, which denoted technological advance, social flux, and unregulated modernisation. However, most Europeans were confident that modernisation in Europe could take a different, but equally effective, path.

Because the USA was not considered a political or military threat, European concerns about American economic dominance rarely entered the domain of foreign policy. This explains, in part, the difference between political reactions to German and American economic growth before the First World War.

Despite the rise of protectionism in the late nineteenth century and the rhetoric accompanying trade wars, international commerce continued to flourish. The networks of the global economy were malleable, as Sven Beckert shows in his study of how the cotton industry adjusted during and after the American Civil War. Cotton consumption doubled between 1860 and 1890 and doubled again in the following thirty years.[16] States and businesses recognised they had an interest in maintaining an effective global trade system. German exports to the USA grew by 75 per cent between 1899 and 1913, while American exports to Germany grew by 316 per cent. The USA enjoyed a massive trade surplus and German exporters urged their government to seek a reduction in American tariffs. In 1907, at a meeting of the League of Farmers, Georg Ottel, the editor of *Deutsche Tageszeitung*, argued that a trade war with the USA was preferable to 'a rotten, mouldy peace'. His was a minority view. As the Chancellor, Hohenlohe, noted in 1900, a trade war with the USA was a 'greater danger than an internal conflict between the government and

---

[14] Cited in Hartmut Pogge von Strandmann, ed., *Walther Rathenau: Industrialist, Banker, Intellectual, and Politician. Notes and Diaries, 1907–1922* (Oxford, 1985), p. 154.

[15] Jacques Portes, *Fascination and Misgivings: The United States in French Opinion, 1870–1914* (Cambridge, 2000), pp. 370–77.

[16] Sven Beckert, *Empire of Cotton: A Global History* (New York, 2014), pp. 275–79.

the agrarians'.[17] Trade between Germany and Russia doubled between 1904 and 1911, falling back slightly before the First World War. German exports to Britain grew from £26 million in 1880 to £80.4 million in 1913, while British exports, including re-exports, grew from £30.4 million to £60.4 million in the same period.

Trade wars were rare in the last decade of peace. This was possibly because there were no major tariff negotiations between the great powers after the Russo-German trade treaty of 1904. German tariffs remained set by the Bülow Tariff Act of 1902. Because Germany was at the centre of European (though not global) trading patterns, stability in the Reich's tariffs created stability in the trading system. There were occasions when commercial antagonisms surfaced – the Russian press referred bitterly to the 1904 trade treaty with Germany during the press war in the spring of 1914. For the most part, commercial relations between the great powers remained stable and encouraged contemporaries to see international trade as one of the bonds of peace.

In the 1840s, Cobden had argued that free trade would bring nations together, replace war with commercial rivalry, and undermine the dominant political position of the aristocracy, who pursued and benefited from war. His vision of free trade had been defeated by the 1880s at the very latest, but some of his other hopes for economic and political change were closer to realisation. The increase in world trade led some contemporaries to argue that commercial exchange made war between the great powers impossible, or certainly self-defeating from an economic point of view. Indeed, commercial rivalry had replaced war. McKinley, speaking the day before he was assassinated by the anarchist, Leon Czolgosz, told his audience that 'isolation is no longer possible or desirable . . . no nation can any longer be indifferent to another . . . Though commercial competitors we are, commercial enemies we must not be.'[18] Nicholas Murray Butler, the president of Columbia University and a leading American pacifist, argued that the European aristocracy, whose social and political position was rooted in war and power politics, was being displaced by a cosmopolitan elite, who rejected war. This was a contentious claim – arguably the European aristocracy was the most cosmopolitan element in any national society and they also played a full role in commercial life. Nonetheless, it was significant that some soldiers feared that modern

---

[17] Torp, *Herausforderung der Globalisierung*, pp. 331–42; Andreas Etges, *Wirtschaftnationalismus. USA und Deutschland im Vergleich (1815–1914)* (Frankfurt, 1999), p. 298.

[18] Cited in Frank Ninkovich, *The Wilsonian Century: US Foreign Policy since 1900* (Chicago, 1999), p. 25.

life, with its emphasis on material gain and commercial profit, had eroded 'the spirit of self-sacrifice. The spirit of the times looks upon war as an avoidable evil and militates directly against the kind of courage that despises death.'[19]

Jan Bloch, a Polish-Russian banker who employed Witte in his railway company, and Norman Angell, a British journalist, wrote two widely read tomes, arguing that modern commercial life made war a less viable instrument of great power politics. 'The banker, the merchant, and, in general, the commercial classes', argued Angell in 1913, 'are doing the real work of peace, though they will not wear the laurels.'[20] Economic self-interest, not moral considerations, dictated the preservation of peace. Around Europe, industrialists subscribed to Angell's view. The leading magnates of the day had no interest in a general war, which would disrupt trade patterns. Friedrich Thyssen, who had invested large sums in the French mining industry, argued in the special issue of *Nord und Süd* on Anglo-German relations: 'The last decade has created a series of international relations and understandings, so that one can well claim, that the national economy becomes increasingly international from day to day. I am convinced that, in this era of the internationalisation of national economies, trade and commerce, international relations between nations are founded, in the first instance, on an economic basis, and therefore must be regulated on an economic basis.'[21] Firms such as AEG, Siemens, and Renault had large investments and plants abroad, which were likely to be lost in a general war. Businessmen were prominent members of transnational groups, which aimed to promote better relations between the great powers. In February 1908, the Deutsch-Französische Wirtschaftsverein and the Comité commerciale franco-allemande (Franco-German Commercial Committee) were set up as sister committees to support economic cooperation.

Hugo Stinnes, who was to make a fortune from the wartime and post-war inflation in Weimar Germany, had no interest in fomenting a great power conflict, which would ruin his business interests abroad. In 1913, he bought minefields in northern England, hardly the investment of a man who foresaw war. Similarly, financial and industrial elites in St Petersburg supported the import of foreign capital and considered peace a necessary prerequisite for continued economic growth. The

[19] Wilhelm Balck, cited in Antulio Echevarria, *After Clausewitz: German Military Thinkers before the Great War* (Laurence, 2000), p. 80.
[20] Cited in Paul Laity, *The British Peace Movement, 1870–1914* (Oxford, 2001), p. 190.
[21] Klaus Wilsberg, *Terrible ami – amiable ennemi. Kooperation und Konflikt in den deutschfranzösischen Beziehungen 1911–1914* (Bonn, 1998), pp. 208–18, 223–24.

patterns of international commerce before 1914 did not suggest a desire for war. Of course, other businessmen had a different view of international economic relations, as they clamoured for tariffs, but demands for tariffs were some way short of hoping for war.

By the early twentieth century, probably 1906 at the latest, the tariff system, which emerged in the 1870s, had stabilised. The victory of the free trade Liberals over the tariff reformers of the Conservative party in the 1906 election, the settlement of the Russo-German trade treaty in 1904, and the German Tariff Act of 1902 mark, in reverse order, the moments when the international trading system stabilised. The first years of the twentieth century witnessed a burst of fear about American exports, but by the eve of the First World War, President Woodrow Wilson reduced tariffs as part of a programme of domestic political reforms. Protection from foreign competition, revenue raising, and concerns about the economic basis of national security had influenced the adoption of tariffs. Protection slowed down the growth of world trade, but it still continued to grow at a faster rate than the world economy. The creation of a protectionist system from the 1870s had sparked some belligerent rhetoric and trade wars, but it was accommodated relatively easily within the framework of the international system. Trade wars never threatened to escalate into military conflict. Further, they normally followed political trends, rather than anticipated them. Finally, many commentators saw international trade as a force for peace, rather than as a stimulus to war. It was only after the outbreak of war in July 1914 that calls for large, autarchic economic units became a feasible political option. Even then, in the midst of war, as Soutou has shown, untangling the threads of world trade patterns was difficult. It took the First World War *and* the Depression to achieve the end of the first era of globalisation.

Capital, Financiers, and International Relations

Foreign investment represented another side of economic globalisation in the nineteenth century. Britain was by far the largest lender, with $18.3 billion in overseas investments in 1914. France followed with $8.6 billion, then Germany with $5.6 billion, and the USA with $3.4 billion. Other countries, such as Belgium, had significant foreign investments as well. These foreign investments created a dense network of economic and political relationships, which were particularly unbalanced when the financiers of a great power lent to a much weaker state – British and French loans to Egypt and Turkey, for example. Foreign investment could create political interests, but in general, finance was used as an instrument in great power politics, rather than determining the alignments of the great powers.

The relationship between bankers and politicians was a contentious issue in contemporary politics, and these debates have seeped into historians' assessments of the role of finance in international politics before the First World War. In the British case, Cain and Hopkins have argued that a system of 'gentlemanly capitalism' emerged, in which the interests of government and bankers were fused into one. This fusion occurred at several levels. Bankers and their relations entered politics and sat in the cabinet, while politicians had large overseas investments; 37 per cent of Gladstone's portfolio was in Egyptian stock in the summer of 1882, when Britain occupied the country. They constituted one social network, which made it easy for bankers and politicians to meet on a regular basis. Second, they shared similar attitudes to political economy. They upheld the principles of a balanced budget, low government expenditure, and the defence of property. 'Gentlemanly capitalism' led British governments to identify the national interest with the financial interest of the City. In foreign policy terms, this meant the security of British overseas investments, the promotion of global trade, and the maintenance of peace between the great powers. In short, bankers did not need to prompt the government to adopt certain foreign policies, because politicians and bankers thought in similar ways. The concept of 'gentlemanly capitalism', which Hopkins and Cain use to explain British imperial expansion, particularly in Egypt and South Africa, has been subjected to considerable criticism.

The British state had its own autonomous strategic interests, which could, but did not always, coincide with those of British financiers. Salisbury lamented that the British government was unable to pressure banks into lending in the same ways as the continental great powers. In legal terms, this was true; in political terms, the British government began to intervene more regularly to direct loans towards the service of their foreign policy. In the late 1890s, the Foreign Office worked closely with the Hong Kong Bank, supporting its loans to China. In doing so, the Foreign Office had to overcome resistance from the Treasury, which saw this as a dangerous precedent for government interference in capital markets. When negotiating a loan to Russia in 1905, Lord Revelstoke of Barings Bank stayed at the British embassy in St Petersburg. The involvement of British finance in the loan to Russia after the revolution was strongly supported by Grey. The government also supported William Knox D'Arcy, who acquired the concession for oil drilling in Persia. In 1909, the Anglo-Persian Oil Company floated on the London Stock Exchange. On 20 May 1914, the British government, following the demands of the navy to secure a source of oil supplies, became a shareholder in the company. In each case, political, not financial, interest was the dominant factor. The Foreign Office perspective trumped the doubts of the Treasury, the guardian of financial stability.

In France, government control over foreign loans was regulated by a decree issued in 1880, which allowed the Finance Ministry to stop the placement of a foreign loan on the Paris money market. The Finance Ministry was supposed to consult with the Quai d'Orsay before taking action. There were no restrictions, however, on the movement of capital abroad. Financiers also made an important contribution to political life in the Third Republic. Caillaux and Rouvier, two leading financiers, served as premiers and in other cabinet posts.

Caillaux and Rouvier considered France's financial power to be an essential element of her great power status. With a tinge of regret, Caillaux told the Senate in 1900: 'We have become little by little the financial clearing house of the whole world.'[22] Almost half of French savings were invested abroad, meaning that relatively little remained to invest in the domestic economy. This might have hindered industrial growth; on the other hand, the lack of industrial growth prompted the export of large sums of capital. If the slow rate of industrial growth in France weakened her great power position, her financial strength was widely recognised as fundamental to her great power status. The payment of the war indemnity imposed after the Franco-Prussian War by 1873 was an achievement that astonished Bismarck. It signalled that French financial power would be instrumental in the pursuit of her foreign policy aims. Whereas only 5.2 per cent of British foreign investments were in Europe in 1914, 52 per cent of French foreign investments were in Europe. As a proportion of French foreign investment, investments in colonies declined from 4.33 per cent in 1882 to 3.4 per cent twenty years later. 'The financial prosperity of France is, perhaps, the principal cause of its moral situation and its prestige in Europe', the president of the Budget Commission, Lockroy, noted in 1895.[23] Foreign loans were a powerful tool in the international system between 1871 and 1914. China, Turkey, the Balkan states, North African states, and Latin America, where countries jostled for influence, all required foreign loans. Finance was a more subtle and effective instrument for exerting influence in these regions than large battalions and French diplomacy benefited from the prestige of French banking.

[22] Jean-Claude Allain, *Joseph Caillaux. Le défi victorieux* (Paris, 1978), pp. 302–11.
[23] Pierre Guillen, *L'expansion, 1881–1898* (Paris, 1984), pp. 53–60.

In the late nineteenth century, Germany began to export capital. Its stronger industrial economy and close links between banks and industry meant that a considerable amount of German capital was invested at home. Institutions such as Deutsche Bank and Dresdner Bank, as well as smaller merchant banks, became important overseas investors around the turn of the century. As in Britain and France, bankers had close connections to political leaders. Bismarck had a close relationship with Bleichröder, while Arthur Gwinner and Karl Helfferich of Deutsche Bank were close to diplomatic and political circles. Instances such as Bismarck's decision to ban a Russian loan from the Berlin money market in 1887 demonstrate the close control that government could exert on foreign investments. However, the German Foreign Office never regarded finance as an instrument of foreign policy in the same way as the Quai d'Orsay. Bankers were often critical of German foreign policy. Hansemann, of the German-Asiatic Bank, denounced Holstein as a 'clumsy hippopotamus' when the latter tried to put together a Franco-Russian-German consortium to lend to China in 1895, in a move clearly directed against Britain – Hansemann wanted to cooperate with the British bank, Hong Kong Bank. Mendelsohn & Company were infuriated by Bülow's decision to block German participation in a loan to Russia in 1906. Equally, financial interests rarely dictated German foreign policy. The Ottoman Empire, where Germany had significant investments and projects, was unable to get German diplomatic support during the 1908 Bosnian crisis and during the war against Italy in 1911/12. In these crises, maintaining the Triple Alliance, not the value of foreign investment, was the German Foreign Office's priority.

In the western hemisphere, the USA also began to use its financial power to pursue its strategic goals. 'The policy has been characterised as substituting dollars for bullets', President William Taft declared in his Annual Message in 1912. 'It is one that appeals alike to idealistic humanitarian sentiments, to the dictates of sound policy and strategy, and to legitimate commercial aims... The United States has been glad to encourage and support American bankers, who were willing to lend a helping hand to financial rehabilitation.'[24] The financial problems of countries such as Venezuela, which owed large sums to European creditors, threatened American interests in the western hemisphere. Roosevelt's declaration that the USA would uphold and enforce these obligations was designed to stave off European intervention. The government intervened to appoint financial advisers and to encourage foreign

---

[24] Cited in Emily Rosenberg, *Financial Missionaries to the World: The Politics and Culture of Dollar Diplomacy, 1900–1930* (Cambridge, MA, 1999), p. 1.

202 The Origins of the First World War

investment. Strategy and commercial interests fused as the USA consolidated its hegemonic position.

The lines of international financial politics and great power strategic interests were sometimes aligned, sometimes ran in parallel, and sometimes diverged in different directions. Bankers could operate independently of foreign offices, but they could rarely bend foreign policy to their own interests. Instead, governments determined the national interest and tried, with some success, to bend bankers to their strategy.

The financial relationship between France and Russia stands out as the most significant case where relations between two great powers were fashioned on the basis of financial diplomacy. Whether Russian foreign policy was manipulated by French loans remains a contentious issue. As Guernaut, a senior official at the Ministry of Finance, pointed out in January 1905, France had almost as much to lose as Russia, if the Tsarist regime went bankrupt: 'If there is a credit default, the ruin of Russia is certain . . . the ruin of the debtor will cause major damage for the creditor.' Siegel's recent study has argued that Russia indebtedness became a form of power, a lever which successive Russian statesmen used to influence French financial and foreign policy.[25] Between 1889 and the First World War, French bankers issued fourteen loans to Russia, totalling 11.7 billion francs. By the time of the first major loan in September 1891, diplomatic and military negotiations between the two powers were well advanced. Ribot and Rouvier used the loan to strengthen the Franco-Russian relationship. The politicisation of French loans was evident in the loan at the turn of the century. By the late 1890s, support for the alliance had declined in France amongst the public and the bankers. Moreover, investors preferred industrial shares, which offered better returns than loans to the Russian state. Delcassé put pressure on the bankers to make loans to Russia, enabling him to maintain the Franco-Russian alliance.

The tensions between political and financial considerations became evident in the years just before the Russo-Japanese War. Strikes and social unrest caused apprehension amongst French investors. Aware that the security of their loans rested on the political, as well as economic, stability of the Tsarist regime, French banks advised their agents in Russia against provocative policies towards Japan in the Far East. Crédit Lyonnais warned the Russian government that 'our first consideration must be our security'. French loans in 1904 came with high interest rates and were linked to Russian orders from French industrialists. The refusal of French financiers to make a loan in March 1905, following news of the Russian army's defeat at the battle of Mukden, was one of

[25] Girault, *Emprunts russes*, p. 22; Siegel, *Peace and Money*, pp. 10, 213–14.

the most significant causes of the strained relations between the two allies in the first half of 1905. German bankers made a loan to Russia, under pressure from Bülow, as the German Chancellor tried to forge a Russo-German alliance. If financially motivated decisions threatened to derail the Franco-Russian alliance, political and financial calculations salvaged it. The Russian government required so much money that French banks were bound to play a central role in the financial rescue of the Tsarist regime. In France, the prospect of a Russo-German alliance concentrated minds. 'Henceforth, the financial imperialism of France', an editorial in the influential *Le Temps* argued, 'must be the exact basis of its power. Our diplomacy, disappointed by the results of its policy based on sentiment and practised to this day, has the responsibility of basing itself on the considerations and interests of an economic order, whose achievements ensure other advantages and replace all other successes.'[26] Using its financial power, France secured Russian support against Germany in Morocco and rebuilt its diplomatic position. From 1905, however, Russian statesmen looked to diversify their sources of capital. 'The more equally the debt of a state is distributed among its creditors', Kokovtsov told J. P. Morgan in 1905, 'the wider the scope of capital it can avail itself of – the more stable and independent is its financial situation and the less subordinate it is to casual conjectures by the different money markets.'[27]

Further loans in 1909 and 1913 consolidated the alliance. French finance was integral to Russian industrial growth, railway building, and rearmament. In June 1913, a loan was made conditional on the construction of strategic rail lines in western Russia, aimed at speeding up mobilisation against Germany. Kokovtsov agreed to these conditions in June, but retreated from them somewhat by the end of the year. Once Russia had recovered from defeat and revolution, her economy began to grow, making it an attractive place to invest. A French banking agent, Verneuil, predicted in July 1913 that Russia's economic growth in the first half of the twentieth century would match that of the USA in the late nineteenth century. Had the alliance not existed, French banks would probably have lent a good deal of money to Russia in any case. Equally, some of the decisions made by the Russian government – on the construction of railroads, for example – were not solely related to French loans. Russian military strategy, which became more offensively orientated in 1912, required more railways running westwards.

Financial diplomacy was used to strengthen the bonds of the Triple Alliance, although it was never as important to internal workings of that

---

[26] Girault, *Emprunts russes*, p. 424.
[27] Cited in Siegel, *Peace and Money*, p. 75.

alliance, when compared to the Franco-Russian alliance. The withdrawal of French capital from Italy in the late 1880s led the Crispi government to turn towards Germany, where the government ordered reluctant bankers to step into the breach. 'I have no confidence in the Italians', Bleichröder told the French ambassador, Jean Herbette. 'They are going bankrupt and I do not see how patriotism obliges me to ruin myself with them.'[28] German-born bankers Otto Joel and Federico Weil were influential in the Banca Commerciale Italiana, set up in Milan in 1894. It marked the beginning of Italy's recovery from a banking crisis, which had led to the collapse of major banks in the late 1880s and early 1890s. However, German bankers never aimed to control the Italian banking system. Nonetheless, a nationalist backlash in Italy against German economic domination arose in the years before the First World War. In fact, from 1911 onwards, Italian industrial and banking interests became more closely aligned with those in Britain and France, presaging Italy's entry into the war in 1915 on the side of the Allies.

Germany's financial relations with Austria-Hungary were complicated by their divergent economic interests. The two countries were economic rivals, as well as political allies. In the Balkans and the Ottoman Empire, divisions became obvious. In 1908, Karl Helfferich was dismayed by German support for the Austrian annexation of Bosnia, as it cut across good relations with the Ottoman Empire, which were essential to the construction of the Baghdad railway. Deutsche Bank invested in Romanian oilfields, which sold crude oil to the Royal Navy in the Mediterranean, one of Germany's and Austria-Hungary's potential enemies. German bankers continued to invest in Serbia and even sold arms to the country after the Balkan Wars, though they believed that Serbia was too weak to act aggressively against Austria-Hungary. On the other hand, the Habsburgs were blocked from raising money on the French markets, so they were more reliant on German finance. German industry also had a large presence in Austria. In general, there was little coordination of economic and financial policy by either government, while German bankers preferred to work with French and British colleagues, who had access to more plentiful supplies of capital.

Political considerations could shape financial and business rivalries, but bankers were, more often than not, willing to put aside the differences between the great powers to concentrate on making a penny or two. There were struggles between governments and bankers for control of the leverage of capital in foreign policy. In the first decade of the twentieth century, cooperation between bankers was prevalent, before

---

[28] Girault, *Emprunts russes*, p. 213.

financial nationalism, to use Poidevin's term, emerged in the four years before the war. Bankers, then as now, sought to spread the risk by forming international groups. This was particularly evident in countries such as China and Turkey, which had a high risk of default. In 1902/3, French and German bankers cooperated to consolidate Turkish debt. There was competition between different international banking groups, rather than between national banks. In the Ottoman Empire, Deutsche Bank cooperated with the Banque Impériale Ottomane, but opposed the Dresdner Bank. French and German bankers were enthusiastic supporters of the Baghdad railway, although the French government was concerned about Russian opposition. Arthur Gwinner of Deutsche Bank told William II that the pan-German claims about colonisation in Asia Minor threatened to make the Baghdad railway a German project, which would undermine the necessary international financial support. This is precisely what happened. In the wake of a press campaign, which portrayed the Baghdad railway as a German threat to British interests, Lansdowne refused to give government backing to British financiers who were interested in participating in the project. Without finance, the project stalled.

In the aftermath of the First Moroccan crisis, German and French companies and banks embarked on a number of collaborative projects in North Africa. Paul Leroy-Beaulieu and Edmond Théry, influential economists, advocated a Franco-German economic rapprochement after the Moroccan crisis. Etienne, the leading figure in the French colonial movement and a businessman, met William II at Kiel in 1907 to discuss common French and German commercial interests, including in Morocco.[29] In 1907 an Anglo-Franco-German consortium, Union des Mines Marocaines, was established to exploit Moroccan mineral resources. The 1909 agreement between France and Germany, which acknowledged German economic interests in Morocco, was emblematic of the improved relations between the two countries. An attack by the German businessman Mannesmann on the Union des Mines Marocaines in 1910 and 1911 was one of the triggers for the Second Moroccan crisis. However, both German diplomats and other business figures, such as Rathenau, had little sympathy for Mannesmann's willingness to play the nationalist card in order to advance his business interests.

In the four years before the war, international financial cooperation became more difficult, though not impossible. The Quai d'Orsay played a leading role in destroying the financial entente between financiers in the two countries. In the summer of 1910, Djavid Bey, the Ottoman

[29] Raymond Poidevin, Les relations économiques et financières entre la France et l'Allemagne de 1898 à 1914 (Paris, 1969), pp. 236–37, 418.

Finance Minister, travelled to Paris to finalise an agreement with Crédit Mobilier. The French government intervened, demanding that the Ottoman Empire take a loan from Banque Impériale Ottomane, according to which the French bank would effectively administer the Ottoman budget. The Quai d'Orsay feared that French loans to Turkey would be spent on German goods, unless safeguards were built into the loan agreement. Djavid Bey refused to accept these conditions, whereupon German diplomats identified an opportunity to make a loan to the Ottoman Empire, depriving France of and bolstering German influence in the process. German banks, however, were less happy at the prospect of ending cooperation with their French colleagues and bearing the whole risk.

In 1912 and 1913, financial rivalry spread to the Balkans. French loans were often tied to ordering war matériel from French armaments manufacturers, such as Schneider-Creusot. French diplomats used financial leverage to try to loosen Bulgaria and Romania from the Triple Alliance, though they failed in both cases. However, French loans to Greece and Serbia increased the ties of these two states to the Triple Entente. The combination of loans and arms to Serbia was a particular threat to Austria-Hungary. The conclusion of a loan between Dresdner Bank and the Bulgarian government on the eve of the war tied Bulgaria more closely to Germany and Austria-Hungary.

Before concluding that financial relations roughly mirrored political relations on the eve of the war, it is worth noting important instances of cooperation, which cut across the alliance system, in late 1913 and early 1914. In late 1913, Britain, France, and Germany rejected a request from the Russian government for a seat on the Ottoman Public Debt Council. This Council had been set up in 1881 to ensure the repayment of creditors and controlled part of the Ottoman budget. It was supposed to act in the interests of creditors, not great powers. On this basis, Russia had no justification for a seat and its membership would have transformed the Ottoman Public Debt Council into an instrument of great power politics. The cooperation of France, Britain, and Germany in rejecting Russia signalled their common economic interests in the Ottoman Empire. This cooperation was enhanced by a series of agreements in early 1914 between Germany and France and between Germany and Britain, which paved the way for the construction of the Baghdad railway. On 15 February 1914, Deutsche Bank and the Banque Impériale Ottomane signed an agreement, which was followed by one in June signed by Lichnowksy and Grey in London. These agreements divided the Ottoman Empire into zones of economic interest. Cooperation in 1914 aimed at disentangling interests, rather than coordinating them.

By 1911, John Hobson, a vociferous critic of financial capitalism during the Boer War, had changed his views about the relationship between financiers, war, and peace. 'That which Christianity, justice, and humane sentiment have been impotent to accomplish through nineteen centuries of amiable effort', he argued, 'the growing consolidation of financial interests seems likely within a generation to bring to consummation, namely, the provision of such a measure of international government as shall render wars between the great civilised powers in the future virtually impossible.'[30] Hobson was not blind to potential threats to great power peace, but he did not identify the financial elite as bellicose.

Certainly, European bankers were conscious that war between the great powers was a fearful possibility, while tensions and crises were part and parcel of international affairs. Writing to his cousin in Paris as the naval crisis broke in September 1908, Nathaniel Rothschild noted that 'Germany will continue to develop her army and her navy and hopes to be so strong by land and by sea that she will always be able to have her own way. The natural consequence is that other nations will have to remain armed to the teeth too.'[31] Karl Helfferich and Max Warburg pointed out that financial preparations for war were almost as important as military ones. During the Second Moroccan crisis, a major financial panic in early September demonstrated the nervousness of bankers about the frailties of the international system.

On the other hand, economic rationality suggested that a great power war was unlikely, and certainly unwelcome. Ernst Agahd, a director of a Russian bank in the Far East, pointed out that a general war would end in bankruptcy, not victory for any of the participants. In early 1914, the Berliner Handelsgesellschaft was confident that the great powers did not want war and, despite the division of Europe into two armed blocs, would cooperate to avoid war. 'In this [cooperation across the divisions of the blocs] and in the conviction of the powers, that any war amongst the European states must lead to a world war with unforeseeable consequences, lies the most certain guarantee for the maintenance of peace and the most calming prediction for the new year.'[32]

Bankers were close to diplomatic and political circles and they used their contacts to try to ease tensions in the international system. During the First Balkan War leading bankers, such as Paul von Schwabach, Alfred de Rothschild, and Max Warburg, urged Britain and Germany to

---

[30] Cited in P. J. Cain, *Hobson and Imperialism: Radicalism, New Liberalism, and Finance, 1887–1938* (Oxford, 2002), p. 194.

[31] Barth, *Deutsche Hochfinanz*, p. 439.

[32] Ibid., p. 450.

restrain their respective partners, Russia and Austria-Hungary. Two close friends – Ernst Cassel, a British banker, and Albert Ballin, the Hamburg shipping magnate – tried to facilitate the improvement of Anglo-German relations before the war. Ballin had supported the construction of the German navy under Tirpitz, as a necessary instrument in 'the brutal struggle of nations for light and air'. The fleet was to promote trade, an interest which Germany shared with Britain. In 1908, Ballin began to distance himself from Tirpitz, as he considered the navy sufficiently large and was concerned by British reaction to the German fleet, of which he had learned much through Cassel. Cassel, like Ballin, was well connected to diplomatic as well as business circles and both men used their networks to try to defuse, without much success, tensions over the naval race. In July 1914, the two men tried to avert war, but once again, commercial considerations proved too weak in the face of political and military rivalries.

Those who argued that economic factors would either lead to war or prevent one overestimated the importance of economic concerns in great power politics. Commercial and financial issues rarely determined policy; instead, governments, even the British government, which traditionally had a laissez-faire approach to the international economy, saw finance and trade as instruments of foreign policy. Economic levers were a valuable addition to a state's armoury of diplomatic weapons. Pressure could be applied and influence gained without the risk of mobilising military power. Britain, France, Germany, and to a lesser extent, because of the nature of its foreign policy interests, the USA were able to exploit their economic power to bolster their political influence. Alexandre Millerand, the French Minister of Public Works, told Sciences Po graduates in 1909 that 'If it is true that influence follows the fleet, it is also true that influence follows business.'[33] Around the globe, from South America to China, trade and loans sustained great power influence. Gunboats and troops could always be dispatched, if needed, to enforce trade agreements and financial contracts. Of these great powers, financial power was most significant to French foreign policy.

Russia, Italy, and Austria-Hungary did not possess the same calibre of financial and commercial leverage as the other major powers. Arguably, in the years before the outbreak of war, their relative economic weakness led them to adopt riskier policies. Russia's frustration at being unable to put financial pressure on the Ottoman Empire in late 1913, when it failed

[33] Cited in Philip Nord, 'Social Defence and Conservative Regeneration: The National Revival, 1900–14', in Robert Tombs, ed., *Nationhood and Nationalism in France: From Boulangism to the Great War, 1889–1914* (London, 1991), p. 214.

to acquire a seat on the Ottoman Public Debt Commission and failed to get France to withhold loans from Turkey during the Liman von Sanders crisis, set the scene for Sazanov's decision to adopt a more assertive foreign policy in early 1914. Similarly, in 1912, Austria-Hungary failed to force Serbia to join a customs union, which would have left the emerging Balkan state dependent on the Habsburg empire. The customs union was unlikely to succeed because Serbia had already freed itself from Austro-Hungarian economic dominance during the Pig War of 1906. Moreover, Serbia had developed new export markets and had access to French financial markets. The failure of Berchtold's customs union plan meant Austria-Hungary could only use military power to defend its position in the Balkans. While Italian businesses had interests in the Balkans, the Ottoman Empire, and North Africa, these were so weak compared to the financial and commercial strength of Britain, France, and Germany, that Italy had no effective economic lever in its foreign policy.

The development of the international economy had its own dynamics, which were often independent of great power politics. To the extent that the two intersected, economic factors mainly served to preserve peace. The trade wars and financial rivalries never threatened to escalate into a military conflict. Governments were aware of the increasing economic interdependence of nation-states, even if they sought to soften the impact of economic competition by raising tariffs. Governments tried to mobilise bankers and capital to serve their foreign policy interests, rather than taking instructions from the financial elite. The commercial and financial elite recognised that peace between the great powers was a pre-condition of continued economic growth and they used their influence, such as it was, to resolve diplomatic crises. Economic rivalries ebbed and flowed, but these rivalries were largely framed by political concerns. The financial cooperation between bankers in France, Germany, and Britain had frayed slightly in the years before the war, but there were few signs in the international economy, let alone any desire amongst financiers and businessmen, for war in the summer of 1914.

6   The July Crisis

The military commander of Bosnia, General Oskar Potiorek, had pressed the Archduke Franz Ferdinand to make a trip to the recently annexed province. A visit would help the integration of Bosnia into the Habsburg empire. The Archduke, however, was a reluctant visitor, and even tried to cancel the trip in mid-April on account of the Emperor's fading health. 'The thing is not particularly secret', Franz Ferdinand allegedly told the Countess von Harrach, 'because it would not surprise me, if a couple of Serbian bullets awaited me.'[1] Just after one o'clock on 28 June 1914, the Archduke and his wife, Sophie, were assassinated. Gavrilo Princip, a Bosnian of Serbian descent, carried out the attack. Princip was a member of the Young Bosnia movement, an exponent of a Greater Yugoslav state, rather than a greater Serbian nationalist, but he had links with an extreme Serbian nationalist group, Unity or Death, which in turn had links to the Black Hand organisation and certain elements in the Serbian army. The most notable supporter was Colonel Dimitrijevic, nicknamed the 'Bull' (Apis), who supplied the group with guns and allowed them to move weapons across the Serbo-Austrian border in June 1914. The prime minister, Pasič, tried to prevent the transfer of military supplies, as he rightly feared it could end up provoking an Austro-Hungarian attack, but he was unable to impose the authority of his government on Dimitrijevic and other officers. By 28 June, Princip was in Sarajevo to assassinate the Archduke.

News travelled fast in the era of the telegraph and the radio. The assassination was framed in different ways across Europe, starting a process whereby initially Serbia and Austria-Hungary, but later all belligerents sought to establish the legitimacy of their actions. Josef Redlich, the Austrian scholar and liberal, immediately called the assassination a 'world historical event', which demonstrated that peaceful coexistence between the Habsburg empire and aggressive Serbian nationalism was

---

[1] Günther Kronenbitter, *'Krieg im Frieden'. Die Führung der K. u. K. Armee und die Großmachtpolitik Österreichs-Ungarns 1906–1914* (Munich, 2003), p. 459.

impossible.[2] When the French president, Poincaré, heard of the assassination, he simply stayed at the Longchamps racecourse outside Paris. From this perspective, the assassination was a tragedy, but hardly an event that justified war. Assassinations of leading politicians were quite common in Europe before 1914. In some ways, the murder was less of a threat to Austria-Hungary's great power status than the changes that had taken place over the course of the Balkan Wars; but we should also bear in mind that the assassination of the heir to the throne, in a state whose stability rested to some extent on an ageing monarch, was a serious challenge, compounded by the political changes of the previous years.

So why did the July crisis turn out differently to the previous crises? One answer is that the July crisis was simply a trigger. A detailed account of the crisis might be interesting, but the course for a general war had been set much earlier, either as a result of the growing tensions in the international system or because a government had consciously decided to use one of the periodic crises to launch a war. The most recent works on the origins of the war, however, emphasise the importance of the July crisis, the contingency of decision-making, and the systemic character of the crisis.[3] Decisions were made by a small group of men and their aims, assumptions, perceptions, and choices require careful scrutiny. The crisis was highly complex, as different bureaucracies, personalities, and networks within and between the key states interacted, often with unintended consequences. Once scholars 'open the black box and stop anthropomorphising countries', as John Vazquez puts it, concepts of 'rational decision-making' and uniform understandings of a putative national interest become less convincing and the highly contingent nature of the crisis becomes increasingly evident.[4]

The previous chapters have emphasised the restraints on war within the international system, though they have indicated some developments that made war a more likely outcome of the July crisis than had a similar assassination taken place in, say, December 1910. That said, a general war was not inevitable after the assassination. A series of decisions taken in the capitals of the great powers interacted with each other, as the crisis escalated from an assassination to a local war to a European war

[2] Fritz Fellner, ed., *Schicksalsjahre Österreichs, 1908–1919. Das politische Tagebuch Josef Redlichs* (Böhlau, 1953), vol. I, p. 235.
[3] Christopher Clark, *The Sleepwalkers: How Europe Went to War in 1914* (London, 2012); Jack S. Levy and John A. Vasquez, eds, *The Outbreak of the First World War: Structure, Politics and Decision-Making* (Cambridge, 2014); Annika Mombauer, *Die Julikrise. Europas Weg in den Ersten Weltkrieg* (Munich, 2014); Thomas Otte, *July Crisis: The World's Descent into War, Summer 1914* (Cambridge, 2014).
[4] John A. Vasquez, 'The First World War and International Relations Theory: A Review of Books on the 100th Anniversary', *International Studies Review*, 16 (2014), pp. 624–25.

and ultimately to a world war, once Britain entered the lists in August 1914. Other outcomes were considered throughout the crisis – a localised conflict, a conference, and guarantees of territorial integrity were bandied about as alternatives to a general war. Miscalculation, risk-taking, and ultimately an unwillingness to back down characterised the decision-making in European capitals. Decisions made in one capital, which were intended to produce a certain result, often resulted in decisions in other capitals and outcomes wildly at variance with the original intention. Each side hoped that the prospect of catastrophic war would lead the other side to back down. Ultimately leaders made conscious decisions to go to war, but the world war begun in 1914 was nobody's preferred outcome. To assess why the July crisis ended in war, it is necessary to ask why the other options were not pursued and why the restraints were cast aside.

The Ultimatum

Grief was not the dominant emotion in court circles in Vienna when news of the assassination arrived. The Archduke was widely disliked, on account of his personality and his dovish views on foreign policy. His death removed a significant restraint on the war party in Vienna. 'The world does not know', Alexander von Hoyos, one of the leading proponents of war within the Ballhausplatz, told Redlich, 'that the Archduke was always against the war. So, through his death, he has helped us to the decision, which he would never have taken, as long as he lived.'[5] Conrad, who had called for a war for seven years, renewed his appeals. However, he was not necessarily confident of victory and he expected Russia to support Serbia. 'It will be a hopeless struggle', he told his lover, Gina von Reininghaus, 'but it must be pursued because so old a monarchy and so glorious an army cannot go down ingloriously. So I look forward to a gloomy [trübe] future and a gloomy end to my life.'[6] The following day Conrad met Berchtold. The Austro-Hungarian foreign minister refused to mobilise immediately, though he signalled his approval of some form of punitive measures against Serbia. On 30 June, Berchtold met the powerful Hungarian premier, Count István Tisza. He opposed a war against Serbia on the grounds that Austria-Hungary needed to build diplomatic support within the Balkans and to ensure Bulgaria and Romania sided with the Dual Alliance. Moreover, he feared that any annexations of Serbian territory would merely increase the number of Slavs within the

[5] Fellner, ed., *Schicksalsjahre*, p. 239.
[6] Cited in Kronenbitter, '*Krieg im Frieden*', p. 462.

empire, exacerbating the paralysing ethnic divisions. He was to be the most significant opponent of a war policy in Vienna in early July.

Berchtold had set aside his doubts and embraced a war policy by time he met Franz Joseph on 30 June. This was the second decisive change in the upper echelons of the Austrian elite, following the assassination of the Archduke. Figures, such as Leon von Bilinski, the Finance Minister who had favoured rapprochement with Serbia, now supported war. 'The Serb responds only to violence', he told two generals in early July, 'a diplomatic success would make no impression in Bosnia and would be more damaging than anything else.'[7] Berchtold had verged towards a military solution of the conflict between Serbia and Austria-Hungary since October 1913. His colleagues in the Ballhausplatz and the prospect of German support confirmed his policy. A younger generation of Austro-Hungarian diplomats, led by Hoyos, were forceful advocates of a war policy. Hoyos was at the centre of efforts to secure German support, even before he travelled to Berlin on 4 July. He was in contact with Dietrich von Bethmann Hollweg, the nephew of the German Chancellor and Victor Naumann, a German journalist, who assured the Austrian diplomat of German support in a war against Serbia. However, these informal contacts merely paved the way for Hoyos's mission to Berlin.

In Berlin, William II believed that Austria-Hungary had to take decisive action against Serbia. 'The Serbs must be dealt with, and soon', he noted on 30 June.[8] Hoyos came to Berlin with a personal letter, which he had crafted, from Franz Joseph to William II. The Austrian diplomat argued that the Habsburg empire and Serbia could no longer co-exist peacefully. His aim was to secure German support for any Austro-Hungarian action in the Balkans. Both the Kaiser and the Chancellor in meetings on 5 July assured him of German support, offering the famous blank cheque. While Hoyos believed that the current moment offered the best opportunity for Austria-Hungary to defeat Serbia, he also asked his German counterparts whether 'a later point would be preferable from the European point of view'. This betrayed the Austro-Hungarian focus on the Balkans, while giving Germany responsibility for the broader consequences of Habsburg measures against Serbia. 'Bethmann Hollweg told me that it was not Germany's affair to give us advice regarding our policy towards Serbia. It [Germany] would cover our backs with all its power and fulfil its alliance duties in every way, if we found it necessary to act against Serbia. If I wanted to know his personal view regarding the opportunity of the

---

[7] Cited in Otte, *July*, p. 52.
[8] Jürgen Angelow, *Kalkül und Prestige. Der Zweibund am Vorabend des Ersten Weltkrieges* (Cologne, 2000), p. 447.

moment, he would tell me that if war was inevitable, then the current time was better than a future one.'[9]

In the July crisis, Austria-Hungary had seized the initiative from Germany. This marked a departure from the pattern of alliance diplomacy during the Balkan Wars, when Berlin had retained almost complete control of the alliance. In the second half of 1913, Austria-Hungary had begun to adopt a unilateral approach to international politics, issuing ultimatums without consulting the other great powers or even Berlin. The alliance system had sustained great power peace during the Balkan Wars, because Germany had refused to underwrite an Austro-Hungarian war policy against Serbia. Arguably, the Dual Alliance had broken down, in terms of the day-to-day functioning of great power diplomacy, in 1913 and 1914, as Austria-Hungary adopted a unilateral approach to the Balkans, often without prior discussion with the German government. In the July crisis, the alliance was reconstituted on terms more favourable to Austro-Hungarian interests in the Balkans.

The granting of the blank cheque did not result from a coherent discussion of policy amongst German leaders. Decisions were reactive and spontaneous. Nonetheless, German leaders shared certain assumptions about the crisis in early July. They were prepared to cede the initiative within the alliance to Austria-Hungary for two reasons. First, German diplomats were concerned that the Habsburg empire was on the verge of collapse. Given that it survived four years of war, this assessment of Austrian weakness was wide of the mark. However, it encouraged German leaders to take drastic action to rescue the creaking empire. Second, the value of the Austro-Hungarian alliance to Germany had increased in May and June 1914, following the breakdown of the Anglo-German détente. In his report of the meeting with Hoyos, Bethmann Hollweg argued that 'our own vital interests demand the maintenance of Austria intact'.[10]

German leaders also believed that strong support for Austria-Hungary offered the best chance of localising the war by deterring Russia from aiding Serbia. They considered the possible escalation of the crisis if Russian supported Serbia, but the prevailing opinion was that Russia would not intervene in a military conflict. Colonel Plessen, a member of William II's military cabinet who attended the meeting on 5 July noted in his diary: 'Amongst us, the view is that the sooner the Austrians get going against the Serbians the better and that the Russians – although friends

[9] Fritz Fellner, 'Die Mission Hoyos', in Wilhelm Alff, ed., *Deutschlands Sonderung von Europa 1862–1945* (Frankfurt, 1984), pp. 312–13.
[10] Bethmann Hollweg memorandum, 5 July 1914, in Immanuel Geiss, ed., *July 1914: The Outbreak of the First World War: Selected Documents* (London, 1967), vol. I, p. 85.

of Serbia – will not join in.'[11] Admiral Eduard von Capelle, another figure close to William II in 1914, did not think that Russia would support Serbia, 'as the Tsar could not support murderers of monarchs and Russia was neither financially nor militarily ready for war'.[12] Habsburg and German leaders believed that Serbia was a criminal state, which had placed itself outside the moral and normative order of European politics. Bethmann Hollweg's report of 5 July made clear that he preferred that the Austro-Serbian conflict not escalate into an international conflict. German civilian (and some military) decision-makers did not perceive Russia's financial and military weakness in 1914 as a window of opportunity to launch a preventive war, justified on the flimsy pretext of the assassination of the Archduke. Instead, in Berlin's view, Austria-Hungary had a legitimate opportunity to strike at Serbia, while Russian weakness was likely to ensure the maintenance of peace between the great powers. On the other hand, the mere fact that Russia's reaction was considered suggested that German leaders acknowledged the risk of a general war. If Russia were to react to an Austro-Hungarian attack on Serbia, then – in the reasoning of German leaders – this would simply confirm that the war party had already gained the upper hand in St Petersburg and would have gone to war in the near future in any case.

The assumption of Russian weakness and consequent pusillanimity was a risky one. It informed the policy of calculated risk, which Bethmann Hollweg adopted, and which his close adviser, Kurt Riezler, had articulated in two books before the war. According to Riezler, the risks of war outweighed the benefits. States armed, not as a preparation for war, but as a means of forcing concessions from other states. To succeed, the threat of the use of force had to be credible. The opposing side would make concessions as long as its vital interests were not harmed. Bethmann Hollweg calculated that whereas an attack, sponsored by institutions within Serbia, on the Habsburg monarchy would be considered a vital interest to Austria-Hungary, a punitive war undertaken by Austria-Hungary against Serbia would not be considered a vital interest to Russia. The asymmetry of interests, coupled with the risks of war, would restrain Russia.[13] The blank cheque, therefore, was issued on the assumption that a war between Austria-Hungary and Serbia could probably be localised.

[11] Diary entry, 5 July 1914, in ibid., p. 87.
[12] Diary entry, 6 July 1914, in Michael Epkenhans, ed., *Albert Hopman. Das ereignisreiche Leben eines Wilhelminers. Tagebücher, Briefe, Aufzeichnungen 1901–1920* (Munich, 2004), pp. 382–84.
[13] Andreas Hillgruber, *Deutsche Großmacht und Weltpolitik im 19. und 20. Jahrhundert* (Dusseldorf, 1979), pp. 91–104.

Assured of German support, the Austrian Council of Ministers met on 7 July. Whether Austro-Hungarian leaders thought Russia would hold back from giving military support to Serbia is a matter of debate; it is significant, however, that discussions in Vienna continued to ignore the broader European dimension. At the meeting, Conrad called for a surprise attack against Serbia, but Berchtold won general support for his proposal that an unacceptable ultimatum be delivered to Belgrade, which would effectively bring about a war and give Austria-Hungary some diplomatic cover. Tisza continued to search for a diplomatic victory, centred on the creation of an anti-Serbian Balkan League. Berchtold, on the other hand, had had enough diplomatic victories, none of which had secured the Habsburg empire against the Serbian challenge. But Tisza was in a powerful position and Berchtold could not simply overrule him. Instead, a decision was delayed.

Over the following week, Tisza's mind changed. First, one of Tisza's main concerns was the position of Romania in a future war, as there was a large Romanian minority living in the Siebenburg region of Hungary. Between 7 and 14 July, his envoy to Vienna, Count István Burian, convinced him that Romania would stay out of the war, owing to German intervention in Bucharest. A failure to act against Serbia, on the other hand, might encourage Romania to stake out its claims to Hungarian territory. The Habsburg empire, therefore, had to make an example of Serbia, *pour encourager les autres*. A second factor was a report from the ambassador in Berlin, Count Ladislaus Szögény, which seemed to ensure that Germany would deter Russia from entry, Britain would stay out, and Serbia, tarred as a regicide state, was isolated throughout Europe. Under pressure from the German government, Austro-Hungarian leaders met again on 19 July to draft the ultimatum. The previous day Hoyos told an official at the German embassy that the ultimatum would be drafted in such a way 'that a state, which was self-confident and had dignity, could not possibly accept it'.[14] The ultimatum read like a charge sheet, condemning the Serbian government for tolerating 'acts of terrorism' and 'the criminal doings of diverse societies and associations directed against the Monarchy.'[15] Vienna depicted Serbia as a menace to the European order.

The Austro-Hungarian government then delayed the delivery of the ultimatum to Belgrade until 23 July. This delay was necessary to enable the gathering of the harvest – and to ensure that Poincaré, on one of his regular state visits to St Petersburg, would have left the Russian capital

[14] Angelow, *Zweibund*, pp. 456–47.
[15] Geiss, ed., *July Crisis*, pp. 142–46.

and be at sea. Once the ultimatum was delivered, the ball was briefly in Pasič's court. Serbia's reply has recently been called a 'masterpiece of diplomatic equivocation'.[16] The difficulty in forging a reply owed much to the unresolved relationship between army and state in Serbia. While Pasič wanted peace, in order to consolidate Serbian gains from the two Balkan Wars, figures like Dimitrijevic were able to wield significant influence. There is some evidence that the Serbian government adopted a less conciliatory stance in the confident expectation of Russian support.[17] Pasič was prepared to dissolve radical nationalist groups if necessary. The Serbian response to the ultimatum accepted all but one of Austria-Hungary's conditions, the right of the Austro-Hungarians to conduct their own investigation on Serbian territory. This constituted an enormous infringement of Serbian sovereignty. While the Serbian reply recognised the criminal dimension of the assassination, it demanded its sovereign rights to investigate the crime. Serbia, due to its 'pacific and moderate policy during the Balkan crisis' and the 'sacrifice she has made in the exclusive interest of European peace', had earned the right to be treated as an equal sovereign state. Understandings of security – on both sides – were interwoven with normative claims about the rules and principles of the European order.

Pasič's refusal to accept this final part of the ultimatum was what Berchtold expected and wanted. The Habsburg envoy, Vladimir von Giesl, did not even bother to ask for instructions from his government when he received the Serbian reply on 25 July at 6 p.m. Within minutes, he had broken off diplomatic relations and boarded the train for Vienna. Three days later, Franz Joseph declared war on Serbia.

From Regional War to Continental War

Between the delivery of the ultimatum and the German declarations of war against Russia and France on 1 and 3 August, the conflict escalated from a Balkan to a continental war. Given that Germany had already committed to supporting Austria-Hungary on 5 July, the major decisions were taken in St Petersburg and, to a lesser extent, Paris. That is not to say that German leaders were inactive during this period. They sought to deter Russia and then France, while attempting to keep Britain out of the war. The meeting of 5 July had given primacy to the preservation of the alliance over the maintenance of peace in German policy, and this remained the case throughout the July crisis. The assumption that

[16] Clark, *Sleepwalkers*, p. 464.
[17] Ibid., pp. 462–63.

Russia would leave Serbia to its fate was tested to destruction and the implications of the blank cheque, given on 5 July, became clearer. During this phase of the July crisis, the balance within the Triple Entente shifted to Russia. In previous crises, Britain had clearly been the dominant power within the Triple Entente, able to restrain France and Russia. During his visit to St Petersburg, Poincaré and Sazonov agreed on joint action to maintain peace and restrain Austria-Hungary, two incompatible goals. The Triple Entente momentarily collapsed during late July. Russian leaders were confident, but not certain of French support, when they ordered partial and later full mobilisation, while France decided to fulfil its alliance obligations to Russia without being sure of Britain's stance. Only when Britain entered the war was the Triple Entente restored. The treaty of 5 September 1914, when each of the three powers agreed not to make a separate peace marked the conclusion of this process of the unmaking and remaking of the bloc.

The second important feature of this period was the increasing influence of soldiers and military considerations in the decision-making process. In the early part of July, soldiers had been present at the moments of decision, but they had not influenced any of the decisions. Bethmann Hollweg and Berchtold had considered military factors, such as the long-term military strength of Russia. Without wishing to resuscitate the old 'war by timetable' thesis, the pressures of military mobilisation shaped the options open to statesmen. Soldiers argued that diplomacy was superseded by the requirements of military necessity. In other words, national security rested solely on military defence. Soldiers and political leaders had very different understandings of the dynamics of the crisis. Where political leaders saw mobilisation as a means of signalling their intentions, soldiers viewed mobilisation as the prelude to war. These different understandings meant that decisions often had unintended consequences.

When the terms of the ultimatum became known on 24 July, the entente powers were unanimous in considering them extreme. The most important choice now lay with the Russian government. On receiving the terms, Sazonov declared war to be inevitable and blamed German support for encouraging Austria-Hungary's extreme measures. Before convening the ministerial council, he met with George Buchanan, the British ambassador, who adopted a non-committal pose. The Russian foreign minister found Maurice Paléologue, the French ambassador, much more supportive of his policy of standing firm against Germany and Austria-Hungary. Paléologue played an important role during the crisis, as Poincaré was at sea until 29 July. The French diplomat had an inflated sense of self-importance, was an ardent advocate of the Dual

Alliance, and entertained exaggerated suspicions of German malignity. He doctored telegrams in order to make Russia appear as conciliatory as possible. By shaping the information transmitted to Paris, he influenced, though did not determine, policy. Sazonov also met with General Yanushkevich before he met with his fellow ministers. Sazonov's policy was based on a firm military response and the support of France and Britain. In that respect, it mirrored the Austro-Hungarian and German policy, so that very little room remained for manoeuvre between two opposed blocs, prepared to use military force.

At the meeting of 24 July, Sazonov made clear his preference for supporting Serbia. He argued that further concessions in the Balkans would mark the collapse of Russian prestige and influence in the region. Compromise would be regarded as supine. While there were doubts about Britain's position and the condition of Russian finances, the general tone of the meeting was summed up by the influential Minister of Agriculture, Krivoshein. 'He thought that the only hope of influencing Germany was to show them, by making a firm stance, that we had come to the end of the concessions we were prepared to make. In any case, we should take all the steps, which would enable us to meet an attack.'[18] Prestige was a term that had been bandied about in diplomatic exchanges and the press for decades. Although, as the currency of great power politics, it was invested with deep significance, statesmen had stopped short of risking war against another great power to maintain prestige. The meeting of the Council of Ministers, by elevating the defence of Russia's great power prestige into a justification for war, departed from the culture of decision-making in previous crises.

In geopolitical terms, the western Balkans were not a vital strategic interest to Russia. Constantinople, the Straits, Poland, and Bulgaria were essential buffer zones in Tsarist Russia's strategy. The other great powers had, or believed they had, clear territorial and geopolitical interests at stake in the July crisis. Austria-Hungary's existence was challenged by Serbia, Germany and France fought to preserve allies and alliances fundamental to their security, and Britain entered the war to maintain the balance of power in Europe. These material security interests were also imbricated with particular understandings of the principles of the international order, such as sovereignty, international law, and the norm against preventive war. Russian decision-makers emphasised an ideological dimension to foreign policy – the historical mission of emancipating the Balkan Christians and Slavs from foreign rule – but this reading of

[18] Cited in D. C. B. Lieven, *Russia and the Origins of the First World War* (London, 1983), pp. 141–44.

security interests was particular to Russia, rather than a potential basis for a set of shared principles underpinning the European order. Nicolas de Basily, a leading official in the Foreign Office, warned the Austrian military attaché: 'you commit a serious error of calculation in supposing the fear of revolution will prevent Russia from fulfilling its national duty'.[19] However, it must be noted that these ideological and cultural factors had always been present in Russian foreign policy, including the Bosnian crises and the two Balkan Wars. Their importance in the July crisis was contingent on other developments, notably the increase in Russian military strength, the consolidation of the Triple Entente, and the growing influence of public opinion.

On 25 July, the Tsar began to prepare orders for partial mobilisation, which were issued the following day. The military districts of Kiev, Odessa, Kazan, and Moscow were mobilised. These were clearly directed against Austria-Hungary, not Germany. Even the Warsaw military district, which bordered Austria and Germany and was vulnerable to an Austrian offensive, was not mobilised. The significance of Russia's partial mobilisation remains contentious. A recent study by David Alan Rich points to some of the problems and misunderstandings that affected Russian military and political decision-making between 25 and 30 July. Partial mobilisation was designed to serve a specific political end – the deterrence of Austria from an offensive. By only mobilising against Austria-Hungary, Sazonov sought to reassure Germany that Russia was not about to start a general war. Indeed, neither Bethmann Hollweg nor Moltke saw the partial mobilisation of 26 July as an immediate threat to Germany. However, the plans for partial mobilisation ran roughshod over Russian mobilisation plans. Danilov, who was not involved in the decision for partial mobilisation, had forged Schedule 19 on the assumption that in the next war Russia would fight Austria-Hungary and Germany. At this point, the mobilisation plans, once triggered, placed enormous pressure on diplomacy. Sazonov, Sukhomlinov, and Yanushkevich, none of whom was familiar with the intricacies of Russian war planning, saw in partial mobilisation an instrument crafted to a specific political purpose. There was, as Otte has argued, 'a mobilization gap', which would be exposed if German forces tested deterrence.[20] The immediate needs of diplomacy were at odds with the absolute nature of Schedule 19. But despite Danilov's concerns, partial mobilisation held from 26 to 30 July. Russian leaders, like their counterparts in Vienna and Berlin, still hoped that a general war could be avoided.

[19] Ibid., p. 86.
[20] Otte, *July*, p. 246.

All three great powers, Austria-Hungary, Germany, and Russia, counted on the other side backing down, leaving little room for compromise at this point. On the same day that Nicholas II authorised partial mobilisation, Grey decided to revive that tried and trusted instrument of crisis management, the Concert of Europe. He issued an invitation to the governments of France, Germany, and Italy to instruct their ambassadors to meet with him in London with a view to finding a resolution to the crisis – or at the very least to buy time to find a solution. He sought to forestall military measures, although Russia had embarked on partial mobilisation. It was significant that he did not extend the invitation to either Austria-Hungary or Russia, whereas in 1912 he had initially hoped these two powers could collaborate to resolve the crisis in the Balkans. Now, he was relying on the alliances to restrain the two powers. However, the basis of the Concert – the restraint of allies and Anglo-German cooperation – had broken down. Britain was no longer in a position to restrain Russia. Buchanan had made it clear to Sazonov, in their meeting on 24 July, that Britain had 'no direct interests in Serbia and public opinion in England would never sanction a war on her behalf'. But this had not deterred the Tsar from ordering partial mobilisation. If Britain was unable to restrain her entente partner, Germany was unwilling to restrain Austria-Hungary. Finally, Bethmann would not countenance a Concert solution, rejecting Grey's proposal for the ambassadorial conference in London. The German Chancellor doubted whether Britain could or would effectively restrain Russia. He stuck to his deterrence strategy in the hope that British and French leaders would get the Russian government to back down.

France barely tried to restrain Russia at all during the crisis. To do so would have been to cast doubt on the alliance, a repudiation of Poincaré's policy since becoming premier in January 1912. French leaders did not want a war, but considered the risk of one preferable to the collapse of their Russian alliance. Nonetheless, a prematurely aggressive move by France would have laid the government open to accusations that it provoked the war, damaging both domestic support and the possibility of British intervention in the war. Joffre's calls for preparatory measures were routinely rejected by his political masters. On 21 July, the Supreme War Council had met, but had not discussed the possibility of a war arising out of the July crisis. Only three days later did the Minister of War, Messimy, mention the possibility of war to Joffre, but even on 28 July, the minister refused to allow Joffre to take preparatory measures until Poincaré returned. France's military posture remained defensive, though its diplomacy was more forthright. On 27 July, Poincaré signalled continued French loyalty to Russia, when he sent a telegram to St Petersburg, declaring he would support Russian efforts to solve the crisis. Poincaré was committed to a policy of firmness in the crisis, which he hoped would strengthen the alliance with Russia and maintain peace – in that order of priority.

Austria-Hungary, however, was not to be diverted from her course. On 28 July, Austria-Hungary declared war on Serbia. Habsburg mobilisation was painfully slow, but initial fighting took place on 28 and 29 July. Conrad accelerated Austro-Hungarian mobilisation against Serbia, but left the empire more exposed to a Russian attack. The possibilities for avoiding a general great power war were narrowing by the day. One potential option was the 'halt at Belgrade', which would involve the Austrian occupation of the Serbian capital until the investigation of the assassination had been completed. Otte argues that the proposal 'offered a realistic framework' for resolving the crisis.[21] It did, but it required considerable sacrifices, particularly from the Russian point of view. William II conjured up the proposal on 28 July 1914 in an attempt to prevent a general European war. In William II's view, the Habsburg occupation of Belgrade would satisfy the requirements of great power honour, the territory would serve as a 'forfeit' (Pfand) to be used in further negotiations, and the limited extent of the occupation signalled that Serbia would be restored to its full integrity. Berchtold had no interest in the proposal, nor did several German leaders. Berchtold doubted it would resolve the chronic tensions between Serbia and Austria-Hungary and feared the eventual retreat of occupying Habsburg forces would weaken Austro-Hungarian prestige in the Balkans. Owing to Austro-Hungarian opposition it was hardly a viable option. Nor did Russian leaders view it as feasible. When Pourtalès, the German ambassador, asked Sazonov to propose a compromise solution on 30 July, the Russian foreign minister replied that Austria had to recognise the European dimensions of the quarrel and eliminate from the ultimatum all infringements of Serbian sovereignty.[22] The Halt in Belgrade, however, concept would have involved the presence of Habsburg troops in occupying Serbian territory, a massive violation of sovereignty. Sazonov had already suggested on 24 July that Serbia not offer any resistance, but the Pašič regime had rejected such a course. Moreover Sazonov's proposal demanded Austria-Hungary recognise the European rather than the local character of the crisis. Such a course was unacceptable to Berchtold.

In Vienna, St Petersburg, and Berlin, the pressures for full mobilisation escalated on 28 and 29 July. The Habsburg declaration of war

---

[21] Ibid., p. 347.
[22] Ibid., p. 426.

7. Crowds in front of the Winter Palace, St Petersburg, 29 July 1914 (IWM Q 81828). As the July crisis entered its final phase, crowds gathered in capitals around Europe. This picture shows the range of popular reactions. Some were jubilant, flinging their hats in the air; many others were sombre, recognising the catastrophe a general war would cause.

had effectively thrown down the gauntlet to Russia. In St Petersburg, Danilov argued that if Russia attacked Austria-Hungary, it would also end up fighting Germany. In other words, the partial mobilisation aimed at deterring Austria-Hungary had failed and the Tsar had to order full mobilisation. The Tsar dithered until 30 July, when he issued orders to mobilise all military districts. Rich points out that this did not mean Russian units would cross the border into Germany. In Berlin, Moltke argued that Germany could not take the risk of standing by while the Russian army gained a vital advantage in the speed of mobilisation. However, the German mobilisation plan meant war on two fronts. Whereas the Russian and French mobilisation plans were designed to concentrate the troops, the German mobilisation plan was designed to launch a strike in western Europe. The pattern of the crisis was becoming clear. Each decision, while not aimed at provoking a general war, accepted the risk of one, and precipitated a decision in another capital, which worsened the crisis and reduced the possibility of a peaceful resolution. War plans, which had been largely irrelevant in previous crises, were based on the assumption of a general war. Once politicians and soldiers moved to implement them, the dynamic of the crisis changed.

On 31 July Germany declared 'a state of threatened war', the final step before mobilisation and the declaration of war. On the same day, Germany issued an ultimatum to Russia to draw back from its general mobilisation within twelve hours. Germany also asked France if it would remain neutral in the case of a war between Germany and Russia. Bethmann Hollweg did not expect France to declare its neutrality, but just in case it did, he also demanded that France surrender its fortresses at Verdun and Toul to German occupation until the end of the Russo-German war. The demands were designed to give Germany the excuse to declare war, unless, and this was highly unlikely, the partners in the Dual Alliance backed down at the last moment. As expected, the French and Russian governments rejected the demands. On 1 August, Germany declared war on Russia. Two days later, Berlin declared war on France.

From Continental War to World War

At his meeting with the reserved Buchanan on 24 July, Sazonov had predicted that Britain would have to join a continental war sooner or later. For ten days, Sazonov's prediction hung in the balance, before Britain declared war on Germany on 4 August. Historians continue to disagree over the main determinants of British foreign policy during these ten days. Whereas Otte sees Grey as an honest broker, seeking a peaceful resolution to the crisis, Clark argues Grey's diplomacy continually favoured his entente partners, France and Russia, and never offered a genuine basis for a deal with Germany. Douglas Newton's recent study goes much further, charging Grey, Asquith, and Churchill with undermining constitutional restraints, deceiving colleagues, and allowing the crisis to escalate by failing to restrain Russia and mobilising the British fleet. Both Clark and Newton draw to a certain extent on the earlier work of Keith Wilson, who argued that British policy was determined by a fear of Russian expansion in Central Asia. Supporting Russia in Europe ensured her friendship in Central Asia – even at the cost of conflict with Germany. Offering a wholly different perspective, Isabel Hull argues that the British entry to war was shaped in part by the 1839 treaty of guarantee to Belgium and a belief in international law.[23]

Grey's policy during the July crisis was shaped by his fading hopes of maintaining peace, the threat of German hegemony in Europe, the

---

[23] Douglas Newton, *The Darkest Days: The Truth behind Britain's Rush to War, 1914* (London, 2014); Hull, *Scrap*, pp. 16–50.

continuing divisions over foreign policy within the Liberal cabinet, and the need to secure public support for any war. His calculations that British reserve might restrain Russia and France and the possibility of British entry might deter Germany were misplaced in the July crisis. He had warned the Russian ambassador, Benckendorff, not to count on British support, while also warning the German ambassador, Lichnowsky, against assuming British neutrality. But this failed to make any impact on German or Russian policy. Grey was no longer the arbiter of the international system as he had been in late 1912. By 29 July, he had come to accept that the question now revolved around whether Britain would enter the war.

At a cabinet meeting on 29 July, the divisions within the cabinet became apparent. Grey and Churchill favoured entering a general war, while a 'peace party', headed by one of the grand old men of the Liberal party, John Morley, was opposed. There was a large group of undecideds, including the prime minister, Asquith. Opposition to war drew on longstanding suspicions of Tsarist Russia, well-founded concerns that war would destroy liberalism, and the geopolitical argument that the balance of power in Europe was of no concern to Britain. Grey and Churchill, on the other hand, could point to the German threat to British security in Europe and naval supremacy. Foreign and naval policy had persistently troubled the unity of the Liberal cabinet since the 1908/9 naval crisis and Asquith again tried to hold his cabinet and the party together. The preservation of Liberal unity involved a series of steps in which British high politics and foreign policy intersected. It slowed down the process of decision-making, it alarmed the French government, and it gave a burst of momentary hope to William II. But it also meant that when Britain entered the war, it did so with the overwhelming support of the population and the unity of the political elites.

The first step in this dance came on 31 July 1914, when Grey asked the German and French governments to guarantee Belgian neutrality. The latter was willing to do so, but Germany could not, unless it abandoned its war plan. Grey was well aware of this, as military and naval aid to Belgium in the case of a German invasion had been discussed by policy makers since 1906. It was a note designed to be rejected.

However, the next proposal was startling and has become known as the 'misunderstanding of 1 August'. Early on the morning of 1 August, Grey met Lichnowksy. He suggested that if Germany did not launch an offensive in the west against France, Britain would guarantee French passivity. Grey's purpose in making this offer remains contentious. To a certain extent, however, the purpose of Grey's offer was a red herring. Grey was in no position to guarantee French neutrality. Even if the British government decided to stay out of the war, the French army had still mobilised. The proposal was significant for the reaction that it elicited in Berlin. It seemed to offer Germany the opportunity of a one-front war. William II called for a halt of the offensive in the west. 'To general astonishment', Moritz von Lyncker, the head of the Kaiser's military cabinet, noted, 'Moltke declared that the march to the west could not be halted and that, despite all, France had to be overcome in war. At this point, an extremely lively and dramatic discussion took place. Moltke, very excited and with quivering lips, insisted on his point of view. In vain the Chancellor and the Kaiser and everyone else tried to persuade him, until Falkenhayn took him aside and a calmer discussion between the two of them took place in the corner of the room.'[24] Moltke's successful opposition to halting the offensive in the west has often been seen as the epitome of German militarism, the moment when the demi-gods of the General Staff overruled the civilian politicians and even the Kaiser in the name of their vaunted mobilisation schedules. There is something to be said for this interpretation, provided that one remembers it was the first occasion on which the General Staff succeeded in overcoming the aims of the civilian government and that the orders for mobilisation had already been issued. It was an exceptional moment, hardly emblematic of the broader pattern of civil–military relations in Germany.

In any case, Moltke argued, with considerable justification, that Grey's promise of French neutrality was worthless. The British Foreign Secretary had made a promise which he could not possibly honour. French policy in the July crisis was based on the maintenance of the Russian alliance. On 1 August, Grey warned Cambon that the British government would not commit to entry to the war. Cambon stumbled, white-faced, into Nicolson's office, asking whether the word 'honour' had disappeared from the English language. What was significant about this episode is that Grey's wavering did not affect French policy. Moltke's analysis was correct. France was committed to war, with or without Britain. Of course, the French government were desperate to get British support, but there was no discussion in Paris about leaving Russia in the lurch. Even had Moltke been able to reverse the offensive in the west, leave a small covering force, and concentrate German units on the Russian front, this would have left western Germany dangerously exposed to a French offensive. Poincaré might have restrained an offensive for a few days, but Russian pressure would surely have led to a French attack in early August. By

---

[24] Lyncker's diary entry, 1 August 1914, in Holger Afflerbach, ed., *Kaiser Wilhelm II als Oberster Kriegsherr im Ersten Weltkrieg. Quellen aus der militärischen Umgebung des Kaisers 1914–1918* (Munich, 2005), p. 132.

the evening of 1 August, Britain withdrew the offer, blaming it on a 'misunderstanding'.

Grey nudged the cabinet closer to war as he set a series of conditions on British neutrality, which Germany could not meet without tearing up its war plan – respecting Belgian neutrality and refraining from attacking France. He was also able to use the naval agreement of 1912, whereby the British fleet guarded the French Channel coast and the French concentrated their fleet in the Mediterranean, to move closer to war. On 2 August, with the threat of Grey's and Asquith's resignation hanging over the government, the cabinet agreed that the British fleet should defend French coasts, if they were attacked by the German fleet. Had Grey and Asquith resigned, the Liberal government would have collapsed, to be replaced, in all probability by the Unionists, headed by Andrew Bonar Law. Bonar Law and other members of the Unionist front-bench let Asquith, Churchill, and Grey know that they would support the Liberal government if it entered the war. This changed the political calculus at Westminster. If the Unionists came to power, then British entry to the war was certain. This made Liberal opposition to entry almost pointless. All that Liberal opponents of the war could achieve was the collapse of their government and loss of control over British policy once war was declared. If Britain was going to enter the war, most Liberals thought, better that it should do so under a Liberal, rather than a Unionist, government.

Asquith used a letter from Bonar Law at a cabinet meeting on 2 August. The cabinet agreed to the naval defence of France's northern coast and it also agreed to a suggestion from one of its more junior members and opponents of the war, Herbert Samuel, that a minor violation of Belgian territory by German troops would not constitute a sufficient cause for British entry to war. The issue of Belgian neutrality was important in holding the Liberal party together and uniting British public opinion. The Belgian question linked a range of issues, including the security of the English Channel, the sanctity of treaties, and notions of national honour and obligation. 'The threatened invasion of Belgium had set the nation on fire from sea to sea', said Lloyd George on 3 August 1914.[25] Lloyd George used it to hold the radicals together within the party. Grey's speech to the House of Commons on 3 August stressed that Britain could not tolerate the domination of Europe by one power and that her credibility in world politics was at stake. The balance of power in Europe and the maintenance of the ententes, particularly the one with France, were the determining factors in Grey's policy. On 4 August, after

[25] J. Paul Harris, 'Great Britain', in Richard Hamilton and Holger Herwig, eds, *The Origins of the First World War* (Cambridge, 2003), pp. 287–89.

Germany rejected a British ultimatum to withdraw from Belgium, His Majesty's Government declared war.

Britain's entry into the war transformed the conflict into a global one. Fighting spread to Africa, Japan joined the war in the Far East, seizing some German colonies, and soldiers from the French and British empires bolstered their armies in Europe. However, many states managed to remain out of the war. Italy, which had not been consulted by her alliance partners, was not under any obligation to enter and had no vital interest at stake in the July crisis. The USA, secure in the western hemisphere, was under no pressure to enter the war. Some of the Balkan states, Bulgaria and Romania, managed to stay out of the conflict for a few years, while the Ottoman Empire only joined the war on the side of Germany in November 1914. In western and northern Europe, the Dutch, Danish, and Swedish governments declared their neutrality, though they bent their policy to preserve the goodwill of Germany and forestall any invasion.

That the July crisis ended in war was the outcome of a series of decisions, none of which individually was motivated by a desire for war, but all of which risked a general war. Yet war was partly, but not simply, the grotesque outcome of a sequence of miscalculations. The great powers refused to draw back from the consequences of their decisions, even when they had the opportunity and when it became clear that the general war that few of them wanted was becoming increasingly likely. The reason for their failure to retreat was that war was no longer the worst possible option. The will to peace, which had sustained international stability for several decades, had broken down in late 1913 and 1914. Shifts in the international system, the arms race, and the perceived rise of radical nationalist opinion were the proximate causes of the erosion of the bonds of peace. The coincidence of the July crisis with these factors caused the outbreak of the First World War.

The July crisis was not simply a trigger for world war. Had – and this is, of course, speculative – Princip lost his nerve on 28 June and the Archduke and his wife returned to Vienna, a major crisis would have been avoided. It is also likely that some time would have passed before another major crisis occurred. At worst, diplomats expected a war between the Ottoman Empire and Greece at some point in 1914. By 1915, it was likely that relations between the great powers would have changed yet again. Anglo-Russian relations were increasingly poor in Central Asia, Britain, France, and Germany were cooperating in the Ottoman Empire, the arms race had slowed, though Russia had just launched its 'Big Programme', due for completion in 1917, and the influence of radical nationalist opinion was likely to wane, as the French elections of 1914 demonstrated. In the summer of 1914, Tyrrell had planned to meet Jagow to discuss consolidating the improvement of Anglo-German relations that had taken place since 1911, but the German Foreign Secretary's wedding meant the meeting was postponed, another alternative never explored. There were still severe problems, notably the deterioration of relations between Serbia and Austria-Hungary, confrontation between Russia and Germany in the Ottoman Empire, and growing concern in Germany and Austria-Hungary about the growth of Russian military power. The international system evolved constantly and the pressures on peace may (or may not) have eased. The point is that the assassination of the Archduke on 28 June came at a moment when leaders in three capitals, Vienna, St Petersburg, and Berlin, were least disposed to the preservation of peace.

7   Conclusion

Much of this book has suggested that a general war was not an inevitable, or even a probable, outcome of international rivalries before 1914. Between 1871 and 1914, the international system was able to accommodate vast economic, social, and cultural changes. The maintenance of peace was a fundamental condition for many of these changes, particularly economic globalisation. Peace also facilitated cooperation on everything from agreements on scientific standards to the development of international associations to promote sport. The international system did not remain static, but evolved considerably during the forty-four years separating the Franco-Prussian War and the outbreak of the First World War. Imperial expansion and the shift in the relative power of the great powers put pressure on the international system. However, these changes were accommodated by a combination of cooperation, alliances, ententes, and armaments. There were periodic crises, particularly in the final years of peace, but these were resolved without the recourse to general war. Every political system – domestic and international – endures crises. The test of a system lies not in its ability to prevent crises, but in its ability to resolve them. The fact that crises recurred in the same areas – the Balkans, North Africa, and the Far East – is testimony to the fact that solutions were based on compromise, not a final settlement of differences. A final reckoning of these differences would have led to war.

Viewing international relations before 1914 as the prelude to war places historical research into something of a teleological tunnel. Histories privilege conflict at the expense of restraint, crises at the expense of their solutions, recklessness at the expense of compromise. Of course, these were important features of international politics in this period. Nonetheless, an awareness of the different possibilities and the open-ended, contingent nature of history enables a broader and more nuanced understanding of international politics before the First World War. The history of international relations in this period is not simply an account of the origins of the war, but also of the maintenance of peace. It is a history of achievements, as well as of ultimate failure. Both require explanation and the explanation of one enhances our understanding of the other.

There were powerful restraints on a general war between the great powers before 1914. Statesmen accepted that war was a legitimate instrument of policy, but none embraced it as a creative force in human affairs. Wars were associated with upheaval and revolution, as they had been since the 1790s. Governments were loath to risk war, given the financial costs and political dangers. Even 'small wars' had become risky affairs by the late nineteenth century. Civilian leaders differed markedly in their views on war from their generals and radical nationalist groups. These viewed war in positive terms, as inevitable events, by which societies could progress. In its most radical form, war became an end in itself. The outcome – victory or defeat – was secondary to fighting. On this reading, war had been loosened from its political moorings. It was no longer an instrument of policy, it was an objective in its own right. However, this view was not widely shared. Civilian leaders managed to control their militaries, sometimes with great difficulty. Final decisions on foreign policy lay with civilian government, though figures such as Tirpitz could exercise influence on the direction and tone of foreign policy. While calls for preventive wars emanated regularly from generals, these were routinely dismissed. Perhaps it was a sign of weakness that the generals, who opposed the foreign policy of the civilian government, were not dismissed. However, when Conrad returned to the post of Chief of the General Staff in 1912, his calls for a war against Serbia were ignored by Berchtold. War was the policy instrument of last resort. Only in defence of a vital interest was war with another great power considered justifiable.

The great powers had few conflicting vital interests, although their ambitions collided around the globe. Vital interests were, first and foremost, the existence of the state, its territorial integrity, and its great power status. While the great powers had territorial claims against each other – France's claim to the lost provinces of Alsace and Lorraine, Italian irredentist claims against Austria – these claims never formed part of the practical politics of foreign policy. Only during the First World War did these claims become part of a realistic political agenda. The defence of Britain's route to India against Russian encroachments might also be considered a vital interest, which brought Britain and Russia to the brink of war in 1878. Thereafter, the Ottoman Empire became less important to British strategy, easing tensions between the two states. The lack of directly conflicting territorial claims meant that state- and nation-building wars, as had happened in the 1850s and 1860s, were highly unlikely. Many crises centred on the competition for influence, which could be resolved by negotiation. Great power status was a more nebulous vital interest, wrapped up in the term 'prestige'. But even when prestige was at stake, statesmen mostly pulled back from war. The very vagueness of the term allowed for retreat.

The need for popular support in any general war confirmed the cautious approach of statesmen. Governments were aware that war needed to be justified to those who would fight in it and pay for it. Popular militarist movements, the public spectacle of military and naval parades, and stories of heroism in war novels and the press did not transform European societies in belligerent, militarist camps. People read war novels (as they do today) for many different reasons, pleasure being one of them. The same could be said of attendance at the great military and naval displays. The largest parties in Europe were distinctly anti-militarist – the SPD in Germany and the Liberals in Britain, as well as the left in France. They would support war in very limited circumstances. For the most part, public attitudes towards war were grounded in notions of defensive patriotism. Politicians were sensitive to the circumstances in which a war could be justified to the populace. The influence of radical nationalism on international politics was limited, though it increased on the eve of the First World War.

The development of an integrated global economy was one of the most dramatic developments in the late nineteenth century. It was facilitated by a revolution in transport and communications, but it was also underpinned by the stability of the international system and the power of the leading states to integrate a still largely rural world into the logic of a global capitalist economy. Foreign investment and trade flourished in the expectation of peace, and, in turn, they fastened the bonds of peace around the globe. Tariff wars and financial rivalries were conducted with a rhetorical violence that was never likely to lead to war. Financiers, industrialists, and merchants had a stake in the maintenance of peace between the great powers. In particular, bankers used their diplomatic contacts to try to ease international tensions. War would disrupt patterns of economic life that had brought profits. Politicians were aware that the economic consequences of war would be dire, even if they were uncertain about the precise extent of the upheaval.

The structures of the international system sustained peace between the great powers for over four decades. The alliance system, although its purpose changed between the 1870s and the 1910s, generally functioned as a restraint on war. Alliances provided a modicum of security for their members, were defensively orientated, and restrained states from pursuing overly aggressive policies. Great powers did not wish to be dragged into conflicts in which they had no vital interests at stake. Time and again, great powers made it clear that they would only support their ally in a defensive war. Alliances also acted as a deterrent against attack. Unlike the 1850s and 1860s, great powers knew that they could not pick off their rivals in a series of separate and limited wars. By making a general war the very likely outcome of a war between two great powers, alliances actually reduced the risk of war in Europe. Security and restraint characterised the internal workings of the two alliance systems. Nor did the division of Europe into two separate blocs prevent cooperation between great powers on opposite sides of the divide. Cooperation on secondary issues could ease tensions between great powers. It also facilitated the brief revival of the Concert of Europe in 1912 and 1913. On the other hand, cooperation could also provoke tensions and suspicions within an alliance, which required careful handling. But these were part and parcel of the nods and winks that oiled the wheels of diplomacy before 1914. The international system remained flexible and complex, belying the simple division of the great powers into two separate blocs.

The most significant transformation in the international system after 1871 was the expansion of European rivalries to the far reaches of the globe. A global balance of power emerged. This transformation was achieved without a great power war. The diversion of expansionist energies outside Europe maintained the peace within it. Great powers were compensated for the gains their rivals made. Imperial competition did not become a zero-sum game. Cooperation, compensation, and restraint towards other great powers characterised the foreign policy of imperialism. The resolution of crises around the globe schooled a generation of diplomats in managing confrontations between the great powers. If expansion helped to sustain the peace, it came at the expense of non-European powers or weaker Europeans states, such as Portugal and Spain. Europe's expansion into Africa and Asia was often violent. Governments were much quicker to resort to violence against states and societies outside the circle of the great powers. Arguably the great powers' ready recourse to violence against 'barbaric' and 'semi-civilised' societies reinforced their own self-perception as 'civilised' states, which could settle disputes through reason and negotiation. By 1911/12, most of the major imperial disputes had been resolved. Revolution in China and the collapse of state structures in central America in 1911 precipitated neither a great power conflict nor a serious international crisis, whereas a decade earlier, rivalries in these regions had embroiled the great powers in disputes. This relative stability was partly because the minds of European statesmen were firmly fixed on Europe. It also owed much to the more stable settlements at which the great powers had arrived – the division of China into spheres and the establishment of American hegemony in the western hemisphere.

'Was it inevitable? Might the Great War not have taken place and would the history of the twentieth century thereby have been transformed?' Jean-Jacques Becker's response to these rhetorical questions betrayed his irritation with the line of argument advanced here. 'Absurd questions or at least anti-historical, because the Great War did take place. It is the duty of the historian to try to analyse what happened.'[1] Yet only by understanding how peace was preserved in Europe until 1914 is it possible to understand why the July crisis ended in war. The history of the origins of the war also requires an analysis of the loosening of the bonds of peace, as Paul Schroeder has pointed out in several important articles.[2] Starting with the July crisis, it is clear that the mechanisms that had preserved peace amongst the great powers either failed or served to provoke war. The Concert, proposed by Grey, was rejected without a second thought by Bethmann Hollweg. Allies failed to restrain each other as they had in previous crises. Austria-Hungary seized the initiative within the Dual Alliance, while Russia did likewise in the Triple Entente, which briefly collapsed before Britain's entry to the war. There was no prospect of adequate, face-saving compensation for Russia if Austria-Hungary achieved its ambition of crushing Serbia. Military pressures played a role late in the day; no longer did mass conscript armies act as a deterrent. Instead, their mobilisation put pressure on the decision-making process. Concerns about public reaction to war led politicians to craft their decisions with a view to justifying war in the public domain. Governments could manipulate the narrative of events to persuade their own public to support a war waged in the name of national defence. Financial and commercial issues played a marginal role in the discussions about war and peace in 1914. Efforts of financiers to influence the diplomatic process were futile. In other words, factors that preserved great power peace for four decades were either irrelevant or were twisted to cause war in the circumstances of the July crisis.

None of the great powers wanted a general war in 1914, but, with the exception of Italy, they were all willing to risk it. This was the marked difference with previous crises, when at most one power or one bloc had been willing to risk war. Their decisions interacted with each other so that the crisis escalated. Austria-Hungary's decision to destroy Serbia, backed by Germany, prompted Russia to begin partial mobilisation on 26 July with a view to deterring an Austro-Hungarian offensive. Russian and Austro-Hungarian aims were mutually incompatible and left no room for

---

[1] Jean-Jacques Becker, *L'année 1914* (Paris, 2004), p. 3.
[2] Paul Schroeder, *Systems, Stability, and Statecraft: Essays on the International History of Modern Europe*, ed. Robert Jervis, David Wetzel, and Jack Levy (Basingstoke, 2004).

negotiation. As Russia mobilised, Germany followed. Whereas Russian mobilisation was one step short of war, German mobilisation was effectively a declaration of war. Owing to the Schlieffen plan, itself a product of the fear of a two-front war, Germany attacked France as well as Russia. France, which held back its troops ten kilometres from the border, had no option but to fight. Britain had more room for manoeuvre, but Grey's ambiguous messages alternately caused despair and hope in Berlin. Once the German army went on the offensive in western Europe, Britain could not remain out of the war, as the balance of power in Europe, one of the foundations of its security, was in peril.

What is striking about the decisions taken in the July crisis is that governments conceived of them as defensive – not the methods used, but the aims they hoped to achieve. They also considered themselves to be defending often contradictory principles – European values, international law, and sovereignty. For Austria-Hungary, its existence appeared to be at stake, at the mercy of a 'criminal state'. In St Petersburg, the Tsar and his advisers feared that Russia's great power status was at stake, but leaders also invoked the rights of state sovereignty. In Germany, upholding Austria-Hungary's great power position had become a vital interest, the sole means of preserving Germany's long-term independence, which was threatened by the encirclement of the Triple Entente. Poincaré reasoned in a similar way about the necessity of the Russian alliance to French security. Britain aimed to uphold the balance of power and international treaty law. Once war started, government aims were radicalised, but it is misleading to read war aims backwards into pre-war policy. If each power could conceive that its aims were defensive, then this signified that the international system could no longer accommodate the tensions between the great powers. Great powers could only preserve their vital interests at the expense of another power's vital interests. In other words, the maintenance of great powers' vital interests had become mutually incompatible, leading to a general war.

Why did this happen in 1914, as opposed to an earlier date? War was the result of an accumulation of decisions, each one of which individually was not designed to provoke war, but which interacted with other decisions to destroy the foundations of peace. Between late 1912 and June 1914, a series of decisions on future foreign policy was made in Vienna, St Petersburg, and Berlin, which reflected fears that each great power's position was deteriorating and could only be rescued by a more assertive foreign policy. An assertive foreign policy risked war, but this risk was outweighed by the fear that, in the future, their position would become progressively worse. Moreover, there was also the hope, even expectation, that the other side would back down in the face of an assertive military stance. Of all the great powers, it was Austria-Hungary that most clearly defected from the practices and norms of the international system. The concentration on its position in the Balkans, the subordination of European perspectives to its contest with Serbia, and the issuing of ultimatums, backed by the threat of military force, were rooted in Austro-Hungarian weakness.

Taking a longer view, the collapse of the Ottoman Empire in Europe weakened the international system. This accelerated from 1908, as the great powers came to a series of agreements and made gains at the expense of the Ottoman Empire. Austria-Hungary's annexation of Bosnia in 1908 and Italy's annexation of Tripoli in 1911 were the two most obvious moments when the great powers acted to destroy the Ottoman Empire. But the Anglo-Russian entente of 1907 and subsequent cooperation in the Balkans, Germany's ill-advised Moroccan policy, and French willingness to support Italian expansion in North Africa in return for Italian support over Morocco were policies that ended up destroying the Ottoman Empire. While the great powers were strong enough to destroy the Ottoman Empire, they were too weak and too divided to manage the successor states in the Balkans. The international system became less stable from 1908, and this instability accelerated in the wake of the Second Moroccan crisis in 1911, which spawned the Italian attack on the Ottoman Empire in Libya and the subsequent Balkan Wars. Moreover, Habsburg foreign policy makers saw in the decline of the Ottoman Empire a premonition of their own fate, a multi-ethnic empire, facing multiple challenges, and let down by an international system more interested in hacking it to pieces than in preserving it as a mainstay of the European system and great power peace. These crises also weakened the sense of shared norms that had underpinned great power peace since the 1870s. The inviolability of treaties, the rights of the great powers, and the practices of multilateral crisis management were worn bare. The nationality principle emerged and small states declared their sovereign equality, the basis for a new normative environment. A general war was by no means inevitable from 1908 or 1911 onwards, but it had become more likely, especially after the latter date.

Other features of international politics reinforced the possibility of war. From 1911, the arms race in Europe escalated, as Germany, France, and Russia responded to each other's military challenge by increasing military expenditure and manpower. Other states, including the Balkan ones, also joined the race, so that states in Europe were locked in a web of escalating armaments. Diplomacy was militarised and the concept of the window of opportunity gained ground, as governments feared they would be unable to keep pace in the arms race with their rivals.

At the same time, radical nationalist opinion gained ground. Radical nationalists not only put pressure on their own governments to act more aggressively, they also inspired fear in other governments. The fear that governments could not control or resist radical nationalist demands was unfounded, but as an assumption it became part of the foreign policy calculus. French and Russian leaders feared pan-Germans, German leaders feared pan-Slavs and revanchists. Governments proclaimed their peaceful intentions, but diplomats paid increasing attention to the aggressive articles in the radical national press. They either believed that these campaigns were inspired by the government or they feared the state would be unable to hold these passions at bay. Radical nationalist agitators fed off each other's campaigns, contributing to the damaging uncertainty and distrust in international politics.

Economic issues hardly contributed to great power tensions in the years before the war. Although there were signs of economic nationalism in Russia and France on the eve of the war, this had a very limited impact on foreign policy. Commercial and financial cooperation continued right up to the eve of war, while bankers and businessmen tried to avert war at the last moment.

While it is important to examine the history of international relations between the 1870s and 1914 from the perspective of the First World War, it is also possible to locate this history within a broader chronological framework. The idea that the First World War marked the 'seminal catastrophe' of the twentieth century and that it marked the beginning of the end of European dominance of the international system makes it difficult to look beyond 1914, to identify continuities. The forty-four years of great power peace were slightly longer than the thirty-nine years of peace that followed the Napoleonic Wars. Not until 1989, as the Cold War entered its denouement, was there such a long period of peace between the great powers. Indeed, one of the most significant developments of the modern international system has been the decreasing number of general great power wars. While great power wars occurred frequently after the Peace of Westphalia, the eighteenth century was characterised by increasingly lengthy periods of great power peace. Of course, this was an uneven process, but the trend towards the maintenance of peace and the absence of great power wars has been one of the most significant developments in modern European history.

It has also been one of the least explained. While it is beyond the scope of the book to offer an explanation for this change in the international system, this long-term development offers a useful perspective from which to view great power politics before the First World War. Peace between the great powers was founded on numerous factors, all of which have a long history, beginning before 1871 and enduring beyond 1914. The growing financial costs, the domestic political consequences, and the moral condemnation of war made military force a less effective instrument of great power politics. Diplomatic institutions, such as the Concert of Europe and ambassadorial conferences, which aimed to prevent war breaking out, were established by the early eighteenth century. From the post-1815 period, alliances were no longer signed as a prelude to war, but were used to serve defensive purposes and to stabilise international politics. The idea of military power as a deterrent to war, rather than an instrument of war, reached its apogee during the nuclear politics of the Cold War. Economic interdependence and globalisation have tightened the bonds of peace in Europe after 1945 and around the world more recently. International organisations, which emerged in the last great age of globalisation in the late nineteenth century, handle important humanitarian, technical, and scientific issues of global concern, from human rights to health. While some transnational networks were and are violent – terrorist groups and criminal gangs for instance – many more promote better relations between different societies. Popular attitudes to war, especially major systemic wars, have become increasingly negative. The failure to maintain peace in 1914 was a catastrophe, but the war that followed the long peace was framed, in large part, as a war to remake a more peaceful world. Peace in its many guises became the yardstick by which policy, action, and result in the international system were judged. The history of international relations before 1914 is both the history of the origins of the First World War and a history of the international system as it is today.

Bibliography

Aarbakke, Vemund, *Ethnic Rivalry and the Quest for Macedonia, 1870–1913* (New York, 2003)

Abbenhuis, Maartje, *An Age of Neutrals: Great Power Politics, 1815–1914* (Cambridge, 2014)

Adams, Iestyn, *Brothers across the Ocean: British Foreign Policy and the Origins of the Anglo-American Special Relationship, 1900–1905* (London, 2005)

Afflerbach, Holger, *Der Dreibund. Europäische Großmacht- und Allianzpolitik vor dem Ersten Weltkrieg* (Vienna, 2002)

Falkenhayn. Politisches Denken und Handeln im Kaiserreich (Munich, 1996)

ed., *Kaiser Wilhelm II als Oberster Kriegsherr im Ersten Weltkrieg. Quellen aus der militärischen Umgebung des Kaisers 1914–1918* (Munich, 2005)

Afflerbach, Holger, and Stevenson, David, eds, *An Improbable War? The Outbreak of World War I and European Political Culture before 1914* (Oxford, 2007)

Ahmad, Feroz, *The Young Turks: The Committee of Union and Progress in Turkish Politics, 1908–1914* (Oxford, 1969)

Aksakal, Mustafa, '"Not by Those Old Books of International Law, but Only by War": Ottoman Intellectuals on the Eve of the Great War', *Diplomacy and Statecraft*, 15, 3 (2004): 507–49

Alff, Wilhelm, ed., *Deutschlands Sonderung von Europa 1862–1945* (Frankfurt, 1984)

Allain, Jean-Claude, *Joseph Caillaux. Le défi victorieux* (Paris, 1978)

Andrew, Christopher, *Théophile Delcassé and the Making of the Entente Cordiale: A Reappraisal of French Foreign Policy, 1898–1905* (London, 1968)

Angelow, Jürgen, *Kalkül und Prestige. Der Zweibund am Vorabend des Ersten Weltkrieges* (Cologne, 2000)

Ansari, Sarah, 'The Sind Blue Books of 1843 and 1844: The Political "Laundering" of Historical Evidence', *English Historical Review*, 120, 2 (2005): 35–65

Antier, Chantal, 'Le recrutement dans l'empire colonial français, 1914–1918', *Guerres mondiales et conflits contemporains*, 230 (2008): 5–22

Ascher, Abraham, *P. A. Stolypin: The Search for Stability in Late Imperial Russia* (Stanford, 2001)

The Revolution of 1905: Russia in Disarray (Stanford, 1988)

Bachmann, Klaus, *Ein Herd der Feindschaft gegen Rußland. Galizien als Krisenherd in den Beziehungen der Donaumonarchie mit Rußland (1907–1914)* (Munich, 2001)

Baechler, Christian, and Müller, Klaus Jürgen, eds, *Les tiers dans les relations Franco-Allemandes* (Munich, 1996)

Bairoch, Paul, 'Europe's Gross National Product, 1800–1975', *Journal of European Economic History*, 5, 2 (1976): 273–340

'International Industrialization Levels from 1780 to 1980', *Journal of European Economic History*, 11, 2 (1982): 269–334

Barth, Boris, *Die deutsche Hochfinanz und die Imperialismen. Banken und Außenpolitik vor 1914* (Stuttgart, 1995)

Baumgart, Winfried, *Europäisches Konzert und nationale Bewegung. Internationale Beziehungen 1830–1878* (Paderborn, 1999)

Beasley, W. G., *Japanese Imperialism, 1894–1945* (Oxford, 1987)

Becker, Frank, 'Strammstehen vor der Obrigkeit? Bürgerliche Wahrnehmung der Einigungskriege und Militarismus im Deutschen Kaiserreich', *Historische Zeitschrift*, 227, 1 (2003): 87–113

Becker, Jean-Jacques, *L'année 1914* (Paris, 2004)

1914: Comment les français sont entrés dans la guerre (Paris, 1977)

Becker, Jean-Jacques, and Audoin-Rouzeau, Stéphane, *La France, la nation, la guerre, 1850–1920* (Paris, 1995)

Beckert, Sven, *Empire of Cotton: A Global History* (New York, 2014)

Bellanger, Claude, Godechot, Jacques, Guiral, Pierre, and Terrou, Fernand, eds, *Histoire générale de la presse française de 1870 à 1940* (Paris, 1972)

Bitsch, Marie Thérèse, *La Belgique entre la France et l'Allemagne, 1905–1914* (Paris, 1994)

Blouet, Brian, ed., *Global Geostrategy: Mackinder and the Defence of the West* (Abingdon, 2005)

Bloxham, Donald, *The Great Game of Genocide: Imperialism, Nationalism, and the Destruction of the Ottoman Armenians* (Oxford, 2005)

Bobroff, Ronald, *Road to Glory: Late Imperial Russia and the Turkish Straits* (London, 2006)

Boemeke, Manfred, Chickering, Roger, and Förster, Stig, eds, *Anticipating Total War: The German and American Experiences, 1871–1914* (Cambridge, 1999)

Bönker, Dirk, *Militarism in a Global Age: Naval Ambitions in Germany and the United States before World War I* (Ithaca, NY, 2012)

Bosworth, Richard, *Italy and the Approach of the First World War* (London, 1983)

Braybon, Gail, ed., *Evidence, History, and the Great War: Historians and the Impact of 1914–1918* (Oxford, 2003)

Brechtken, Magnus, *Scharnierzeit 1895–1907. Persönlichkeiten und internationale Politik in den deutsch-britisch-amerikanischen Beziehungen vor dem Ersten Weltkrieg* (Mainz, 2006)

Bridge, F. R., *Great Britain and Austria-Hungary, 1906–1914: A Diplomatic History* (London, 1972)

Brown, Michael E., Coté, Owen R., Lynn-Jones, Sean M., and Miller, Steven E., eds, *Theories of War and Peace: An International Security Reader* (Cambridge, MA, 2000)

Cain, P. J., *Hobson and Imperialism: Radicalism, New Liberalism, and Finance, 1887–1938* (Oxford, 2002)

Cecil, Lamar, *Albert Ballin: Business and Politics in Imperial Germany, 1888–1918* (Princeton, 1967)

Charmley, John, *Splendid Isolation? Britain and the Balance of Power, 1870–1914* (London, 1999)

Clark, Christopher, *The Sleepwalkers. How Europe Went to War in 1914* (London, 2012)

Clark, Ian, *Globalization and Fragmentation: International Relations in the Twentieth Century* (Oxford, 1997)

Clark, Martin, *Modern Italy, 1871–1995* (London, 1996)

Clemens, Gabriele, ed., *Nation und Europa. Studien zum internationalen Staatensystem im 19. und 20. Jahrhundert* (Stuttgart, 2001)

Cobb, Stephen, *Preparing for Blockade: Naval Contingency for Economic Warfare, 1885–1914* (Farnham, 2013)

Conrad, Sebastian, *Globalisierung und Nation im Deutschen Kaiserreich* (Munich, 2006)

Conze, Eckart, '"Wer von Europa spricht, had Unrecht". Aufstieg und Verfall des vertraglichen Multilateralismus im europäischen Staatensystem des 19. Jahrhunderts', *Historisches Jahrbuch* (2001)

Cosson, Olivier, *Préparer la grande guerre. L'Armée française et la guerre russo-japonaise (1899–1914)* (Paris, 2013)

Cosson, Olivier, 'Expériences de guerre et anticipation à la veille de la Première Guerre mondiale: Les milieux militaires franco-britanniques et les conflits extérieurs', *Revue de l'Histoire Moderne et Contemporaine*, 50, 3 (2003)

Crampton, R. J., *Bulgaria* (Oxford, 2007)

The Hollow Détente: Anglo-German Relations in the Balkans, 1911–1914 (London, 1980)

Crépin, Annie, *Défendre la France. Les français, la guerre, et le service militaire de la guerre de Sept Ans à Verdun* (Rennes, 2005)

Daunton, Martin, *Trusting Leviathan: The Politics of Taxation in Britain, 1799–1914* (Cambridge, 2001)

Deist, Wilhelm, *Flottenpolitik und Flottenpropaganda. Das Nachrichtenbureau des Reichsmarineamtes 1897–1914* (Stuttgart, 1976)

Deringil, Selim, *The Well-Protected Domains: Ideology and the Legitimation of Power in the Ottoman Empire, 1876–1909* (London, 1999)

Di Paolo, Pietro, 'The Spies Who Came in from the Heat: The International Surveillance of the Anarchists in London', *European History Quarterly*, 37, 2 (2007): 189–215

Diószegi, Istn, *Die Außenpolitik der Österreich-Ungarischen Monarchie, 1871–1877* (Vienna, 1985)

Droz, Jacques, *Les causes de la première guerre mondiale* (Paris, 1973)

Duggan, Christopher, *Francesco Crispi: From Nation to Nationalism* (Oxford, 2002)

Dülffer, Jost, *Im Zeichen der Gewalt. Frieden und Krieg im 19. und 20. Jahrhunderte*, ed. Martin Kröger, Ulrich Soénius, and Stefan Wunsch (Cologne, 2003)

Dülffer, Jost, Kröger, Martin, and Wippich, Rolf-Harald, *Vermiedene Kriege. Deeskalation von Konflikten der Grossmächte zwischen Krimkrieg und Ersem Weltkrieg* (Munich, 1997)

Duroselle, Jean-Baptiste, *Clemenceau* (Paris, 1988)

Echevarria, Antulio, *After Clausewitz: German Military Thinkers before the Great War* (Laurence, 2000)

Edwards, E. W., *British Diplomacy and Finance in China, 1895–1914* (Oxford, 1987)

Ehlert, Hans, ed., *Der Schlieffenplan. Analysen und Dokumente* (Paderborn, 2006)

Eley, Geoff, *Reshaping the German Right: Radical Nationalism and Political Change after Bismarck* (New Haven, CT, 1980)

Epkenhans, Michael, ed., *Albert Hopman. Das ereignisreiche Leben eines Wilhelminers. Tagebücher, Briefe, Aufzeichnungen 1901–1920* (Munich, 2004)

Etges, Andreas, *Wirtschaftnationalismus. USA und Deutschland im Vergleich (1815–1914)* (Frankfurt, 1999)

Fellner, Fritz, ed., *Schicksalsjahre Österreichs, 1908–1919. Das politische Tagebuch Josef Redlichs*, vol. I (Böhlau, 1953)

Ferenczi, Caspar, *Außenpolitik und Öffentlichkeit in Rußland, 1906–1912* (Husum, 1982)

Ferguson, Niall, *The Pity of War* (London, 1998)

'Public Finance and National Security: The Domestic Origins of the First World War Revisited', *Past and Present*, 142 (1994): 141–68

Findlay, Richard, and O'Rourke, Kevin, *Power and Plenty: Trade, War, and the World Economy in the Second Millennium* (Princeton, 2007)

Fischer, Fritz, *Germany's War Aims in the First World War*, with an introduction by James Joll (London, 1967)

War of Illusions: German Policies from 1911 to 1914 (London, 1975)

Foch, Ferdinand, *Des principes de la guerre* (Paris, 1996)

Foley, Robert, *German Strategy and the Path to Verdun: Erich von Falkenhayn and the Development of Attrition, 1870–1916* (Cambridge, 2005)

ed., *Alfred von Schlieffen's Military Writings* (London, 2003)

Forsbach, Ralf, *Alfred von Kiderlen-Wächter (1852–1912)*, 2 vols. (Göttingen, 1997)

Förster, Stig, 'Der deutsche Generalstab und die Illusion des kurzen Krieges, 1871–1914. Metakritik eines Mythos', *Militärgeschichtliche Mitteilungen*, 54 (1995): 61–95

'Im Reich des Absurden: die Ursachen des Ersten Weltkrieges', in Bernd Wegner, ed., *Wie Kriege entstehen. Zum historischen Hintergrund von Staatenkonflikten* (Paderborn, 2000), pp. 211–52

Der doppelte Militarismus. Die deutsche Heeresrüstungspolitik zwischen Status-Quo-Sicherung und Aggression 1890–1913 (Stuttgart, 1985)

Forsyth, Douglas, *The Crisis of Liberal Italy: Monetary and Financial Policy, 1914–1922* (Cambridge, 1993)

Frevert, Ute, ed., *Das neue Jahrhundert. Europäische Zeitdiagnosen und Zukunftsentwürfe um 1900* (Göttingen, 2000)

Fridenson, Patrick, ed., *The French Home Front, 1914–1918* (Providence, RI, 1992)

Friedberg, Aaron, *The Weary Titan: Britain and the Experience of Relative Decline, 1895–1905* (Princeton, 1988)

Fuller, William C., *Civil–Military Relations in Imperial Russia, 1881–1914* (Princeton, 1985)

Strategy and Power in Russia, 1600–1914 (New York, 1992)

Gaddis, John Lewis, *The Long Peace: Inquiries into the History of the Cold War* (Oxford, 1989)

Gall, Lothar, *Bismarck: The White Revolutionary, 1871–1898* (London, 1986)

Garrigues, Jean, *La République des hommes d'affaires (1870–1900)* (Paris, 1997)

Gattrell, Peter, *Government, Industry, and Rearmament in Russia, 1900–1914: The Last Argument of Tsarism* (Cambridge, 1994)

Geiss, Imanuel, *Studien über Geschichte und Geschichtswissenschaft* (Frankfurt, 1972)

ed., *July 1914. The Outbreak of the First World War: Selected Documents* (London, 1967)

Geppert, Dominik, *Pressekriege. Öffentlichkeit und Diplomatie in den deutsch-britischen Beziehungen, 1896–1912* (Munich, 2007)

Geppert, Dominik, and Gerwarth, Robert, eds, *Wilhelmine Germany and Edwardian Britain: Essays on Cultural Affinity* (Oxford, 2008)

Geppert, Dominik, Mulligan, William, and Rose, Andreas, eds, *The Wars before the Great War: Conflict and International Politics before the Outbreak of the First World War* (Cambridge, 2015)

Geyer, Dietrich, *Russian Imperialism: The Interaction of Domestic and Foreign Policy, 1860–1914* (Leamington Spa, 1987)

Geyer, Martin, and Paulmann, Johannes, eds, *The Mechanics of Internationalism: Culture, Society, and Politics from the 1840s to the First World War* (Oxford, 2001)

Gienow-Hecht, Jessica C. E., and Schumacher, Frank, eds, *Culture and International History* (Oxford, 2003)

Gilbert, Bentley B., 'Pacifist to Interventionist: David Lloyd George in 1911 and 1914', *Historical Journal*, 28, 4 (1985): 866–86

Gildea, Robert, *Barricades and Borders: Europe 1800–1914*, 3rd edn (Oxford, 2003)

Girardet, Raoul, *L'idée coloniale en France de 1871 à 1962* (Paris, 1972)

Le nationalisme français, 1871–1914 (Paris, 1966)

Girault, René, 'Les Balkans dans les rélations franco-russes en 1912', *Revue Historique*, 253 (1975): 172–83

Emprunts russes et investissements français en Russie 1887–1914 (Paris, 1973)

Godsey, William, *Aristocratic Redoubt: The Austro-Hungarian Foreign Office on the Eve of the First World War* (Cambridge, 1999)

Golder, Frank A., *Documents of Russian History, 1914–1917* (London, 1927)

Grand, Alexander de, *The Italian Nationalist Association and the Rise of Fascism in Italy* (Lincoln, NE, 1978)

Guillen, Pierre, *L'expansion, 1881–1898* (Paris, 1984)

'Les questions coloniales dans les relations franco-allemandes à la veille de la première guerre mondiale', *Revue Historique*, 248 (1972)

Hajimu, Masuda, 'Rumors of War: Immigration Disputes and the Social Construction of American–Japanese Relations, 1905–1913', *Diplomatic History*, 33, 1 (2009): 1–37

Hamer, D. A., *John Morley: Liberal Intellectual in Politics* (Oxford, 1968)

Hamilton, Richard, and Herwig, Holger, eds, *The Origins of the First World War* (Cambridge, 2003)

eds, *War Planning 1914* (Cambridge, 2009)

Hanotaux, Gabriel, *La guerre des Balkans et l'Europe, 1912–1913* (Paris, 1914)

Hardtwig, Wolfgang, ed., *Politische Kulturgeschichte der Zwischenkriegszeit* (Göttingen, 2005)

Hawkins, Angus, *British Party Politics, 1852–1886* (Basingstoke, 1998)

Hayne, M. B., *The French Foreign Office and the Origins of the First World War, 1898–1914* (Oxford, 1992)

Haywood, Geoffrey, *Failure of a Dream: Sidney Sonnino and the Rise and Fall of Liberal Italy* (Florence, 1999)

Helmreich, Jonathan E., 'Belgian Concern over Neutrality and British Intentions, 1906–1914', *Journal of Modern History*, 4 (1964): 416–27

Herrmann, David, *The Arming of Europe and the Making of the First World War* (Princeton, 1996)

'The Paralysis of Italian Strategy in the Italo-Turkish War, 1911–1912', *English Historical Review*, 104 (1989)

Hewitson, Mark, *Germany and the Origins of the First World War* (Oxford, 2004)

National Identity and Political Thought in Germany: Wilhelmine Depictions of the French Third Republic, 1890–1914 (Oxford, 2000)

Hildebrand, Klaus, *Das vergangene Reich. Deutsche Außenpolitik 1871–1945* (Stuttgart, 1995)

Hillgruber, Andreas, *Deutsche Großmacht und Weltpolitik im 19. und 20. Jahrhundert* (Düsseldorf, 1979)

Hobson, J. M., 'The Military-Extraction Gap and the Wary Titan: The Fiscal Sociology of British Defence Policy, 1870–1913', *Journal of European Economic History*, 22, 3 (1993): 461–506

Hoetzsch, Otto, ed., *Die internationalen Beziehungen im Zeitalter des Imperialismus*, 1st series, vol. I (Berlin, 1931)

Holmes, T. H., 'The Reluctant March to Paris', *War in History*, 8, 2 (2001): 208–32

Holquist, Peter, 'Violent Russia, Deadly Marxism? Russia in the Epoch of Violence, 1905–1921', *Kritika: Explorations in Russian and Eurasian History*, 4, 3 (2003): 627–52

Hölzle, Erwin, ed., *Quellen zur Entstehung des Ersten Weltkrieges. Internationale Dokumente 1901–1914* (Darmstadt, 1978)

Hopkins, A. G., ed., *Globalization in World History* (London, 2002)

Horn, Martin, and Imlay, Talbot, 'Money in Wartime: France's Financial Preparations for the Two World Wars', *International History Review*, 27, 4 (2005): 709–53

Howard, Christopher, ed., *The Diary of Sir Edward Goschen, 1900–1914* (London, 1980)

Howe, Anthony, *Free Trade and Liberal England, 1846–1946* (Oxford, 1997)

Hull, Isabel V., *A Scrap of Paper. Breaking and Making International Law during the Great War* (Ithaca, NY, 2014)

Hutton, Patrick, 'Popular Boulangism and the Advent of Mass Politics in France, 1886–1890', *Journal of Contemporary History*, 11, 1 (1976): 85–106

Iliasu, A. A., 'The Cobden-Chevalier Commercial Treaty of 1860', *Historical Journal*, 14, 1 (1971): 67–98

Iriye, Akira, *Japan and the Wider World: From the Mid-Nineteenth Century to the Present* (London, 1997)

James, Harold, *The End of Globalization: Lessons from the Great Depression* (Cambridge, MA, 2001)

Jeffery, Keith, *Field Marshal Sir Henry Wilson: A Political Soldier* (Oxford, 2006)

Johansen, Anja, 'Violent Repression or Modern Strategies of Crowd Control: Soldiers as Riot Police in France and Germany, 1870–1914', *French History*, 15, 4 (2000): 400–420

Joll, James, 'The 1914 Debate Continues: Fritz Fischer and His Critics', *Past and Present*, 34 (July 1966): 100–113

The Second International, 1889–1914 (London, 1955)

Joll, James, and Martel, Gordon, *The Origins of the First World War* (Harlow, 2007, 3rd edn, London, 1992, 2nd edn)

Joly, Bertrand, *Déroulède. L'inventeur du nationalisme français* (Paris, 1998)

'La France et la revanche, 1871–1914', *Revue d'histoire moderne et contemporaine*, 46, 2 (1999): 325–47

Kagan, Frederick, and Higham, Robin, eds, *The Military History of Tsarist Russia* (Basingstoke, 2002)

Kalmykov, Andrew D., *Memoirs of a Russian Diplomat: Outposts of the Empire, 1893–1917* (New Haven, 1971)

Kammen, Michael, ed., *The Past before Us: Contemporary Historical Writing in the United States* (Ithaca, NY, 1980)

Keiger, John, *France and the Origins of the First World War* (London, 1983)

Raymond Poincaré (Cambridge, 1997)

Kennan, George, *The Decline of Bismarck's European Order: Franco-Russian Relations, 1875–1890* (Princeton, 1979)

The Fateful Alliance: France, Russia, and the Coming of the First World War (Manchester, 1984)

Kennedy, Paul, 'The Costs and Benefits of British Imperialism, 1846–1914', *Past and Present*, 125 (1989): 186–92

The Rise of the Anglo-German Antagonism, 1860–1914 (London, 1980)

The Rise and Fall of the Great Power: Economic Change and Military Conflict from 1500 to 2000 (London, 1988)

ed., *The War Plans of the Great Powers, 1880–1914* (London, 1979)

Kennedy, Paul, and Nicholls, Anthony, eds, *Nationalist and Racialist Movements in Britain and Germany before 1914* (London, 1981)

Kießling, Friedrich, *Gegen den großen Krieg? Entspannung in den internationalen Beziehungen 1911–1914* (Munich, 2002)

'Österreich-Ungarn und die deutsch-englischen Détentebemühungen', *Historisches Jahrbuch*, 116, 1 (1996)

Koch, H. W., ed., *The Origins of the First World War: Great Power Rivalry and German War Aims*, 2nd edn (London, 1984)

Kolb, Eberhard, *Der Weg aus dem Krieg. Bismarcks Politik im Krieg und die Frieden-sanbahnung, 1870–71* (Munich, 1989)

Kos, Franz-Josef, *Die politischen und wirtschaftlichen Interessen Österreich-Ungarns und Deutschland in Südosteuropa 1912/13* (Vienna, 1996)

Koss, Stephen, *The Rise and Fall of the Political Press in Britain*, vol. I, *The Nineteenth Century* (London, 1981)

Sir John Brunner: Radical Plutocrat, 1842–1919 (Cambridge, 1970)

Kowner, Rotem, ed., *The Impact of the Russo-Japanese War* (London, 2007)

Kramer, Alan, *Dynamics of Destruction: Culture and Mass Killing in the First World War* (Oxford, 2007)

Kronenbitter, Günther, *'Krieg im Frieden'. Die Führung der k. u. k. Armee und die Großmachtpolitik Österreichs-Ungarns 1906–1914* (Munich, 2003)

Krumeich, Gerd, *Armaments and Politics in France on the Eve of the First World War* (London, 1984)

Lahme, Rainer, 'Das Ende der Pax Britannica: England und die europäische Mächte 1890–1914', *Archiv für Kulturgeschichte* (1992)

Deutsche Außenpolitik 1890–1894. Von der Gleichgewichtspolitik Bismarcks zur Allianzstrategie Caprivis (Göttingen, 1990)

Laity, Paul, *The British Peace Movement, 1870–1914* (Oxford, 2001)

Lambert, Nicholas, 'British Naval Policy, 1913–1914: Financial Limitation and Strategic Revolution', *Journal of Modern History*, 67, 3 (1995): 596–626

Sir John Fisher's Naval Revolution (Columbia, SC, 1999)

Planning Armageddon. British Economic Warfare and the First World War (Cambridge, MA, 2012)

Lassman, Peter, and Speirs, Ronald, eds, *Weber: Political Writings* (Cambridge, 1994)

Lebovics, Hermann, *The Alliance of Iron and Wheat in the Third French Republic, 1860–1914* (Baton Rouge, 1988)

Lehmann, Hartmut, ed., *Paths of Continuity: Central European Historiography from 1933 to the 1950s* (Cambridge, 1994)

Lenin, V. I., *Imperialism, the Highest Stage of Capitalism: Collected Works*, vol. XXII (Moscow, 1964)

Leroy-Beaulieu, Paul, *Les États-Unis au XXe siècle* (Paris, 1904)

Levy, Jack S., and John A. Vasquez, eds, *The Outbreak of the First World War: Structure, Politics and Decision-Making* (Cambridge, 2014)

Lieven, Dominic, *Empire: The Russian Empire and Its Rivals* (London, 2000)

'Pro-Germans and Russian Foreign Policy, 1890–1914', *International History Review*, 11, 1 (1980): 34–54

Russia and the Origins of the First World War (London, 1983)

Lindemann, Thomas, *Die Macht der Perzeptionen und die Perzeptionen von Macht* (Berlin, 2000)

Lippmann, Walter, *Public Opinion* (New York, 1922)

Lohr, Eric, and Poe, Marshall, eds, *The Military and Society in Russia, 1450–1917* (Leiden, 2002)

Lorrain, Sophie, *Des pacifistes français et allemands. Pionniers de l'entente francoalle-mande, 1870–1925* (Paris, 1999)

Loth, Wilfried, and Osterhammel, Jürgen, eds, *Internationale Geschichte. Themen – Ergebnisse – Aussichten* (Munich, 2000)

Lowe, C. J., and Marzari, F., *Italian Foreign Policy, 1870–1940* (London, 1975)

MacKenzie, David, *Serbs and Russians* (New York, 1996)

MacKenzie, John M., ed., *Popular Imperialism and the Military, 1850–1950* (Manchester, 1992)

Marsh, Peter, *Britain and the First Common Market, 1860–1892* (New Haven, CT, 1999)

Martel, Gordon, *Imperial Diplomacy: Rosebery and the Failure of Foreign Policy* (Kingston, 1986)

Matsumoto-Best, Saho, 'British and Italian Imperial Rivalry in the Mediterranean, 1912–1914: The Case of Egypt', *Diplomacy and Statecraft*, 18, 2 (2007): 297–314

Mayer, Martin, *Geheime Diplomatie und öffentliche Meinung. Die Parlamente in Frankreich, Deutschland und Großbritannien und die erste Marokkokrise, 1904–1906* (Düsseldorf, 2002)

Mayeur, Jean-Marie, and Reberioux, Madeleine, *The Third Republic from Its Origins to the Great War, 1871–1914* (Cambridge, 1987)

McDonald, David McClaren, *United Government and Foreign Policy in Russia, 1900–1914* (Cambridge, MA, 1992)

McMeekin, Sean, *The Russian Origins of the First World War* (Cambridge, MA, 2012)

McReynolds, Louise, *The News under Russia's Old Regime: The Development of a Mass-Circulation Press* (Princeton, 1991)

Mehlinger, Howard, and Thompson, John, *Count Witte and the Tsarist Government in the 1905 Revolution* (Bloomington, 1972)

Menning, Bruce W., 'Pieces of the Puzzle: The Role of Iu. Danilov and M. V. Alekseev in Russian War Planning before 1914', *International History Review*, 25, 4 (2003)

Metzler, Gabriele, *Großbritannien – Weltmacht in Europa. Handelspolitik in Wandel des europäischen Staatensystems 1856 bis 1871* (Berlin, 1997)

Meyer, Thomas, *Endlich eine Tat, eine befreiende Tat. Alfred von Kiderlen-Wächters Panthersprung nach Agadir unter dem Druck der öffentlichen Meinung* (Husum, 1996)

Michalka, Wolfgang, ed., *Der Erste Weltkrieg. Wirkung, Wahrnehmung, Analyse* (Munich, 1994)

Miller, Paul C., *From Revolutionaries to Citizens: Antimilitarism in France, 1870–1914* (Durham, NC, 2002)

Mombauer, Annika, 'The First World War: Inevitable, Avoidable, Improbable, or Desirable? Recent Interpretations on War Guilt and the War's Origins', *German History*, 25, 1 (2007): 78–95

'The Fischer Controversy, Documents, and the Truth about the Origins of the First World War', *Journal of Contemporary History*, 48, 2 (2013): 290–314

Helmuth von Moltke and the Origins of the First World War (Cambridge, 2001)

The Origins of the First World War: Controversies and Consensus (London, 2002)

Die Julikrise. Europas Weg in den Ersten Weltkrieg (Munich, 2014)

'Of War Plans and War Guilt: The Debate Surrounding the Schlieffen Plan', *Journal of Strategic Studies*, 28, 5 (2005): 857–85

Mombauer, Annika, and Deist, Wilhelm, eds, *The Kaiser: New Research on Wilhelm II's Role in Imperial Germany* (Cambridge, 2003)

Mommsen, Wolfgang, *Imperial Germany, 1867–1918: Politics, Culture, and Society in an Authoritarian State* (London, 1995)

Morel, E. D., *Truth and the War* (London, 1916)

Morgan, Kenneth, 'Lloyd George and Germany', *Historical Journal*, 39, 3 (1996)

Morgan, Kevin, 'Militarism and Anti-Militarism: Socialists, Communists, and Conscription in France and Britain, 1900–1940', *Past and Present*, 202 (2009): 207–45

Mösslang, Markus, and Riotte, Torsten, eds, *The Diplomats' World: A Cultural History of Diplomacy, 1815–1914* (Oxford, 2008)

Mueller, John, *Retreat from Doomsday: The Obsolescence of Major War* (New York, 1989)

Mulligan, William, 'From Case to Narrative: The Marquess of Lansdowne, Sir Edward Grey, and the Threat from Germany, 1900–1906', *International History Review*, 30, 2 (2008): 273–302

'We Can't Be More Russian Than the Russians: British Policy in the Liman von Sanders Crisis, 1913–14', *Diplomacy and Statecraft*, 17, 2 (2006)

Murray, Bruce, *The People's Budget 1909/10: Lloyd George and Liberal Politics* (Oxford, 1989)

Murray, Williamson, Knox, MacGregor, and Bernstein, Alvin, eds, *The Making of Strategy: Rulers, States, and War* (Cambridge, 1994)

Nasson, Bill, *The South African War, 1899–1902* (London, 1999)

Neilson, Keith, *Britain and the Last Tsar: British Policy and Russia, 1894–1917* (Oxford, 1995)

Neitzel, Sönke, *Kriegsausbruch. Deutschlands Weg in der Katastrophe 1900–1914* (Munich, 2002)

Weltmacht oder Untergang. Weltreichslehre im Zeitalter des Imperialismus (Paderborn, 2000)

Neumatz, Dietmar, 'Das russische Verfassungsexperiment, 1906–1918. Zum Verhältnis von Tradition und Modernität', *Journal of Modern European History*, 6, 1 (2008): 95–102

Newton, Douglas, *The Darkest Days: The Truth behind Britain's Rush to War, 1914* (London, 2014)

Ninkovich, Frank, *The Wilsonian Century: US Foreign Policy since 1900* (Chicago, 1999)

Nish, Ian, *The Anglo-Japanese Alliance: The Diplomacy of Two Island Empires, 1894–1907* (Westport, CT, 1968)

O'Brien, Patrick, 'The Costs and Benefits of British Imperialism, 1846–1914', *Past and Present*, 120 (1988): 163–200

O'Brien, Phillips Payson, *British and American Naval Power: Politics and Policy, 1900–1936* (Westport, CT, 1998)

'The Titan Refreshed: Imperial Overstretch and the British Navy before the First World War', *Past and Present*, 172 (August 2001): 146–69

Offer, Avner, *The First World War: An Agrarian Interpretation* (Oxford, 1989)

Osterhammel, Jürgen, and Petersson, Niels P., *Globalization: A Short History* (Princeton, 2005)

Otte, T. G., *The China Question: Great Power Rivalry and British Isolation, 1894–1905* (Oxford, 2007)

  The July Crisis: The World's Descent into War, 1914 (Cambridge, 2014)

  'A "German Paperchase": The "Scrap of Paper" Controversy and the Problem of Myth and Memory in International History', *Diplomacy and Statecraft*, 18, 1 (2007)

  'Great Britain, Germany, and the Far Eastern Crisis of 1897/8', *English Historical Review*, 110, 5 (1995): 1157–79

  'A Question of Leadership: Lord Salisbury, the Unionist Cabinet, and Foreign Policy-Making, 1895–1900', *Contemporary British History*, 14, 4 (2000): 1–26

Palumbo, Michael, 'German–Italian Military Relations on the Eve of World War I', *Central European History*, 12, 4 (1979): 343–71

Pamuk, Sevket, *The Ottoman Empire and European Capitalism, 1820–1913: Trade, Investment, and Production* (Cambridge, 1987)

Pantenburg, Isabel, *Im Schatten des Zweibundes. Probleme österreichisch-ungarischer Bündnispolitik, 1897–1908* (Vienna, 1996)

Paulmann, Johannes, *Pomp und Politik. Monarchbegegnungen in Europa zwischen Ancien Régime und Erstem Weltkrieg* (Paderborn, 2000)

Pennell, C. R., *Morocco since 1830* (London, 2000)

Petzold, Stephan, 'The Social Making of a Historian in Nazi Germany and the Early Federal Republic: Fritz Fischer's Distancing from Bourgeois-Conservative Historiography', *Journal of Contemporary History*, 48, 2 (2013), 271–89

Pogge von Strandmann, Hartmut, ed., *Walther Rathenau: Industrialist, Banker, Intellectual, and Politician. Notes and Diaries, 1907–1922* (Oxford, 1985)

Poidevin, Raymond, *Les rélations économiques et financières entre la France et l'Allemagne de 1898 à 1914* (Paris, 1969)

Porter, Andrew, '"Gentlemanly Capitalism" and Empire: The British Experience since 1750', *Journal of Imperial and Commonwealth History*, 18, 3 (1990): 265–95

Portes, Jacques, *Fascination and Misgivings: The United States in French Opinion, 1870–1914* (Cambridge, 2000)

Ragsdale, Hugh, ed., *Imperial Russian Foreign Policy* (Cambridge, 1993)

Rauh, Manfred, 'Die britisch-russische Marinekonvention von 1914 und der Ausbruch des Ersten Weltkrieges', *Militärgeschichtlichen Mitteilungen*, 41, 1 (1987): 37–62

Readman, Paul, 'The Conservative Party, Patriotism, and British Politics: The Case of the General Election of 1900', *Journal of British Studies*, 40, 1 (2001): 107–45

Reinermann, Lothar, *Der Kaiser in England. Wilhelm II und sein Bild in der britischen Öffentlichkeit* (Paderborn, 2001)

Reynolds, David, 'International History, the Cultural Turn, and the Diplomatic Twitch', *Cultural and Social History*, 3, 1 (2006): 75–91

Rich, Norman, and Fisher, M. H., eds, *Die Geheimen Papiere Friedrich von Holstein*, 4 vols (Göttingen, 1963)

Rieber, Alfred, *Merchants and Entrepreneurs in Imperial Russia* (Chapel Hill, 1982)

Ritter, Gerhard, *The Schlieffen Plan: Critique of a Myth* (London, 1958)

Röhl, John, *The Kaiser and His Court: Wilhelm II and the Government of Germany* (Cambridge, 1994)

Wilhelm II: The Kaiser's Personal Monarchy, 1888–1900 (Cambridge, 2004)

Wilhelm II. Der Weg in den Abgrund 1900–1941 (Munich, 2008)

Romsics, Gergoly, *Myth and Remembrance: The Dissolution of the Habsburg Empire in the Memoir Literature of the Austro-Hungarian Political Elite* (New York, 2006)

Rose, Andreas, *Zwischen Empire und Kontinent. Britische Außenpolitik vor dem Ersten Weltkrieg* (Munich, 2011)

Rosenberg, Emily, *Financial Missionaries to the World: The Politics and Culture of Dollar Diplomacy, 1900–1930* (Cambridge, MA, 1999)

Rosenberger, Bernhard, *Zeitungen als Kriegstreiber? Die Rolle der Presse im Vorfeld des Ersten Weltkrieges* (Cologne, 1998)

Roth, François, *Raymond Poincaré* (Paris, 2000)

Rüger, Jan, *The Great Naval Game: Britain and Germany in the Age of Empire* (Cambridge, 2007)

Rumpler, Helmut, *Eine Chance für Mitteleuropa. Bürgerliche Emanzipation und Staatsverfall in der Habsburgermonarchie* (Vienna, 1997)

Rumpler, Helmut, and Niederkorn, Jan-Paul, eds, *Der Zweibund 1879. Das deutsch-österreichisch-ungarische Bündnis und die europäische Diplomatie* (Vienna, 1996)

Scheer, Tamara, *"Minimale Kosten, absolut kein Blut". Österreich-Ungarns Präsenz im Sandžak Novipazar (1878–1908)* (Frankfurt, 2013)

Schimmelpenninck van der Oye, David, *Towards the Rising Sun: Russian Ideologies of Empire and the Path to War with Japan* (De Kalb, 2001)

Schmidt, Stephan, *Frankreichs Aussenpolitik in der Julikrise. Ein Beitrag zur Geschichte des Ausbruches des Ersten Weltkrieges* (Munich, 2009)

Schmied-Kowarzik, Anatol, *Die Protokolle des Gemeinsamen Rates der österreichisch-ungarischen Monarchie, 1908–1914* (Budapest, 2011)

Schneider, Irmin, *Die deutsche Rußlandpolitik 1890–1900* (Paderborn, 2003)

Schöllgen, Gregor, 'Kriegsgefahr und Krisenmanagement vor 1914. Zur Außenpolitik des kaiserlichen Deutschland', *Historische Zeitschrift*, 267 (1998)

ed., *Escape into War? The Foreign Policy of Imperial Germany* (Oxford, 1990)

Schröder, Stephen, *Die englisch-russische Marinekonvention. Das deutsche Reich und die Flottenverhandlungen der Tripleentente am Vorabend des Ersten Weltkrieges* (Göttingen, 2006)

Schroeder, Paul, *Systems, Stability, and Statecraft: Essays on the International History of Modern Europe*, ed. Robert Jervis, David Wetzel, and Jack Levy (Basingstoke, 2004).

The Transformation of European Politics, 1763–1848 (Oxford, 1994)

'World War I as Galloping Gertie: A Reply to Joachim Remak', *Journal of Modern History*, 44, 3 (1972): 320–45

Schwengler, Walter, *Völkerrecht, Versailler Vertrag und Auslieferungsfrage. Die Strafverfolgung wegen Kriegsverbrechen als Problem des Friedensschlusses 1919/20* (Stuttgart, 1982)

Seligmann, Matthew, *Spies in Uniform: British Military and Naval Intelligence on the Eve of the First World War* (Oxford, 2006)

  The Royal Navy and the German Threat, 1901–1914: Admiralty Plans to Protect British Trade in a War against Germany (Oxford, 2012)

  'Switching Horses: The Admiralty's Recognition of the Threat from Germany, 1900–1906', *International History Review*, 30, 2 (2008): 239–58

Sexton, Jay, 'The Funded Loans and the Alabama Claims', *Diplomatic History*, 27, 4 (2003): 449–78

Sharp, Alan, and Stone, Glyn, eds, *Anglo-French Relations in the Twentieth Century: Rivalry and Cooperation* (London, 2000)

Siegel, Jennifer, *Endgame: Britain, Russia, and the Final Struggle for Central Asia* (London, 2002)

  For Peace and Money: French and British Finance in the Service of the Tsars and the Commissars (Oxford, 2014)

Smith, Joseph, *The Spanish–American War: Conflict in the Caribbean and the Pacific, 1895–1902* (London, 1994)

Soroka, Marina, *Britain, Russia, and the Road to the First World War: The Fateful Embassy of Count Aleksandr Benckendorff* (Farnham, 2011)

Soutou, Georges Henri, *L'or et le sang. Les buts de guerre économiques de la Première Guerre mondiale* (Paris, 1989)

Spring, D. W., 'Russia and the Franco-Russian Alliance, 1905–1914: Dependence or Inter-Dependence', *Slavonic and East European Review*, 66, 4 (1988): 564–92

Stargardt, Nicholas, *The German Idea of Militarism: Radical and Socialist Critics, 1860–1914* (Cambridge, 1994)

Stein, Olivier, *Die deutsche Heeresrüstungspolitik 1890–1914. Das Militär und der Primat der Politik* (Paderborn, 2007)

Steinberg, John, *The Russo-Japanese War in Global Perspective* (Leiden, 2005)

Steinberg, Jonathan, 'The Copenhagen Complex', *Journal of Contemporary History*, 1, 3 (1966): 23–46

Steiner, Zara, *Britain and the Origins of the First World War* (London, 1977)

  The Foreign Office and Foreign Policy, 1898–1914 (Cambridge, 1969)

Steller, Verena, *Diplomatie von Angesicht zu Angesicht. Diplomatische Handlungsformen in den deutsch-französischen Beziehungen 1870–1919* (Paderborn, 2011)

Sternhill, Zeev, *La droite révolutionnaire, 1885–1914* (Paris, 1997)

Stevenson, David, *Armaments and the Coming of War: Europe, 1904–1914* (Oxford, 1996)

  'War by Timetable? The Railway Race before 1914', *Past and Present*, 162 (February 1999): 163–94

Sumida, Jon, *In Defence of Naval Supremacy: Finance, Technology, and British Naval Policy, 1889–1914* (London, 1989)

Tardieu, André, *La France et les alliances. La lutte pour l'équilibre, 1871–1910* (Paris, 1910)

Taylor, A. J. P., *The Course of Germany History* (London, 1945)
    The Struggle for Mastery in Europe, 1848–1918 (Oxford, 1954)
Thobie, Jacques, *La France impériale, 1880–1914* (Paris, 1982)
Tombs, Robert, ed., *Nationhood and Nationalism in France: From Boulangism to the Great War, 1889–1914* (London, 1991)
Tomes, Jason, *Balfour and Foreign Policy: The International Thought of a Conservative Statesman* (Cambridge, 1997)
Torp, Cornelius, *Die Herausforderung der Globalisierung. Wirtschaft und Politik in Deutschland 1860–1914* (Göttingen, 2005)
Tsuzuki, Chuschichi, *The Pursuit of Power in Modern Japan, 1825–1995* (Oxford, 2000)
Turfan, M. Naim, *The Rise of the Young Turks: Politics, the Military, and Ottoman Collapse* (London, 2000)
Uebel, Thomas, and Cohen, Robert, eds, *Otto Neurath. Economic Writings: Selections, 1904–1945* (Vienna, 2004)
Ullrich, Volker, 'Weltkrieg wider Willen', *Die Zeit*, 2 (2003)
Valone, Stephen J., '"There Must Be Some Misunderstanding": Sir Edward Grey's Diplomacy of August 1, 1914', *Journal of British Studies*, 27 (1988): 405–24
Vasquez, John A., 'The First World War and International Relations Theory: A Review of Books on the 100th Anniversary', *International Studies Review*, 16 (2014): 623–44
Väyrynen, Raimo, ed., *The Waning of Major War: Theories and Debates* (London, 2006)
Verhey, Jeffrey, *The Spirit of 1914: Militarism, Myth, and Mobilization in Germany* (Cambridge, 2000)
Viaene, Vincent, 'International History, Religious History, Catholic History: Perspectives for Cross-Fertilization (1830–1914)', *European History Quarterly*, 38, 4 (2008): 578–607
Vogel, Barbara, *Deutsche Rußlandspolitik. Das Scheitern der deutschen Weltpolitik unter Bülow 1900–1906* (Düsseldorf, 1973)
Vogel, Jakob, *Nationen im Gleichschritt. Der Kult der 'Nation im Waffen' in Deutschland und Frankreich 1871–1914* (Göttingen, 1997)
Walkenhorst, Peter, *Nation–Volk–Rasse. Radikaler Nationalismus im Deutschen Kaiserreich 1890–1914* (Göttingen, 2007)
Wandruszka, Adam, and Urbanitsch, Peter, eds, *Die Habsburger Monarchie im System der internationalen Beziehungen* (Vienna, 1989)
Wank, Solomon, ed., *Aus dem Nachlass Aehrenthal. Briefe und Dokumente zur österreichisch-ungarischen Innen- und Außenpolitik 1885–1912 (Part 2, 1907–1912)* (Graz, 1994)
Wattenberg, Ben, ed., *Statistical History of the United States: From Colonial Times to the Present* (New York, 1976)
Weber, Eugen, *The Nationalist Revival in France, 1905–1914* (Berkeley, 1968)
Weber, Thomas, *Our Friend "the Enemy": Elite Education in Britain and Germany before World War I* (Stanford, 2008)
Webster, R. W., *Industrial Imperialism in Italy, 1908–1915* (Berkeley, 1975)

Wegner, Bernd, ed., *Wie Kriege entstehen. Zum historischen Hintergrund von Staatenkonflikten* (Paderborn, 2000)

Wehler, Hans-Ulrich, *The German Empire, 1871–1918* (Leamington Spa, 1985)

Wesseling, H. L., *Soldier and Warrior: French Attitudes toward the Army and War on the Eve of the First World War* (Westport, CT, 2000)

Westad, Odd Arne, *The Global Cold War: Third World Interventions and the Making of Our Times* (Cambridge, 2005)

Whittam, John, *The Politics of the Italian Army, 1861–1918* (London, 1977)

Williams, Alan, *Republic of Images: A History of French Film-Making* (Cambridge, MA, 1992)

Williamson, Samuel, *Austria-Hungary and the Origins of the First World War* (Basingstoke, 1991)

The Politics of Grand Strategy: Britain and France Prepare for War, 1904–1914 (Cambridge, MA, 1969)

Wilsberg, Klaus, *Terrible ami – aimable ennemi. Kooperation und Konflikt in den deutsch-französischen Beziehungen 1911–1914* (Bonn, 1998)

Wilson, Keith, 'The Anglo-Japanese Alliance of August 1905 and the Defence of India: A Case of the Worst Case Scenario', *Journal of Imperial and Commonwealth History*, 21 (1993): 334–56

'Directions of Travel: The Earl of Selborne, the Cabinet, and the Threat from Germany, 1900–1904', *International History Review*, 30, 2 (2008): 259–72

The Policy of the Entente: Essays on the Determinants of British Foreign Policy, 1904–1914 (Cambridge, 1985)

'Understanding the "Misunderstanding" of 1 August 1914', *Historical Journal*, 37, 4 (1994): 885–89

ed., *Forging the Collective Memory: Government and International Historians through the Two World Wars* (Providence, RI, 1996)

ed., *The International Impact of the Boer War* (Chesham, 2001)

Winzen, Peter, *Bülows Weltmachtkonzept. Untersuchungen zur Frühphase seiner Außenpolitik, 1897–1901* (Boppard am Rhein, 1977)

Das Kaiserreich am Abgrund. Die Daily-Telegraph Affäre und das Hale Interview von 1908 (Stuttgart, 2002)

Witt, Peter Christian, *Die Finanzpolitik des Deutschen Reiches von 1903 bis 1913. Eine Studie zur Innenpolitik des Wilhelminischen Deutschland* (Lübeck, 1970)

Wollstein, Günther, *Theobald von Bethmann Hollweg. Letzte Erbe Bismarcks, erste Opfer der Dolchstosslegende* (Göttingen, 1995)

Zamagni, Vera, *The Economic History of Italy, 1860–1990* (Oxford, 1992)

Zuber, Terence, *Inventing the Schlieffen Plan: German War Planning, 1871–1914* (Oxford, 2002)

Index